# BETWEEN THESE HILLS:
## A CASE FOR THE
## NEW YORK CUMORAH

First Edition

# JONATHAN NEVILLE, MS, JD

**LDS Nonfiction by Jonathan Neville**
*The Lost City of Zarahemla*
*Moroni's America*
*Brought to Light*
*Letter VII: Joseph Smith and Oliver Cowdery Explain the Hill Cumorah*
*The Editors: Joseph, Don Carlos and William Smith*
*Whatever Happened to the Golden Plates?*
*Because of this Theory*
*Mesomania*
*Moroni's America (pocket edition)*
*A Man that Can Translate*
*The 2020 "seeing clearly" trilogy*
*- A Man that Can Translate: Joseph Smith and the Nephite Interpreters (2d edition)*
*- Infinite Goodness: Joseph Smith, Jonathan Edwards, and the Language of the Book of Mormon*
*- Between these Hills: A Case for the New York Cumorah*

———

**Novels by J.E. Neville (LDS)**
*The Joy Helpers*
*Moroni's Keys*
*Among All Nations*
*In Earthly Things*

———

**Novels by Jonathan Neville**
*The Mind Tamer*
*Caught Away*
*The Girl from Helper*
*The Perfect Mother*
*California Blues*
*The Mistake*
*The Clown House*
*The Rule of Equity*

———

**Nonfiction by Jonathan Neville**
Legalines Series:
*Constitutional Law*
*Contracts*
*Property Law*
*Torts*
*Criminal Law*
*Criminal Procedure*
*Civil Procedure*

———

ISBN- 978-1-944200-49-7
Cover Image: Alfred Lambourne *Hill Cumorah* 1893


Museum of the Book of Mormon Press

**MOBOM.org**

DIGITAL
LEGEND

Toll free: 1-877-222-1960
www.digitallegend.com

# BETWEEN THESE HILLS:
## A CASE FOR THE
## NEW YORK CUMORAH

## JONATHAN NEVILLE, MS, JD

DIGITAL
LEGEND

To open-minded people everywhere.

———

At about one mile west rises another ridge of less height, running parallel with the former, leaving a beautiful vale between. The soil is of the first quality for the country, and under a state of cultivation, which gives a prospect at once imposing, **when one reflects on the fact, that here, between these hills, the entire power and national strength of both the Jaredites and Nephites were destroyed.**

By turning to the 529th and 530th pages of the book of Mormon120 you will read Mormon's account of the last great struggle of his people, **as they were encamped round this hill Cumorah.** [1]
(Oliver Cowdery, Letter VII)

———

**Doctrine and Covenants, Section 128**
20 And again, what do we hear? Glad tidings from **Cumorah**! Moroni, an angel from heaven, declaring the fulfilment of the prophets—the book to be revealed. A voice of the Lord in the wilderness of Fayette, Seneca county, declaring the three witnesses to bear record of the book!

---

[1] https://www.josephsmithpapers.org/paper-summary/history-1834-1836/90

———

In my book *Moroni's America*, I recognized four people for their contributions to Book of Mormon studies: John L. Sorenson, John W. Welch, Wayne May, and Rod Meldrum. I repeat that recognition here, but add to them Willard and Rebecca Bean and their family who have done so much to preserve the site and memory of the Hill Cumorah.

I'm also grateful to all the historians who have carefully preserved and compiled Church history resources, with special appreciation for the Joseph Smith Papers project, as well as to all the scientists— archaeologists, anthropologists, geographers, geologists, etc.—whose work continues to inform us. I look forward to even more discoveries.

———

NOTE: For convenience and brevity, I use the capitalized term "Church" to refer to any of the restoration organizations, meaning those who accept the Book of Mormon and the Restoration of the Gospel through Joseph Smith. For historical and practical reasons, I occasionally use the acronym LDS to refer to the Church of Jesus Christ of Latter-day Saints and RLDS to refer to the Reorganized Church of Jesus Christ of Latter Day Saints (now the Community of Christ). I generally use the LDS scriptural citation system.

The notes and links in this book cite the best available sources for the referenced materials, regardless of the editorial stance of the creator(s) of the sources.

Unless otherwise indicated, all **bold** lettering is my added emphasis.

As always, any errors in this book are mine and I encourage you to call them to my attention. I welcome your feedback and thoughts. You can email me at this address: lostzarahemla@gmail.com.

I've learned a lot from readers (and critics) and expect that we will all continue to "instruct and edify each other." (Doctrine and Covenants 43:8)

———

# Table of Contents

## Contents

# Table of Figures

# Preface

Welcome to the magnificent world of the Book of Mormon. People everywhere are curious about the reality of its people and places.

I stipulate that the message of the Book of Mormon is more important than its geography or history. Believers rely on spiritual impressions more than physical evidence. But lingering questions about geography and history impede acceptance of the book as scripture.

After years of thinking of the Book of Mormon in a Mayan setting, in 2014 I learned an alternative concept: the Book of Mormon took place in Ohio, Illinois, Tennessee, and New York. The new perspective led me to blog about Church history and Book of Mormon geography.

My premise: Joseph Smith and Oliver Cowdery taught the truth.

The opposing view: scholars know more about Cumorah, the translation, and other topics than did Joseph and Oliver.

I'm only a minor participant and late comer compared with other well-known scholars, authors, speakers, and their organizations. For decades, they have produced numerous books, articles, web pages, blogs and videos. Yet my simple blogs have generated over 750,000 page views from all over the world.

Why the interest in Cumorah?

Before he obtained the plates, Joseph Smith learned from Moroni that the hill in New York was named Cumorah anciently. Oliver Cowdery learned the name when he and Joseph translated Mormon's book in May, 1829, in Harmony, Pennsylvania. In June, David Whitmer learned the name from a divine messenger who took the Harmony plates back to Cumorah. For the rest of their lives, the fact of Cumorah linked the Book of Mormon to the modern world.

For many believers in the Book of Mormon,[2] Cumorah is part of the

---

[2] Numerically most believers are members of the Church of Jesus Christ of Latter-day Saints (LDS Church), but there are thousands of believers in other faith traditions, including traditional Christian denominations as well as the Community of Christ, the Church of Jesus Christ, The Restoration Church of Jesus Christ of Latter Day Saints, etc. I use "Church" to refer to all of these.

historical reality at the core of their belief in the divine authenticity of the book. Because they believe the book is true spiritually, they believe it must also be true physically.

Other believers accept the book as an inspirational text akin to the parables in the Bible; i.e., it teaches truth but is not a real history. For some, questions about Book of Mormon geography are irrelevant, troublesome, or contentious.

Nonbelievers claim there is no extrinsic evidence to supports its historical claims—at least, not the type of evidence they've been led to expect.

Belief in the historicity of the Book of Mormon is declining, even among members. A survey published in 2019[3] indicated that younger members of the Church of Jesus Christ of Latter-day Saints are less inclined than previous generations to accept the Book of Mormon as an actual history. Only 50% of Millennials believe that.

| Table 1.3 Mormons' Certainty about Specific LDS Teachings, by Generation | | | | |
|---|---|---|---|---|
| % who are "Confident and Know this Is True" | | | | |
|  | Boomers/ Silents | GenXers | Millennials | Delta |
|  | Born before 1965 | Born 1965-1980 | Born since 1981 |  |
| The Book of Mormon is a literal, historical account | 62% | 53% | 50% | -12 |

Figure 1 - Certainty about Book of Mormon

More surprising, perhaps, is that more than 1 in 3 of older generations question whether the Book of Mormon is a literal history.

Regardless of what you believe now, I hope this book will give you insights into why so many people (i) accept the Book of Mormon as an authentic history and (ii) still believe the teachings of the prophets about the New York Cumorah.

---

[3] Jana Reiss, *The Next Mormons* (Oxford University Press, New York, 2019), Table 1.3.

―――――

When Moroni first visited Joseph, he explained there was a "history of the aborigines of this country" that had been "written and deposited" not far from Joseph's home near Palmyra, New York. Moroni told Joseph the hill was called "Cumorah" anciently.

After Joseph translated the abridged plates from Moroni's stone box in the hill, he and Oliver visited Mormon's depository of Nephite records (Mormon 6:6) in another part of the hill.[4]

Mormon chose that location because he knew the Jaredites had built defenses there. The Jaredites, who called the hill Ramah, had chosen the site because of its strategic location. Abundant external evidence corroborates this setting—depending on the underlying assumptions.

For decades, prophets and apostles reaffirmed these teachings about the New York Cumorah. For those of us who grew up in the LDS Church before the 1990s, the New York Cumorah was a well-established given. Newer members, however, know little or nothing about the New York Cumorah. For example, the Church history book *Saints*, volume 1, completely erased Cumorah from the historical record.

Why? What changed?

―――――

In the early 1900s, a book titled *Cumorah Revisited* criticized the prevailing hemispheric model of Book of Mormon geography. This made sense, actually. In the 1842 Wentworth letter, Joseph had replaced Orson Pratt's hemispheric speculation with the declaration that Lehi's remnant were "the Indians that live in this country," a reprise of what Moroni told him the first night. People forgot or ignored that, however.

Consequently, in response to *Cumorah Revisited*, scholars rejected what Joseph and Oliver taught and determined that the Hill Cumorah of Mormon 6:6 could not be located in New York but must be in

―――――

[4] All these references are cited in the body of this book. For one of many detailed discussions, see Cameron J. Packer, "A Study of the Hill Cumorah," https://scholarsarchive.byu.edu/cgi/viewcontent.cgi?article=6007&context=etd

southern Mexico. They developed what I call the Mesoamerican/two-Cumorahs theory (M2C), reasoning that the New York Cumorah was merely a tradition—a false tradition—based on ignorant speculation.

Naturally, the scholars taught M2C to their students, and through the academic cycle, pursuant to Alma 12:9, within two generations the New York Cumorah was forgotten and M2C became the de facto—and ubiquitous—explanation of the Book of Mormon. Bias confirmation has produced plenty of supporting evidence.

If you accept M2C, that's fine with me. If you don't think geography matters, that's also fine with me. I won't persuade you otherwise. I only encourage people to make informed decisions.

———

One thing that attracted me to this topic was what I considered academic abuse of faithful Church members who still believed what the prophets taught. For years, the credentialed class attacked and ridiculed those who disagreed with them about Book of Mormon geography. They sought to censor alternative ideas and evidence that contradicted M2C. I investigated, concluded the scholars were defensive because their work was riddled with logical and factual fallacies, and blogged about the problems I saw. But blogs have limited usefulness.

This presented a dilemma. On one hand, I'm happy for people to believe whatever they want. I don't want to disturb the faith of those whose beliefs are interwoven with M2C. They deserve respect—as do those who disagree with them.

On the other hand, many people are troubled by the rejection of the teachings of the prophets about the New York Cumorah and other topics. Some are troubled by the logical and factual fallacies that I observed and seek an explanation of the Book of Mormon that corroborates and vindicates the teachings of the prophets.

I don't see this as a case of right vs. wrong. Instead, the topic calls for recognizing multiple operating hypotheses. That will lead to mutual understanding and respect, despite disagreement.

Harmony in diversity, leading to the establishment of Zion.

———

From my perspective, just as the Book of Mormon is "the keystone of our religion,"[5] the New York Cumorah is the keystone of the divine authenticity of the Book of Mormon. It is the only specific New World touchstone between the modern era and the ancient Jaredites and Nephites that has been identified by prophets and apostles.

Yet this is not a book about Book of Mormon geography, per se. Originally, I contemplated writing a detailed, evidence-based presentation on why people should embrace the New York Cumorah. There is plenty of material. But by now, we all can see that facts don't really matter. People believe whatever they want and then find facts to reinforce their beliefs.

Instead, I use Cumorah as a case study. You can adapt the principles of analysis and thinking described in this book to explore other topics. I won't try to persuade you or tell you what to think. Naturally, we will review internal and external evidence about the New York Cumorah, but this is not a comprehensive resource.[6] I'll offer information and interpretations you might not have considered. Then you'll make up your own mind by making informed decisions.

**Key point: the New York Cumorah does not determine where other events took place.**

The teachings of the prophets about the New York Cumorah are consistent and persistent. But they have also taught that we cannot specifically identify where other events took place. That makes sense because there are so many real-world locations that may fit the text.

Whatever our beliefs, let us all strive to humbly "receive knowledge from time to time." D&C 1:28. There is surely more to discover—if we're open to it.

---

[5] Quotation from the journal of Wilford Woodruff, attributed to Joseph Smith, Jr.

[6] The Bibliography lists some resources. A visual resource is https://www.mobom.org/known-bom-locations. A comprehensive reference is https://stepbystep.alancminer.com/. If you're interested in my explanation of how the text of the Book of Mormon describes a geographical setting consistent with the New York Cumorah, see my book *Moroni's America*.

# Cumorah in the scriptures

### Mormon, Chapter 6

2 And I, Mormon, wrote an epistle unto the king of the Lamanites, and desired of him that he would grant unto us that we might gather together our people unto the land of **Cumorah** [Camorah, 1830 edition], by a hill which was called Cumorah, and there we could [would 1830 edition] give them battle.

3 And it came to pass that the king of the Lamanites did grant unto me the thing which I desired.

4 And it came to pass that we did march forth to the land of **Cumorah**, and we did pitch our tents around about the hill **Cumorah**; and it was in a land of many waters, rivers, and fountains; and here we had hope to gain advantage over the Lamanites.

5 And when three hundred and eighty and four years had passed away, we had gathered in all the remainder of our people unto the land of **Cumorah**.

6 And it came to pass that when we had gathered in all our people in one to the land of **Cumorah**, behold I, Mormon, began to be old; and knowing it to be the last struggle of my people, and having been commanded of the Lord that I should not suffer the records which had been handed down by our fathers, which were sacred, to fall into the hands of the Lamanites, (for the Lamanites would destroy them) therefore I made this record out of the plates of Nephi, and hid up in the hill **Cumorah** all the records which had been entrusted to me by the hand of the Lord, save it were these few plates which I gave unto my son Moroni.

### Mormon, Chapter 8

2 And now it came to pass that after the great and tremendous battle at **Cumorah**, behold, the Nephites who had escaped into the country southward were hunted by the Lamanites, until they were all destroyed.

**Ether, Chapter 15**

11 And it came to pass that the army of Coriantumr did pitch their tents by the hill **Ramah**; and it was that same hill where my father Mormon did hide up the records unto the Lord, which were sacred.

12 And it came to pass that they did gather together all the people upon all the face of the land, who had not been slain, save it was Ether.

**Doctrine and Covenants, Section 128**

20 And again, what do we hear? Glad tidings from **Cumorah**! Moroni, an angel from heaven, declaring the fulfilment of the prophets—the book to be revealed. A voice of the Lord in the wilderness of Fayette, Seneca county, declaring the three witnesses to bear record of the book!

———

For a list of resources about the Book of Mormon, and Cumorah specifically, see the Bibliography at the end of this book.

# Part One: Why a Case for Cumorah?

Around 100 BC, a lawyer named Alma presented a case before the highest court in the land—a king named Mosiah.

> And now it came to pass that the persecutions which were inflicted on the church by the unbelievers became so great that the church began to murmur, and complain to their leaders concerning the matter; and they did complain to Alma. And **Alma laid the case before their king, Mosiah**.
> And Mosiah consulted with his priests.
> (Mosiah 27:1)

Notice, Mosiah did not make the decision alone. He wisely sought input and advice, other perspectives he might not have otherwise been aware of. Effective decision makers have a certain flexibility that Mosiah exemplified.

That approach to resolving cases is the focus of this book.

This is not a book about geography, Church history, or scriptural interpretation, although it involves those and other elements. Rather, this is a book about how to avoid thinking errors, prioritize values, and solve problems, using the Hill Cumorah as a case study.

One approach: the prophets vs. scholars framework. You can accept the teachings of the prophets and ignore everything else. Or you can parse the teachings of the prophets to find inconsistencies that can be reconciled and rectified only by credentialed experts.

Another approach: you can debate various interpretations of the text and the relevant sciences. I understand the appeal of such approaches—I've done plenty of that myself—but these debates typically just reinforce prior beliefs.

Focusing on who said what and when, or which evidence constitutes a "correspondence" to which interpretation of the text, is an exercise in tail chasing. Ultimately, we can persuade ourselves to believe whatever we want, and we employ a variety of techniques to justify our beliefs. If you're interested in pro and con comparisons, I've included a few in Appendix 4. Appendix 6 includes analysis of the arguments made over the years. But in this book, I hope to offer a case for Cumorah that you may not have considered before.

Because of its provenance, the Book of Mormon presents a case entirely different from the Bible. Although many questions about biblical historicity remain, the main settings are known because they have been continuously occupied and well documented for thousands of years. We all know where Jerusalem is. We know where the Sea of Galilee is. We know where Egypt is, and so forth.

Knowing the geography, however, does not prove the spiritual events took place. We can visit the Sea of Galilee but there is no evidence of miracles that took place in that area. Consequently, although knowing the geography and historicity of the Bible corroborates the message, it does not prove the message is true. Physical settings do not remove the need for faith.

Believing the spiritual events of the Book of Mormon would require faith even if we knew where the events took place. The difference: if we demonstrate the Book of Mormon is an accurate and actual history of real people, then we know for certain it was preserved and translated by the power of God because there is no earthly explanation for Joseph Smith to have produced an accurate history.

Conversely, not knowing where the historical events took place—actually, having no idea where things happened—makes it more difficult to accept the spiritual events.

———

I'm making a case for Cumorah to make space for those who still believe what the prophets have taught, but I don't exclude alternative views that people choose to embrace.

Legal cases are entertaining because they provide fascinating insights into human behavior, but the intrigue comes from uncertainty about the outcome. No one can resist wondering *what happened, who did it,* and *what will happen next?*

Because people are unclear about Cumorah, we could call this the case of the missing Cumorah. I'm not going to "solve" the Cumorah case for you—although I will share my own conclusions. Instead, I'll show you a way to effectively consider variables and possibilities so you can reach your own conclusions.

To make informed decisions, we need not only complete information, but we need to consider alternative explanations and avoid thinking errors—including our own preconceptions. We will seek to understand and explain multiple sides of an issue, pro and con, before we reach a conclusion.

We also recognize that we each have a starting point—a bias, a perspective, a leaning. You have yours and I have mine. I approach this case from the position of a faithful, believing Latter-day Saint with experience and training as a lawyer, educator, businessman, artist, and author, each of which informs my analysis.

I follow this adage: trust, but verify.

I'm also setting aside spiritual knowledge or confirmation, as essential as that is, for the obvious reason that people obtain spiritual convictions of conflicting ideas that they each consider true.

By the end, you may or may not agree with my conclusions—and that's fine with me. You might disagree with me at various points along the way. Also fine. But you will gain some insights into the thinking process that will help you in whatever endeavors you're pursuing.

———

Let's return to the case Alma presented to Mosiah. The result of Mosiah considering multiple perspectives was a ruling that extended beyond the relief Alma sought.

> And it came to pass that king Mosiah sent a proclamation throughout the land round about that there should not any unbeliever persecute any of those who belonged to the church of God. [what Alma desired]

And there was a strict command throughout all the churches that there should be no persecutions among them, that there should be an equality among all men; [the ruling did not apply only to unbelievers]

That they should let no pride nor haughtiness disturb their peace; that every man should esteem his neighbor as himself, laboring with their own hands for their support. [a rule to prohibit religious people from provoking unbelievers]

Yea, and all their priests and teachers should labor with their own hands for their support, in all cases save it were in sickness, or in much want; and doing these things, they did abound in the grace of God. [another rule aimed at complaints from nonbelievers]
(Mosiah 27:2–5)

King Mosiah's judgment is a model of assimilating multiple perspectives with the objective of establishing harmony among diversity. I think a complete airing of the Cumorah case can lead to similar empathetic harmony among believers today.

## What it means to make a case

To "make a case" does not mean to define or reveal objective truth. It means presenting a set of facts and explanations (arguments) to establish a working hypothesis. A plausible scenario. A framework for understanding what we know of reality. An approximation of truth.

The factfinder, such as a judge, jury, commission, etc., weighs the evidence and explanations according to a standard of proof. Whichever party has the burden of proof must present a case that amounts to (i) a preponderance of the evidence, (ii) clear and convincing evidence, or (iii) proof beyond a reasonable doubt.

In the case of Cumorah, each person is the factfinder and each applies the standard of proof he/she deems appropriate. A nonbeliever would likely insist on proof beyond a reasonable doubt to establish the divine authenticity of the Book of Mormon. Some believers would require proof beyond a reasonable doubt to reject the teachings of the prophets, while other believers would require a lesser standard.

Early in their education, lawyers learn they don't understand a case unless and until they can effectively represent two or more sides of the controversy.

After working as a prosecutor, I became a criminal defense lawyer for a time (until one of my clients tried to murder me). A police investigator I had worked with previously asked how I could sleep now that I was defending criminals.

The question surprised me. It seemed natural to me to represent a completely different perspective in these criminal cases, but I recognize my attitude was part of my training and experience. I responded that under the Constitution, everyone is entitled to a defense, but the investigator remained unpersuaded.

There are situations in which a case can be made for a proposition we don't support. But we should understand the case anyway.

The Gospel itself consists of making a case for mortality as part of a broader existence. The Gospel makes a case for trials, challenges, disappointments, etc. as being for our own good. It makes a case for illness, injury, disease. It makes a case for conversion and change and renewal. It makes a case for new perspectives.

## Why Cumorah?

Cumorah is an excellent case study because the debate about Cumorah presents a stark contrast.

Debates about the "narrow neck of land," the location of Sidon and which way it flows, where Lehi landed in the New World, the site of Zarahemla—all of these and more involve interpretation, speculation, inferences, and uncertainty. Except in rare cases, people come out of a debate with their biases confirmed.

It's different with Cumorah.

Cumorah is the only Book of Mormon site that prophets have identified. They have taught the New York Cumorah consistently and persistently for decades. The Cumorah question provides a contrast between the teachings of the prophets and the teachings of the scholars.

There is no other case like it. Evaluating Cumorah forces us to think about how we think.

## Cold cases

A hundred years ago—in 1920—a new edition of the Book of Mormon was published in Salt Lake City by the Church of Jesus Christ of Latter-day Saints. Among other things, it deleted footnotes from the 1879 edition that had explained geographical references in the text.

The 1879 notes, prepared by Elder Orson Pratt, openly speculated about Lehi's landing place, the location of Zarahemla, and the modern identity of the River Sidon.

But the notes did not speculate about the location of Cumorah.

The footnote to Mormon 6:2 declared: "The hill Cumorah is in Manchester, Ontario Co., N. York."[7]

Meetings about Book of Mormon geography were held at Church headquarters in Salt Lake City. People presented their theories. A hemispheric theory. Two limited geography theories, one based on Panama, the other based in Mexico.

The Brethren saw no resolution. The decision was made to not take a position on the issue. In the ensuing 100 years, not much has changed—officially.

In legal terms, Cumorah has become a cold case.

But cold cases can still be solved.

Let me tell you about my experience with such a case.

———

One evening I received a phone call. My youngest brother had been murdered. Some kids found him out in the desert, still alive, but barely. The paramedics tried to save him.

---

[7] See an online version of the 1879 edition here:
https://en.calameo.com/read/0015546559701eea3f55f?page=3

He whispered, "I know who shot me."

They told him to wait for the police.

But he died before they arrived.

Leads in the case fizzled out. It entered the cold case file.

Decades later, new funding arrived. They re-examined the evidence and discovered previously undetected fingerprints on one of the checks from the robbery. A court decision had changed the law to allow testimony from a key witness.

A defendant was identified, charged, and extradited from another state, to the complete shock of his new wife and kids.

I attended the trial.

The key witness testified that one evening many years previously, she had been watching television with her husband. Their baby was asleep.

The news showed a photo of my brother, seeking leads. She told her husband, "I knew that guy. The police interviewed me because I thought it might have been some guys I knew who killed him."

"It wasn't them," her husband said.

"How do you know?"

"Because I killed him."

She had, in fact, married one of the murderers. She had demanded a divorce, but the law of spousal immunity had prevented her from testifying against her former husband.

Now, all these years later, she was testifying about what happened. Her ex-husband was convicted and sentenced.

In this case, as in so many others, the revelations of facts changed worldviews, some quick as a whiplash, others over decades. The changes came, welcome or not, as truth emerged.

The challenge—and fun—of historical research is the realization that the past is, literally, in the past. We can't change the past. The best we can do is discover more facts and offer new (and hopefully more accurate) inferences to reach more accurate conclusions about what actually happened.

From the moment the murderers shot my brother, the facts never changed. What did change was new technology and new focus that allowed the facts to come out.

That's the story of Cumorah, too. It's a cold case that merits another look. In this book we will consider the latest external evidence, but we will also "extradite" witnesses and evidence from the past to enlighten our current understanding.

One example. Like the latent fingerprints uncovered twenty-five years later, a critical clue in the case of Cumorah is the messenger who took the Harmony plates to Cumorah. Why? If you don't know to what I'm referring, we'll discuss it in Part Five: Cumorah and the Two Sets of Plates.

## Shifts in perception

> And they reasoned among themselves, saying, It is because we have no bread.
> And when Jesus knew it, he saith unto them, Why reason ye, because ye have no bread? perceive ye not yet, neither understand?
> (Mark 8:16–17)

Here, Jesus pointed out that poor information led to poor reasoning and a lack of understanding. He offered a shift in perception by providing better information.

Although people have different opinions about many subjects, sometimes our opinions can converge when we access better information. President Russell M. Nelson famously taught that "good inspiration is based upon good information."[8]

| Good inspiration is based upon good information. |
| --- |

We all grow up with perceptions of the world that we inherit from our parents, extended families, peers, and society at large. We take them for granted, like the law of gravity. Sometimes we learn those

---

[8] Russell M. Nelson, April 2018 General Conference, https://www.lds.org/general-conference/2018/04/revelation-for-the-church-revelation-for-our-lives?lang=eng

perceptions were mistakes or misunderstandings.

The Book of Mosiah relates a shift in perception coming from better information that took place when Ammon was captured by King Limhi's guards.

> And now, when Ammon saw that he was permitted to speak, he went forth and bowed himself before the king; and rising again he said: O king, I am very thankful before God this day that I am yet alive, and am permitted to speak; and I will endeavor to speak with boldness;
>
> For I am assured that **if ye had known me** ye would not have suffered that I should have worn these bands. For I am Ammon, and am a descendant of Zarahemla, and have come up out of the land of Zarahemla to inquire concerning our brethren, whom Zeniff brought up out of that land.
> (Mosiah 7:12–13)

"If ye had known me." Limhi's ignorance of Ammon's identity nearly cost Ammon his life. Once he learned the facts, Limhi's perception changed completely.

Usually "old facts" persist despite changed circumstances.

When I was young, we were terrified of Russians.

I was at a scout camp about 10 miles from the Czechoslovakian border when the Russians invaded Czechoslovakia in 1968. Our family visited Berlin and looked over the barbwire wall to see the no-man's-land where people fleeing East Germany were shot to death. At one point in his Air Force career, my father worked for the Special Activities Group in Europe, which was basically an espionage outfit. He interviewed defectors from the Soviet Union. He told us kids that if we saw him in public, we should pretend we didn't know him.

You can imagine what images of Russians I conjured up.

When I was in college, I met an actual Russian for the first time. I remember being nervous to talk with him, but despite his accent, he seemed like an ordinary guy. My perception started to shift.

Still, the Soviet Union was a deadly threat to America.

Changes in geopolitics gave me opportunities for a new and better perspective. Years later, after the Soviet Union disbanded, I traveled to Russia several times on business and worked closely with Russians. I attended Church services in Moscow in a hall that had been the local headquarters for the Communist Party. That was close to whiplash-paced change.

If you've imagined the Book of Mormon in a Mayan setting—and who hasn't, given all the pyramid-themed artwork—you're in for a dramatic change when you begin thinking of Jaredites and Nephites in New York, Ohio, Illinois, Tennessee, and so forth.

Small changes in perspective can have long-lasting impact. Over a dinner of stroganoff in St. Petersburg, my Russian associate mentioned he had visited Antarctica when he served in the Russian Navy.

"I've always wanted to visit Antarctica," I said.

He looked genuinely puzzled. "Why would you want to go there?"

"To see the penguins."

He set down his fork and leaned back in his chair with a disgusted look. "I *hate* penguins."

"How could anyone hate penguins?" I asked, thinking of their tuxedo coloring and the delightful way they walk, hop and swim.

"That's all we had to eat!" he said. "Six months, nothing but penguins."

Years later, when my wife and I visited Antarctica, we watched penguins hop on and off icebergs, slide through pools of water, and generally put on a great show. We went ashore and walked through several penguin colonies.

I discovered why my Russian friend hated penguins. They stink like dead fish!

In Appendix 6 of this book, I discuss some of the scholarly arguments that have been used to reject the New York Cumorah.

———

Regarding Cumorah, my perception dramatically changed when I learned new facts that led to a completely different understanding of both the text of the Book of Mormon and the relevant extrinsic evidence. For decades I envisioned the Book of Mormon in a Mesoamerican setting. Then I learned about a new perspective, popularly called the "Heartland" model, that puts Book of Mormon events in Illinois, Ohio, Tennessee—and New York.

It was a completely new idea for me to learn about the ancient civilizations in what is now the United States.

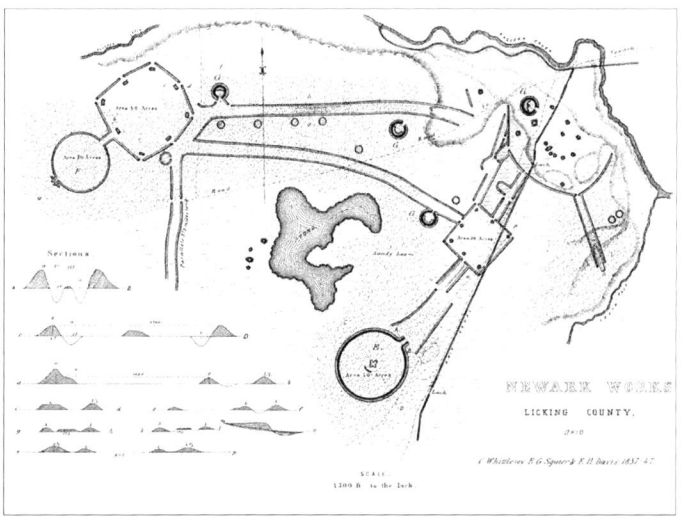

Figure 2 - Earthworks, Newark, Ohio
Squier and Davis engraving, 1848

Alice Beck Kehoe, an anthropologist and archaeologist who has focused on Native Americans in the U.S. and Canada, summarized discoveries into ancient North America.

> Around two thousand years ago, extraordinary constructions appeared on the landscapes of the Ohio Valley. Precisely engineered geometric figures so immense that one encloses a full-size golf course, four-square-mile sets of huge geometric embankments, figures linked by orientation and sight-lines over thirty miles—the scale of Ohio Valley Middle Woodland building is truly stupendous. Nowhere else in the world are there so many,

such exact and cosmically huge geometric constructions of no apparent practical use.[9]

If you're not familiar with these civilizations and their connections with the Book of Mormon, we will review them in Parts Four and Five.

## Simplicity, complexity, simplicity

Oliver Wendell Holmes reportedly observed, "I would not give a fig for the simplicity on this side of complexity. But I would give my life for the simplicity on the other side of complexity."

Typically, we first approach a problem with a naïve simplicity. The more we dig into it, complexity arises from new data, conflicts, obstacles and other challenges. We may study the problem, do our own research, consult experts, etc.

Eventually, on the other side of the complexity, we reach a higher level of understanding. Our views are informed. We have good information. We regain simplicity at a higher level.

The model creates a bell curve.

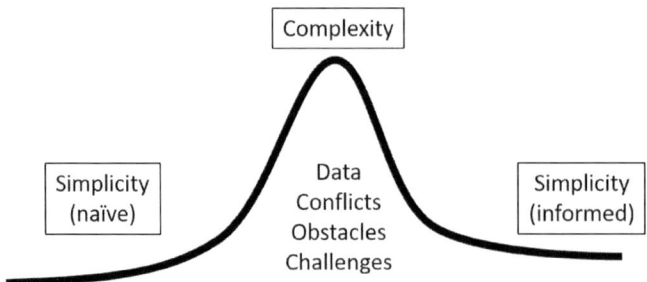

Figure 3 - Simplicity, complexity, simplicity

For lack of information, Limhi simply assumed Ammon was an

---

[9] Alice Beck Kehoe, *America Before the European Invasions*, (Longman, London, UK 2002): 66

enemy. Fortunately for Ammon, Limhi's curiosity led him to seek more information (complexity). Once he discovered the truth, Limhi saw the simple explanation and he was "exceedingly glad." (verse 14)

A good example of this is the question of the translation of the Book of Mormon. Joseph and Oliver taught that Joseph translated with the Urim and Thummim. **Simplicity**. Others said Joseph used a seer stone he put in a hat and didn't even use the plates. **Complexity**.

I worked through the evidence, considering all the data, conflicts, obstacles, and challenges, and ended up with an informed, simple solution: Joseph did translate the plates with the Urim and Thummim. But he also demonstrated the process with the seer stone because he couldn't show people the plates or the Urim and Thummim. Observers related what they saw for specific reasons that made sense at the time. Now, all the historical accounts make sense, and Joseph and Oliver told the truth.[10] As we'll see, Cumorah is another good example of simplicity leading to complexity leading to simplicity.

## Thesis, antithesis, synthesis

Holmes' oft-quoted conceptual model is similar to the framework of thesis-antithesis-synthesis.

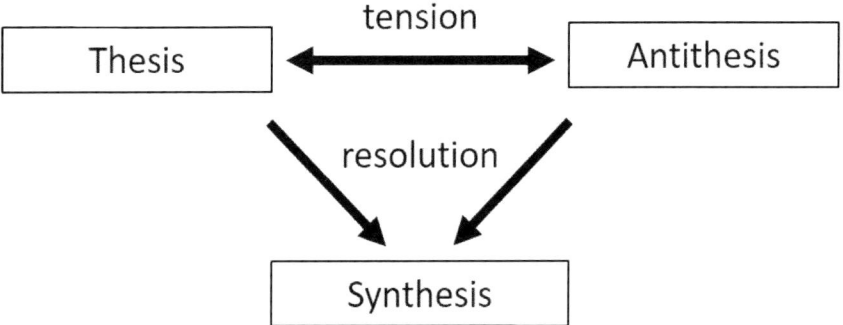

Figure 4 - Thesis, antithesis, synthesis

---

[10] My detailed book about the translation is *A Man that Can Translate*.

You start with an idea—a thesis. An opposite idea arises—the antithesis. You could adopt the thesis or the antithesis, or you could consider both and come up with a synthesis of the two.

The New York Cumorah began with simple declarations from Joseph Smith and Oliver Cowdery—a simple thesis.

The thesis was taught from the pulpit, locally and in General Conference. It was taught in Church magazines and books.

Then, scholars added complexity. They studied the text and determined the distances involved were smaller than previously realized. They assumed most events took place in Central America, and based on that assumption, they sought and found extrinsic evidence from archaeology, anthropology, and other sciences.

Their evidence led them to the conclusion that Cumorah had to be in southern Mexico. They developed the Mesoamerican/two-Cumorahs theory (M2C)—the antithesis of the New York Cumorah.

The antithesis all but obscured the thesis. Decades of persistent advocacy succeeded. Now, few believers even know about the New York Cumorah.

But the tension remains because the historical record is easily available for everyone to see.

Perhaps a synthesis of the prophets and the scholars can lead to resolution of the conflict. By embracing both the prophets and the relevant sciences, we may be able to reach an informed simplicity that sustains what Joseph and Oliver taught all along.

## Sticky ideas (traditions)

I say unto you, my sons, were it not for these things, which have been kept and preserved by the hand of God, that we might read and understand of his mysteries, and have his commandments always before our eyes, that even our fathers would have dwindled in unbelief, and we should have been like unto our brethren, the Lamanites, who know nothing concerning these things, or even do not believe them when they are taught them, because of **the traditions of their fathers, which are not correct.**

(Mosiah 1:5)

Nevertheless, they hardened their hearts, saying unto him: Behold, we know that thou art Alma; and we know that thou art high priest over the church which thou hast established in many parts of the land, according to your tradition; and we are not of thy church, and **we do not believe in such foolish traditions.**
(Alma 8:11)

This juxtaposition of competing traditions is one of the delightful insights in the Book of Mormon. The Nephites said the Lamanite traditions of their fathers were "not correct," a proposition the Lamanites would completely disagree with. Nonbelievers said religious Nephites believed in 'foolish traditions."

Of course, the Nephites claimed their own traditions were correct.

And thousands were brought to the knowledge of the Lord, yea, thousands were brought to believe in the traditions of the Nephites; and they were taught the records and prophecies which were handed down even to the present time.
(Alma 23:5)

Think of your own beliefs. How many are based on traditions you inherited or grew up with? How would you know if they were correct or incorrect, foolish or wise?

A good example is your native language. You inherited that language from your parents and your society. We learn to articulate our thoughts and feelings through the language we inherit. Our language is a filter on reality that affects everything we think we understand.

I grew up in the United States speaking English. I'm writing this book in English. Although I've studied other languages, I'm far more comfortable in English. I can't say I *chose* English because it is more accurate. In fact, once in a while I'll think or say something in French or German because it feels like a better way to express it than in English. But my comfort in English is a result of the tradition I grew up with, not a product of an informed decision.

You can probably relate to one of my family's traditional beliefs. In our family, Chevron gas stations were the enemy. My father refused to go there. He was a pilot in the Air Force and I always assumed the different brands of gasoline were either allies or enemies, so I learned to avoid Chevron.

Later I learned that my father's anti-Chevron bias originated when a Chevron station fixed a flat tire that went flat shortly thereafter. And yet, to this day, I feel an aversion to Chevron gas stations. Whenever there's an alternative, I don't go to Chevron.

———

People everywhere tend to be more comfortable with the traditions they inherited than with other traditions. I have lived in France, Germany, the Philippines, China and Mauritius. I have worked in a dozen other countries and visited dozens more. Everywhere people have traditions that provide social cohesion to make their societies functional.

Fortunately, the modern world enables people to borrow good ideas from other cultures and traditions, but stark differences remain.

In the context of Cumorah, believers have been raised with different traditions. Older people believed Cumorah was in New York. Younger people believe it is in Mexico. An increasing number of believers question whether there ever was a literal hill called Cumorah.

Everyone can get along despite these different traditions. We can serve one another, teach and live correct principles, repent and strive to become more Christlike and help to establish Zion.

Yet, as Alma 23:5 shows, sometimes when people are "brought to believe" in a different tradition, they find greater joy and fulfillment.

## Summary of cases for and against New York

You probably want a summary of the cases for and against New York. I agree it's a good idea to get an overview, even if some of the details are obscure or unclear at this point.

The objective is to pursue unity among diversity. There is no right or wrong answer. You will weigh the various facts and explanations differently from others, but at least you will be making an informed decision. There is no right or wrong answer.

After you read the rest of the book, you can come back here and see if your answers are any different.

### Which Cumorah narrative makes sense to you?

In evaluating the Cumorah alternatives, here is a comparison chart to consider. It lists the alternative explanations of well-known accounts in Church history.

Note that "Mesoamerica" and "M2C" are proxies for *every* theory that places Cumorah somewhere other than in New York. Some people believe Panama is the setting. Others advocate for Baja, Chile, Venezuela—there are many others. Substitute your preference whenever you see Mesoamerica or M2C.

The table presents facts and explanations about the two alternatives so you can compare your own beliefs and make up your own mind. Which do you find more compatible with your beliefs? Which is more compatible with the historical evidence? Which is best corroborated by the sciences?

Circle each box that makes sense to you.

| Cumorah not in New York | Cumorah in New York |
|---|---|
| 1. Mormon and Moroni lived in Mesoamerica. | 1. Mormon and Moroni lived in North America. |
| 2. Mormon wrote his abridgment somewhere in Mesoamerica and hid up all the Nephite records in a repository in the Hill Cumorah (Mormon 6:6), a hill somewhere in southern Mexico, before giving "these few plates" to Moroni. | 2. Mormon wrote his abridgment in western New York and hid up all the Nephite records in a repository in the Hill Cumorah (Mormon 6:6), the hill near Palmyra, New York, before giving "these few plates" to Moroni. |
| 3. Thinking he would not live long, | 3. Thinking he would not live long, |

31

| | |
|---|---|
| Moroni adds a couple of chapters to his father's record. | Moroni adds a couple of chapters to his father's record. |
| Then he travels 3,400 miles to New York, and hides the plates in the stone box, thinking he would not live long. | Then he hides the plates in the stone box he built in the hill Cumorah in New York, separate from his father's depository in the same hill. |
| Or, he keeps the plates with him while he roams around Mesoamerica for decades before taking them to New York. | |
| Or he hides them somewhere else until he is ready to take them 3,400 miles to New York. | |
| Or he transports the plates to New York as a resurrected being. | |
| 4. Later, Moroni retrieves the plates of Ether from the repository in southern Mexico and abridges them. | 4. Later, Moroni retrieves the plates of Ether from the depository in New York and abridges them. |
| He adds the abridgment to his father's abridgment, along with a sealed portion, and hides the plates again in New York. | He adds this abridgment to his father's abridgment, along with a sealed portion and his own commentary, and puts this expanded collection of plates back into his stone box. He returns the original plates of Ether to the depository in the Hill Cumorah in New York. |
| Or, Moroni abridges the plates of Ether right after his father died, and the plates of Ether were among the few his father gave him, and after he abridges them, he returns the original plates to his father's depository. | |
| Or the plates of Ether are the sealed portion. | |
| 5. Later, Moroni returns to the | 5. Later, Moroni returns to the |

| | |
|---|---|
| repository in southern Mexico and gets a sermon and letters from his father. He adds this material to his final comments—the Book of Moroni—and returns to New York to put the finished record back in the stone box.<br><br>Or, Moroni had his father's writings with him all along and kept them with him when he died, so they are buried with him. | depository in New York and gets a sermon and letters from his father. He adds this material to his final comments—the Book of Moroni—finishes the title page, and puts the abridged record back into the stone box. He returns the source material to the depository. |
| 6. Moroni visits Joseph Smith in 1823 and tells him the record was "written and deposited" not far from Joseph's home. But this is a mistake because the record was written in Central America and deposited in New York. Joseph or Oliver misunderstood or erred when they quoted Moroni. | 6. Moroni visits Joseph Smith in 1823 and tells him the record was "written and deposited" not far from Joseph's home. Moroni accurately describes where the record was written. https://www.josephsmithpapers.org/paper-summary/history-1834-1836/69) |
| 7. In early 1827, on his way home from Manchester, Joseph encounters Moroni, who chastises him. When Lucy Mack Smith relates the account, she quotes Joseph saying "as I passed by the hill of Cumorah, where the plates are." Lucy's account is unreliable because she didn't dictate it until 1845, after Joseph was martyred. She merely adopted a false tradition about Cumorah. | 7. In early 1827, on his way home from Manchester, Joseph encounters Moroni, who chastises him. When Lucy Mack Smith relates the account, she quotes Joseph saying "as I passed by the hill of Cumorah, where the plates are." Lucy's account is reliable even though she didn't dictate it until 1845, after Joseph was martyred, because she was an eye witness and had related the history many times during Joseph's lifetime. |
| 8. Parley P. Pratt and David Whitmer both claimed that the hill was called Cumorah anciently, but they were merely relating a false tradition. | 8. Parley P. Pratt and David Whitmer both claimed that the hill was called Cumorah anciently because that's what Joseph and/or Oliver told them. |
| 9a. Joseph Smith obtained the | 9a. Joseph Smith obtained the |

| | |
|---|---|
| abridged record of the Nephites and the Jaredites from Moroni's stone box. | abridged record of the Nephites and the Jaredites from Moroni's stone box. |
| 9b. He translated part of these plates in Harmony and gave them back to Moroni before leaving for Fayette. | 9b. He translated the abridged plates in Harmony and gave them back to a messenger before leaving for Fayette because he was finished with them. |
| 9c. The Lord told him to translate the engravings on the plates of Nephi (D&C 10), even though he had reached the end of the plates (the Title Page) and hadn't yet found these plates of Nephi.<br><br>Or, the Lord told him to translate the engravings on the plates of Nephi but Joseph wasn't using the plates anyway (they were covered with a cloth and he was using a seer stone in a hat) so it didn't matter whether he had the plates of Nephi in Harmony. | 9c. The Lord told him to translate the engravings on the plates of Nephi (D&C 10), but he didn't have those yet. |
| 10. In Harmony or Fayette, Joseph translated the Title Page from the last leaf of the plates. He had it printed and delivered to the U.S. federal district court in New York as part of his copyright application. | 10. In Harmony, Joseph translated the Title Page from the last leaf of the plates. He had it printed and delivered to the U.S. federal district court in New York as part of his copyright application. |
| 11. On the way from Harmony to Fayette, David Whitmer said he, Joseph and Oliver encountered an old man bearing the plates who said he was heading for Cumorah. Joseph said it was one of the three Nephites.<br><br>But David was mistaken because he | 11. On the way from Harmony to Fayette, David Whitmer said he, Joseph and Oliver encountered an old man bearing the plates who said he was heading for Cumorah. Joseph said it was one of the three Nephites.<br><br>This was the messenger who had |

| | |
|---|---|
| conflated the false tradition of the New York Cumorah with another unspecified event.<br><br>Or David misremembered, intentionally misled, etc.<br><br>The *Saints* book omits this account and David Whitmer's explanation that this messenger was one of the Three Nephites who took the Harmony plates to Cumorah because David was confused or wrong. It was actually Moroni. | the Harmony plates and was returning them to the repository in Cumorah because Joseph was finished with them.<br><br>David repeated this account several times, and it was included in an official report to the Quorum of the Twelve by Joseph F. Smith, who interviewed David.<br><br>The *Saints* book omits this account because its editors censored all historical accounts about the New York Cumorah to accommodate M2C. |
| 12. In Fayette, a messenger showed the plates to Mary Whitmer.<br><br>Then the messenger returned the Harmony plates to Joseph.<br><br>The *Saints* book claims this was Moroni because Mary's grandson said his grandmother was mistaken, and because typewritten notes in 1918 attributed to Joseph F. Smith say it was Moroni. | 12. In Fayette, a messenger showed the plates to Mary Whitmer.<br><br>Then the messenger gave Joseph the small plates of Nephi which he had brought from the repository in Cumorah.<br><br>David said the messenger who showed the plates to his mother was the same one who took the plates to Cumorah. Mary Whitmer called him "Brother Nephi." The 3 Nephites were among the 12 disciples, one of whom was named Nephi. |
| 13. In Fayette, Joseph translated the small plates of Nephi (1 Nephi – Words of Mormon). | 13. In Fayette, Joseph translated the small plates of Nephi (1 Nephi – Words of Mormon). |
| 14. Joseph and Oliver Cowdery and others had multiple visions of Mormon's depository in the "real" Hill Cumorah, which is somewhere in southern Mexico. | 14. Joseph and Oliver Cowdery and others actually visited Mormon's depository in the Hill Cumorah in New York and saw the stacks of plates and other Nephite artifacts. |

| | |
|---|---|
| 15. Cumorah cannot be in New York because it is a "clean hill" with no archaeological evidence. | 15. Cumorah is in New York because hundreds of artifacts, including weapons of war, have been recovered from the vicinity of the hill. |
| 16. Cumorah cannot be in New York because it is a glacial moraine that cannot contain a natural cave. | 16. Cumorah is in New York because the man-made room Oliver described can be dug into drumlins such as Cumorah, which are largely clay deposits. An actual room that matches the description given by Brigham Young, Heber C. Kimball, Wilford Woodruff and others has been found there. |
| 17a. In 1834-5, with Joseph's assistance, Oliver wrote a series of essays about Church history, published as letters in the *Messenger and Advocate*. In Letter VII, Oliver wrote that it was a fact that the final battles of the Jaredites and Nephites took place in the mile-wide valley west of Cumorah in New York. Letter VII was republished in the *Times and Seasons* and other publications and copied into Joseph's journal. | 17a. In 1834-5, with Joseph's assistance, Oliver wrote a series of essays about Church history, published as letters in the *Messenger and Advocate*. In Letter VII, Oliver wrote that it was a fact that the final battles of the Jaredites and Nephites took place in the mile-wide valley west of Cumorah in New York. Letter VII was republished in the *Times and Seasons* and other publications and copied into Joseph's journal. |
| 17b. Joseph Smith and Oliver Cowdery never claimed revelation about the location of Cumorah. They merely speculated when they called the hill Cumorah, or they adopted a false tradition started by someone else and misled the Church.<br><br>Joseph later changed his mind and, by writing or approving anonymous articles that never mentioned Cumorah, claimed the Book of | 17b. Joseph Smith and Oliver Cowdery didn't need revelation about the location of Cumorah because they visited Mormon's depository. They may also have had revelations that they didn't write or even relate. E.g., JS-H 1:73-4.<br><br>They did not mislead the Church. Joseph never changed his mind about the New York Cumorah, and never linked the Book of Mormon to Central America, through |

| | |
|---|---|
| Mormon took place in Central America and that only scholars could determine where the Book of Mormon took place. | anonymous articles or otherwise. |
| 18. All the modern prophets and apostles who have identified the Hill Cumorah as the scene of the final battles were speaking as uninspired men.<br><br>They were speculating, giving their own opinions, and they were wrong.<br><br>This includes members of the First Presidency speaking in General Conference. | 18. All the modern prophets and apostles who have identified the Hill Cumorah as the scene of the final battles were affirming what Joseph and Oliver taught and were speaking in their roles as prophets, seers and revelators.<br><br>This includes members of the First Presidency speaking in General Conference. |
| 19a. The two-Cumorahs theory originated with scholars from the Reorganized Church and was adopted and promoted by LDS scholars because it's the only explanation that fits their Mesoamerican-based limited geography theory. | 19a. The two-Cumorahs theory originated with scholars from the Reorganized Church and was adopted and promoted by LDS scholars because it's the only explanation that fits their Mesoamerican-based limited geography theory. |
| 19b. Elder Joseph Fielding Smith was wrong and unqualified when he warned the two-Cumorahs theory would cause members to become confused and disturbed in their faith in the Book of Mormon. | 19b. Elder Joseph Fielding Smith was correct and prescient when he warned the two-Cumorahs theory would cause members to become confused and disturbed in their faith in the Book of Mormon. |
| 20. The scholars' two-Cumorah theory is correct because whenever the current Brethren have a question about the Book of Mormon, they consult the scholars at BYU who promote M2C. | 20. The scholars' two-Cumorah theory doesn't fit the historical record, the affirmative declarations of Joseph and Oliver, or the prophetic statements of numerous modern prophets and apostles. |
| 21. The best way to understand the Book of Mormon is with an | 21. The best way to understand the Book of Mormon is to interpret the |

| abstract map based on the M2C interpretation of the narrow neck of land, etc. | text so it aligns with the New York Cumorah. |

Figure 5 - 3 Cumorah maps

159 - Plausible Locations of the Final Battles

Section 13: Geography in the Book of Mormon

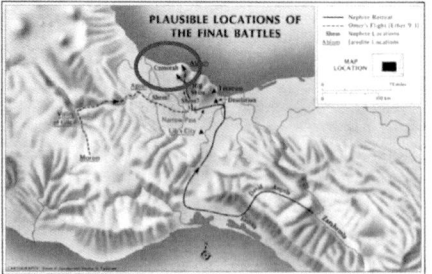

Cumorah: Mesoamerica

Cumorah: BYU abstract map

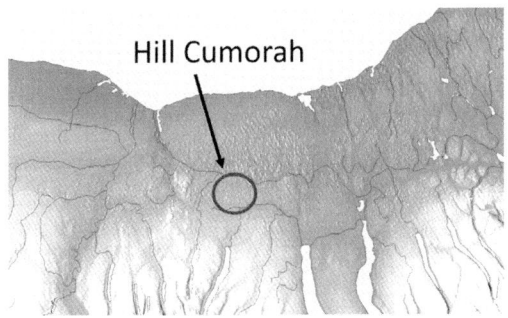

Cumorah: New York

# Part Two: How to view reality

"Truth is knowledge of things as they are, and as they were, and as they are to come." (D&C 93:24)

Philosophers have debated the nature of truth for thousands of years, and the debate continues through the present day. The scriptural definition of truth in Section 93 captures what we want to consider in this book. That definition includes two elements.

1. There is objective truth.
2. We can gain knowledge of objective truth.

By implication, we can:

1. Be ignorant of the truth.
4. Gain knowledge of things that are not true.

Setting aside philosophical objections to these propositions, when we apply this definition to Cumorah, we recognize that, as a matter of objective truth, the final battles of the Jaredites and Nephites either did or did not actually take place. If they did take place, they took place in a specific location.

We may or may not be able to gain knowledge of the truth. We might be ignorant of the truth, and/or we might gain knowledge of things that are not true. The challenge for us is to ascertain where we are in relation to each possibility.

Believers assume the final battles did take place. Nonbelievers assume they did not take place. Both groups can cite evidence to support their positions.

Believers further have different assumptions about where the battles took place and can cite evidence to support their respective positions.

These positions are the "reality" for those who believe them, but reality in this sense is subjective. This is why people can be completely convinced of conflicting realities.

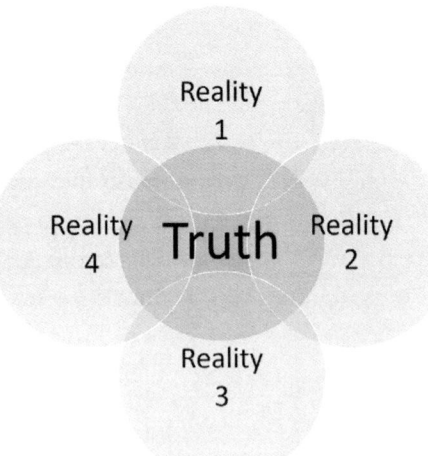

Hopefully, subjective reality overlaps truth to some extent. Sometimes our individual realities overlap and we share a reality.

Humility requires us to remain flexible, with minds as open as we can tolerate. We avoid assuming that our reality is objective truth because that would be the opposite of harmony in diversity.

If you can only imagine or explain the Book of Mormon from one perspective, and you think everyone else is wrong, seek ways to see things from others' points of view. You don't have to agree, but you should understand.

## Assumptions and Conclusions

The ancestors of our conclusions are our assumptions.

The Cumorah case involves competing assumptions. Those who accept the New York Cumorah assume Joseph Smith and Oliver Cowdery spoke the truth about what they saw and heard. Then we seek evidence and interpretations that corroborate that assumption.

Those who reject the New York Cumorah assume Joseph and Oliver made their own unfounded assumptions; i.e., they speculated. Most, but not all, people in this group further assume that Book of Mormon events took place in Central America, specifically Mesoamerica (M2C), and then seek evidence and interpretations that corroborate that assumption.

For example, I think the populations described in the Book of Mormon were relatively small compared with the assumptions made by M2C advocates, but myriad interpretations are possible given the vague references in the text. (See Part 4.)

Our respective assumptions inevitably lead to our respective conclusions. Our perceptions of the truth are usually more perception than truth.

Truth          Perception

As mortal humans, we perceive the world through filters that limit our knowledge of reality. Filters are essential because we cannot absorb everything. We see with our eyes, but our receptors are not capable of seeing the full spectrum of light. We see the perfect amount of spectrum we need to function as human beings. We use instruments to "see" other spectrums. We cannot see very small or very distant objects, so we use microscopes and telescopes to overcome the limits imposed by our visual filters.

Our senses of smell, taste, hearing and touch filter out much of reality. Dogs can smell aromas and hear sounds we cannot.

Think of your senses as metaphors for the mental and spiritual filters—some conscious, some unconscious—that impede or limit our perception and comprehension of truth. These filters include your education and experience, the environment you grew up in, the people you admire and respect, and your peers and social circles.

One way to think of this is the concept of "myside bias."

## Myside bias – bias confirmation

Bias confirmation leads us to (i) embrace information that supports or confirms our assumptions (our biases and beliefs) and (ii) filter out information that contradicts our assumptions. This is why two people can look at the identical information and reach completely different— even opposite—conclusions.

Myside bias has been explained by Keith E. Stanovich:

> People evaluate evidence, generate evidence, and test hypotheses in a manner biased toward their own prior beliefs, opinions, and attitudes…. In determining what to believe, myside bias operates by weighting new evidence more highly when it is consistent with prior beliefs and less highly when it contradicts a prior belief.
>
> This seems wrong, but it is not. Many formal analyses and arguments in philosophy of science have shown that in most situations that resemble real life, it is rational to use your prior belief in the evaluation of new evidence….
>
> What turns this situation into one of inappropriate myside bias is when a person uses, not a belief that prior evidence leads them to think is true, but instead projects a prior belief the person wants to be true despite inadequate evidence that it is, in fact, true. [11]

You can see the implications already. We naturally seek to confirm our own biases—our beliefs—and we usually don't even know we're doing it. Our minds filter out evidence that contradicts what we believe, often to the point that we don't consciously even see such evidence.

---

[11] Keith E. Stanovich, "The Bias that Divides Us," https://quillette.com/2020/09/26/the-bias-that-divides-us/

The false traditions of the Lamanites did not persist because they were obviously false, but because the Lamanites' natural bias confirmation found ways to reinforce those traditions over and over.

Think back to Holmes' simplicity-complexity-simplicity concept. The complexity element often arises because of the work of an expert who uncovers new facts, raises new issues, offers new explanations, etc.

Experts are typically "cognitively sophisticated" in the sense that they have studied topics and disciplined their minds to focus and comprehend complex situations. But that expertise comes with a particular susceptibility to myside bias.

Continuing from the Stanovich quotation above,

> … one particular bias—myside bias—sets a trap for the cognitively sophisticated. Regarding most biases, they are used to thinking—rightly— that they are less biased. However, myside thinking about your political beliefs represents an outlier bias where this is not true. This may lead to a particularly intense bias blind spot among certain cognitive elites.

> If you are a person of high intelligence, if you are highly educated, and if you are strongly committed to an ideological viewpoint, you will be highly likely to think you have thought your way to your viewpoint. And you will be even less likely than the average person to realize that you have derived your beliefs from the social groups you belong to and because they fit with your temperament and your innate psychological propensities.

In Appendix 6, I've provided an overview of some of the most prominent scholarly arguments on the topic of Cumorah. You can decide for yourself how myside bias is a factor in those arguments.

## Thinking errors: Cognitive dissonance

> And he said, Go, and tell this people, Hear ye indeed, but understand not; and see ye indeed, but perceive not. (Isaiah 6:9)

You've probably heard of cognitive dissonance. It's a psychological state that is usually invisible to people who experience it because we create our own reality that, somehow, makes sense to us, even when others do not see or understand that reality.

We can usually spot in others, though.

Cognitive dissonance was one of the triggers that led me to study the Cumorah case. I had accepted M2C for decades before I realized how many times the prophets had taught the New York Cumorah. Because I otherwise accepted what the prophets taught, the discrepancy made me uncomfortable—a classic case of cognitive dissonance.

> In the field of psychology, cognitive dissonance occurs when a person holds contradictory beliefs, ideas, or values, and is typically experienced as psychological stress when they participate in an action that goes against one or more of them. According to this theory, when two actions or ideas are not psychologically consistent with each other, people do all in their power to change them until they become consistent....
>
> They tend to make changes to justify the stressful behavior, either by adding new parts to the cognition causing the psychological dissonance (rationalization) or by avoiding circumstances and contradictory information likely to increase the magnitude of the cognitive dissonance (confirmation bias)[12]

In the case of Cumorah, people who reject the New York Cumorah experience cognitive dissonance because they want to believe the prophets even though those prophets taught the New York Cumorah. Their cognitive dissonance causes them to avoid the contradictory information, usually by taking one or more of these actions:

(i) denying the prophets ever taught that Cumorah was in New York;

(ii) rationalizing that the prophets were merely expressing their own private opinions so they could be wrong without affecting their credibility as prophets on other topics; or

(iii) censoring the teachings about the New York Cumorah, as we see in current lesson manuals, *Saints* volume one, visitors centers, etc.

Some people who accept the teachings of the prophets about the New York Cumorah experience cognitive dissonance because of the lack of evidence of millions, or hundreds of thousands, of dead bodies

---

[12] https://en.wikipedia.org/wiki/Cognitive_dissonance

in the area. We'll discuss that in Part Four, because others of us don't see a problem—we don't think the text declares such high number of participants in the final battles. Others experience cognitive dissonance because they've been taught that Joseph Smith wrote the anonymous articles in the 1842 *Times and Seasons,* but others of us think the evidence shows Joseph had nothing to do with those articles.

As you examine your own views, consider whether, and to what extent, cognitive dissonance may be pushing you toward ignoring relevant evidence or adopting irrational realities.

## Thinking errors: Logical fallacies

You can find lots of different lists of logical fallacies on the Internet. Purdue University has one that I've used with my students. The website summarizes the problem.

> Fallacies are common errors in reasoning that will undermine the logic of your argument. Fallacies can be either illegitimate arguments or irrelevant points, and are often identified because they lack evidence that supports their claim. Avoid these common fallacies in your own arguments and watch for them in the arguments of others.[13]

A common logical fallacy in the case of Cumorah is the circular argument, meaning when someone merely restates the argument instead of proving it with evidence. For example, the basic M2C argument is that the Book of Mormon took place in Mesoamerica because there are so many correspondences between Mayan and Nephite culture. This is a circular argument because the correspondences arise from an interpretation of the text that is driven by the assumption of a Mesoamerican setting.

Another common logical fallacy is ad hominem, which is an attack on the person rather than his/her opinions or arguments.

Other fallacies include the red herring, the straw man, and the appeal to authority or bandwagon appeal. If you're interested, we'll look at

---

[13] https://owl.purdue.edu/owl/general_writing/academic_writing/logic_in_argumentative_writing/fallacies.html

some examples in Appendix 6.

## Multiple working hypotheses

One way to compensate for bias confirmation and other thinking errors is the concept or method of multiple working hypotheses (MMWH). The geologist T.C. Chamberlin described MMWH in 1890. His paper was reprinted in *Science* magazine in 1965.

> There are two fundamental classes of study. The one consists in attempting to follow by close imitation the processes of previous thinkers, or to acquire by memorizing the results of their investigations. It is merely secondary, imitative, or acquisitive study.

> The other class is primary or creative study. In it the effort is to think independently, or at least individually, in the endeavor to discover new truth, or to make new combinations of truth, or at least to develop an individualized aggregation of truth. The endeavor is to think for one's self, whether the thinking lies wholly in the fields of previous thought or not....

> Intellectual methods have taken three phases in the history of progress so far... first, the method of the ruling theory; second, the method of the working hypothesis; and, third, the method of multiple working hypotheses.[14]

The case of Cumorah is well suited for multiple working hypotheses because, whether you accept or reject the New York Cumorah, there are myriad alternative possibilities for other Book of Mormon locations that, in turn, reflect back on the Cumorah question.

---

[14] T.C. Chamberlin, "The Method of Multiple Working Hypotheses," *Science*, 7 May 1965, v148, 3671: 754-759. https://science.sciencemag.org/content/148/3671/754 and http://www.sortie-nd.org/lme/Statistical%20Papers/Chamberlain_1997.pdf.

# Part Three: The History of Cumorah

Think back to Holmes' conceptual model. Applying this approach to the case of Cumorah, we have the original simple concept of the New York Cumorah, as taught by Joseph Smith and Oliver Cowdery. There was one hill Cumorah.

Because much of the information about Cumorah is unknown to modern believers, I'm going to reach back in time and extradite the accounts from history.

According to his mother, Joseph Smith, Jr., referred to the hill near his home in New York as *Cumorah* even before he obtained the plates.

> Presently he smiled, and said in a very calm tone, "I have taken the severest chastisement, that I have ever had in my life". My husband, supposing it was from some of the neighbors, was quite angry; and observed, "I would like to know what business any body has to find fault with you."
>
> "Stop, father, Stop." said Joseph, "it was the angel of the Lord— **as I passed by the hill of Cumorah, where the plates are**, the angel of the Lord met me and said, that I had not been engaged enough in the work of the Lord; that the time had come for the record to <be> brought forth; and, that I must be up and doing, and set myself about the things which God had commanded me to do.[15]

Joseph could have learned the name only from Moroni.

In 1881, David Whitmer gave an interview to the *Kansas City Journal* in which he answered this question:

---

[15] Lucy Mack Smith, *History 1845*, available online at
https://www.josephsmithpapers.org/paper-summary/lucy-mack-smith-history-1845/111

"Did Joseph Smith ever relate to you the circumstances of his finding the plates?"

"Yes, he told me that he first found the plates in the year 1823; that during the fall of 1823 he had a vision, an angel appearing to him three times in one night and telling him that there was a record of an ancient people deposited in a hill near his father's house, **called by the ancients `Cumorah,'** situated in the township of Manchester, Ontario County, N. Y. The angel pointed out the exact spot, and, sometime after, he went and found the records or plates deposited in a stone box in the hill, just as had been described to him by the angel.[16]

In his *Autobiography*, Parley P. Pratt related that Moroni called the hill in New York by the name *Cumorah.*

Heber C. Kimball visited Cumorah in 1832, shortly after his baptism, and recorded that the embankments were still present around the hill.

In 1835, Oliver Cowdery described the hill in New York where Joseph obtained the plates. He wrote:

At about one mile west rises another ridge of less height, running parallel with the former, leaving a beautiful vale between. The soil is of the first quality for the country, and under a state of cultivation, which gives a prospect at once imposing, **when one reflects on the fact, that here, between these hills, the entire power and national strength of both the Jaredites and Nephites were destroyed.**

By turning to the 529th and 530th pages of the book of Mormon you will read Mormon's account of the last great struggle of his people, **as they were encamped round this hill Cumorah.**[17]

The essays Oliver wrote were so important that Joseph had them copied into his personal history. With Joseph's approval, they were republished in the 1841 *Times and Seasons* (Nauvoo) and in *the Gospel*

---

[16] David Whitmer Interview, *Kansas City Journal*, 5 June 1881, republished in the *Millennial Star* 42 (1881): 421-23, 437-439, online at http://whitmercollege.com/published/interviews/kansas-city-journal-1881

[17] https://www.josephsmithpapers.org/paper-summary/history-1834-1836/90

*Reflector* (Philadelphia), also in 1841. The essays were republished in the *Millennial Star*, in a special pamphlet in Liverpool, England, that sold thousands of copies, in *The Prophet* (an LDS newspaper in New York City) in 1844, and in the 1899 *Improvement Era* by Joseph F. Smith, then editor of the magazine and Second Counselor in the First Presidency.

Every one of Joseph's contemporaries and successors in the leadership of the LDS Church who has ever addressed the topic has reaffirmed these teachings about the New York Cumorah. Some of these teachings are included in Appendix 1.

The simplicity of the New York Cumorah did not remain unchallenged, however. Alternative theories arose. The level of complexity increased substantially. Experts disagreed. The topic became contentious. But on the other side of complexity, an informed simplicity is possible when we realize there is abundant evidence that, after all, Joseph and Oliver were correct.

## From one to two Cumorahs

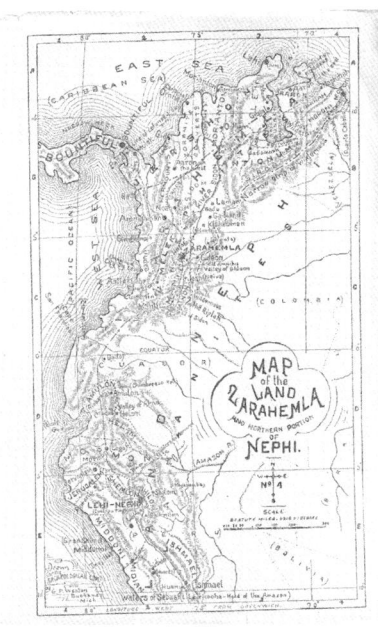

Figure 6 - Weston map

It wasn't until the early 1900s that Cumorah's location changed.

In the late 1800s, the RLDS Committee on American Archaeology arranged for G.F. Weston to prepare six maps of Book of Mormon lands. The Committee reported that "Although the church never officially endorsed the maps, the proposed geographical locations of Book of Mormon cities and lands on the maps made a lasting impression which has been difficult to correct."[18]

You can see that this map Weston prepared depicts the land of Zarahemla in northern South America, basically Colombia and Ecuador, with Panama as the "narrow neck."

Later, RLDS intellectuals decided that Panama was not the "narrow neck" and moved their geography into Mesoamerica.

In 1910, Charles A. Shook published a 589-page book titled *"The Book of Mormon" and the Claims of the Mormons Re-examined from the Viewpoint of American Archaeology and Ethnology.*[19] Shook had been raised in what he called "the Reorganized Mormon Church" but left the faith. In this book, he criticized the Hemispheric theory of Book of Mormon geography, including the idea that all indigenous people in the western hemisphere descended from Lehi.

On March 15, 1911, H.A. Stebbins set forth the theory that all of the events in the Book of Mormon took place in a limited area of Central America. The *Saints' Herald*, a publication of the Reorganized Church of Jesus Christ of Latter-day Saints (RLDS), published Stebbins' article titled "Cumorah Hill." Based on his assumption that Book of Mormon events took place in Central America, he explained:

> Because there now seems to be quite an inquiry as to the original hill Cumorah and its location, and more and more the students of the Book of Mormon are coming up to the idea that the original hill could not have been in New York State, but must have been in Central America, I write of the understanding that I have had during the past eleven years....
>
> I know that in Doctrine and Covenants 10:20 it reads, "glad tidings of Cumorah," but it is in a letter from Joseph Smith, evidently after the idea had become fixed that because records were hidden in Cumorah therefore the one in New York must have been the same hill.
>
> In his "Letters," pages 29, 33, Oliver Cowdery calls it Cumorah: evidently from the same idea, not from any divine or angelic statement that it was

---

[18] Search for "lasting impression: at https://stepbystep.alancminer.com/node/2268
[19] Online at https://archive.org/details/cumorahrevisited00shoorich.

Cumorah. Certainly the idea did not originate with any careful student of the Book of Mormon. There may not ·have been any real study of the book at that time. The book appears to have been largely taken on trust by the old Saints, without great examination or study.[20]

This theory that the Cumorah of Mormon 6:6 is in Central America proposes that there are actually "two Cumorahs." The Cumorah in New York is a misnamed product of a misguided assumption, while the actual Cumorah is in Central America. For simplicity, I refer to this as the Mesoamerican/two-Cumorahs theory, abbreviated as M2C.

In 1917, building on Stebbins' Cumorah theory, another RLDS scholar named L.E. Hills published a map of proposed Book of Mormon lands in Central America. He showed Cumorah in southern Mexico.

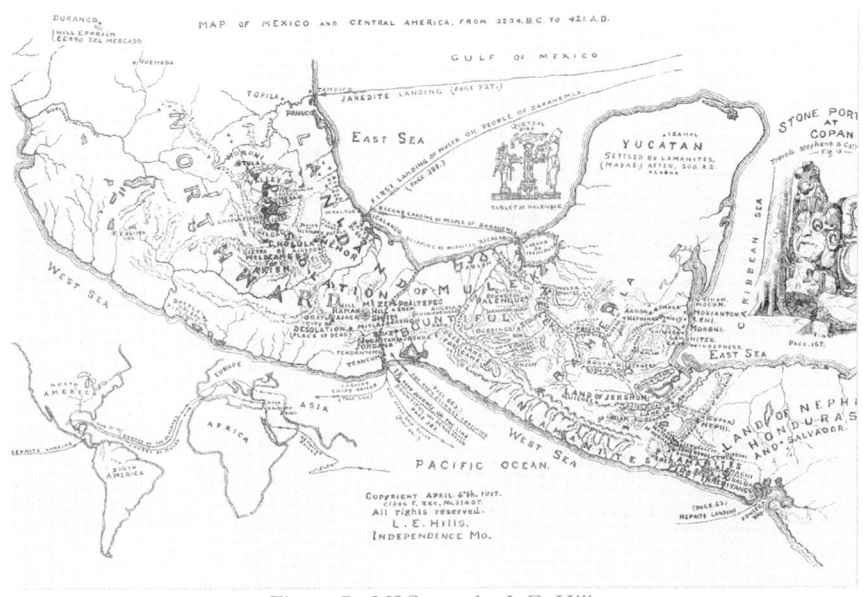

Figure 7 - M2C map by L.E. Hills

[20] Stebbins, H.A., "Cumorah Hill," *The Saints' Herald*, p. 245, 248. http://www.latterdaytruth.org/pdf/100225.pdf

A close-up view of the map shows Cumorah near the "East Sea" which is the Gulf of Mexico.

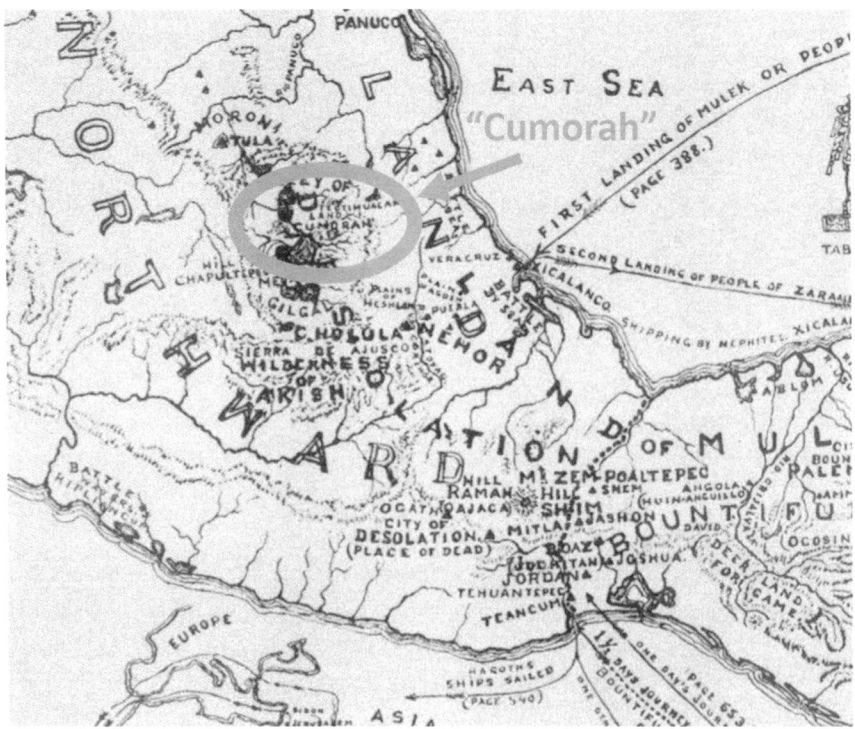

The Hills map has been widely adopted by modern LDS scholars. The Mesoamerican setting it establishes has been portrayed in numerous videos, illustrations, books and articles.

Scholars debate the details, but they follow the basic concept Hills established.

For example, the map currently (as of 2020) posted on the *BYU Studies* web page[21] follows the basic parameters of the Hills map. It depicts Cumorah near the east coast of southern Mexico.

---

[21]     https://byustudies.byu.edu/charts/160-plausible-locations-mesoamerica-book-mormon-places

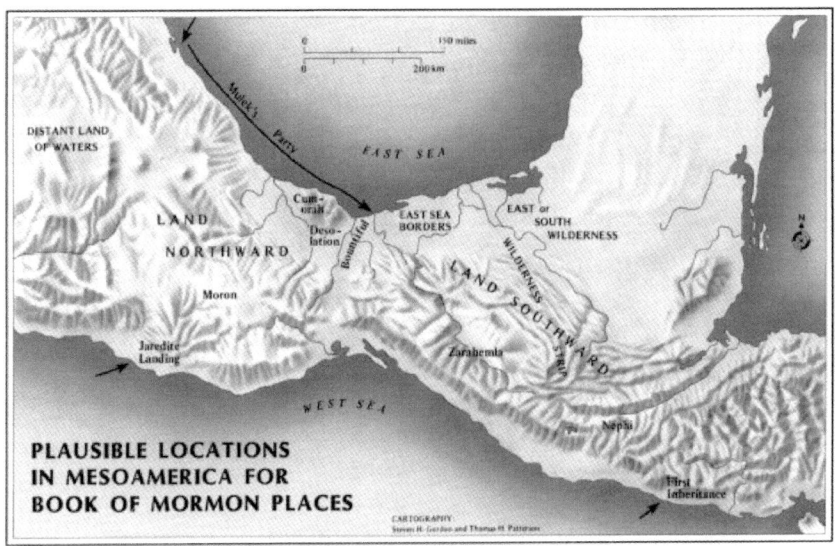

PLAUSIBLE LOCATIONS
IN MESOAMERICA FOR
BOOK OF MORMON PLACES

## RLDS vs LDS context

Hills published his map in the context of an ongoing dispute between the RLDS and LDS churches.

For modern LDS members, it is difficult to put ourselves in the mindset of the LDS vs. RLDS competition from the 1800s, but it was a serious rivalry. Understanding the history adds nuance to the case of the lost Cumorah.

### Joseph Smith III

After Joseph Smith, Jr., died in 1844, there was a power struggle for leadership. While most members of the Church followed Brigham Young (the President of the Quorum of the Twelve) and eventually migrated to Utah. Other members followed various men who claimed a right to succeed Joseph Smith.

Joseph's widow Emma, for example, remained in Nauvoo and believed Joseph's son should succeed him as President of the Church.[22]

---

[22] For a good summary of the diverse groups, see
https://www.lds.org/study/ensign/1979/09/nineteenth-century-break-offs?lang=eng

Figure 8 - Joseph Smith III

On June 6, 1860, Joseph Smith III, son of Joseph and Emma, was ordained President of the Reorganized Church of Jesus Christ of Latter-day Saints (RLDS). He was 27 years old, having been born on November 6, 1832 in Kirtland, Ohio.

He served as President of the RLDS church until he died on December 14, 1914.

Although both churches accepted the Book of Mormon and many of the revelations in the Doctrine and Covenants, they had doctrinal differences and competing historical claims. The RLDS rejected polygamy, claiming Joseph Smith had never taught or practiced the principle. Meanwhile, Brigham Young and other LDS leaders practiced polygamy and claimed Joseph Smith had both taught and practiced the principle.

Figure 9 - Joseph F. Smith

## Joseph F. Smith

Joseph F. Smith, a son of Hyrum Smith, was born in Far West, Missouri, on November 13, 1838.

On July 1, 1866, when Joseph F. Smith was 27 years old, President Brigham Young ordained him an apostle and called him as a counselor in the First Presidency. He served in the First Presidency until he became President of the LDS Church in 1901. He served as President until he died on November 18, 1918.

As cousins, there was both a personal and religious rivalry between Joseph Smith III and Joseph F. Smith. Each claimed to be the rightful successor to Joseph Smith, Jr. The RLDS sent missionaries to Salt Lake City, Utah, who reportedly converted thousands of LDS members.

The most prominent topic of dispute was polygamy, but the question of Cumorah also arose.

The 1879 LDS edition of the Book of Mormon, edited by Elder Orson Pratt, stated in a footnote that the Hill Cumorah was in western New York. Other footnotes acknowledged speculation that Lehi landed in Chile, that the River Sidon was in Colombia, etc.

In 1899, Joseph F. Smith was the Editor of the *Improvement Era*, an LDS publication in Utah. He had been an apostle and member of the First Presidency for 33 years. (Joseph F. Smith served as a counselor in the First Presidency to Brigham Young, John Taylor, Wilford Woodruff, and Lorenzo Snow before becoming President of the Church in 1901.)

In the July 1899 issue of the *Improvement Era*,[23] President Joseph F. Smith published President Cowdery's Letter VII, which declares it is a fact that the Hill Cumorah in New York is the site of the final battles of the Jaredites and Nephites, as well as the location of the depository of Nephite records (Mormon 6:6).[24]

1909, Joseph F. Smith sent Elder George Albert Smith of the Quorum of the Twelve Apostles and his wife Lucy to Palmyra with the assignment of buying the Hill Cumorah and the Joseph Smith Sr. farm. (Geroge Albert Smith was named for his grandfather, a cousin of Joseph Smith Jr.).

Before leaving Salt Lake City, George and Lucy sewed $20,000 in cash into Lucy's skirt. When they arrived in Palmyra, they were able to buy the old Smith farm, but the owner of the Hill Cumorah, Pliny Sexton, refused to sell. Later, he offered to sell at an exorbitant price, but the Church declined to pay that much.

As discussed above, Charles Shook published his book *Cumorah Revisited* in 1910. Stebbins published his article "Cumorah Hill" in 1911.

In 1915, Willard Bean and his wife Rebecca were called as missionaries to live at the Joseph Smith farm. They were the first

---

[23] https://archive.org/stream/improvementera29unse#page/n0/mode/2up

[24] https://archive.org/stream/improvementera29unse#page/652/mode/2up

Church members to live in Palmyra since the early 1830s.

Meanwhile, in 1917, L.E. Hills published his map showing the "real Cumorah" in southern Mexico. In 1924, Hill published *New Light on American Archaeology*,[25] quoting Stebbins extensively regarding the location of Cumorah in Mexico.

Sexton died in 1924. Four years later, the LDS Church purchased the Hill Cumorah. In April 1928 General Conference, President Anthony W. Ivins spoke at length about the Hill Cumorah, re-affirming the teaching of Letter VII and D&C 128:20 that this is the very hill spoken of in Mormon 6:6.[26]

## Debates over the New York Cumorah

Discussions about Book of Mormon geography in the early 1920s led to the deletion of Orson Pratt's footnotes in the 1879 LDS edition that identified known (Cumorah) and speculative (Zarahemla, Sidon) Book of Mormon locations. A committee that included Elders James E. Talmage and George F. Richards heard presentations about geography theories including a hemispheric model and two versions of a limited geography theory, one based in Honduras and another based on Yucatan and Mexico.

In February 1923, Elder Talmage wrote that after listening to these presentations of widely differing opinions, the committee "decided that until we have clearer knowledge in this matter, the Church could not authorize or approve the issuance of any map, chart, or text, purporting to set forth demonstrated facts relating to Book of Mormon lands."[27]

---

[25] See https://babel.hathitrust.org/cgi/pt?id=wu.89058377359&view=1up&seq=5

[26] A summary of his remarks can be found here: http://www.bookofmormoncentralamerica.com/2017/03/conference-classics-president-anthony-w.html

[27] James E. Talmage to Jean R. Driggs, February 23, 1923, James E. Talmage Papers, quoted in https://stepbystep.alancminer.com/node/2257 (search for "purporting"). Also cited in Shannon Caldwell Montez, "The Secret Mormon Meetings of 1922," University of Nevada, Reno (2019), available online at https://scholarworks.unr.edu/bitstream/handle/11714/6712/Montez_unr_0139M_13054.pdf, p. 69. Both references delve into this history in detail beyond the scope

Numerous books and articles on the topic were published from the 1920s to the 1980s. I'll mention four.

Willard Bean, the missionary who lived in Palmyra from 1915 to 1939 and who was instrumental in the purchase of the Hill Cumorah, co-authored a 1948 book titled *Book of Mormon Geography*.[28] This is what I would call a cold case, as we discussed in Part One. The facts Bean cited in his book were well known long before he wrote his book, but they have been largely overlooked today. Some modern scholars dispute these facts of course; we'll discuss that in Part Five.

Bean explained the purpose for the book in the Preface.

> In recent years there has been a tendency among certain students of the Book of Mormon to orientate Book of Mormon cultures far to the south. Many students of the subject are convinced that the three colonies that came to America had their existence in Central America and Mexico. They are thought to have lived within a radius of a few hundred miles of Zarahemla, never pushing northward many miles, certainly not thrusting out their branches as far north as the Great Lakes along our Canadian border.
>
> These students think it unlikely that the Jaredites or Nephites were in North America, and that they surely did not push northward as far as New York state; that the large bodies of water referred to in the Book of Mormon were in Middle America, and that Ramah and Cumorah were in the vicinity of Zarahemla....
>
> The following pages are a plea in defense of the old theory—the interpretation of Joseph Smith, Oliver Cowdery, Orson Pratt, and a countless number of the Authorities of the Church. It is our humble opinion that there is no occasion to fling aside the old interpretation and accept the new, thus restricting the Book of Mormon races to the restricted confines of Central America.

The book quotes early explorers of western New York who found abundant water and wildlife, ancient fortifications, skeletons of people

---

of this book.

[28] McGavin, E. Cecil, and Bean, Willard, *Book of Mormon Geography* (Bookcraft, Salt Lake City, Utah 1948), reprinted by permission by Digital Legend Press (Salt Lake City, Utah 2012).

seven to eight feet tall, and "spearpoints, war hatchets, and other weapons that seem too large for an average sized man to wield." (page 13, citing C. H. Johnson, *History of Erie County*, p. 124.[29]

In 1958, Riley L. Dixon published a book titled *Just One Cumorah*.[30] On page 129, Dixon wrote,

> In the early history of the Church, there was no debate as to where Mormon and Moroni had hidden the plates. But in recent years, however, some students of the Book of Mormon have presumed that the ancient Book of Mormon people never occupied the land north of Mexico and that at the close of the great battles that exterminated the Nephite people the records were buried in some hill near the line between the land of Bountiful and the land of Desolation.

Dixon assumed a hemispheric model, writing on page 133, "Some students have held to the idea that it would have been impossible for the battling armies of Nephites and Lamanites to have moved all the say to New York from their Central American homes. Such a retreat is not at all unreasonable when the time required for the march is taken into consideration."

I mention this book not to make a case for the hemispheric model, but to show that in 1958, the debate over Cumorah was lively.

David A. Palmer published a 1981 book that made a case for two Cumorahs, with the real Cumorah in Mexico.[31]

On page 20, Palmer wrote:

### Designation of the Hill in New York as Cumorah

> There is no record of Moroni having told Joseph Smith that the place where the abridgement was buried was Cumorah, or that the hill was once a great battleground. If this had been the place of those great final battles, it would be rather surprising that it was not mentioned.

---

[29] More discussion of the archaeology of Cumorahland is in Part Four.

[30] Dixon, Riley Lake, *Just One Cumorah* (Bookcraft, Inc., Salt Lake City, UT 1958).

[31] Palmer, David A., *In Search of Cumorah: New Evidences for the Book of Mormon from Ancient Mexico* (Horizon Publishers & Distributors, Bountiful, Utah 1981).

[Note: it is unclear whether Palmer was unaware of what Lucy Mack Smith, David Whitmer and Parley P. Pratt related, or if he dismissed their accounts for unstated reasons.]

We have only the scantiest of inferences that Joseph Smith ever called the hill "Cumorah." (D&C 128:20). However, he does not appear to have corrected Oliver Cowdery, who may have been the one to first name the New York hill "Cumorah." (Cowdery, 1835) [Letter VII]

[Note: presumably Palmer did not know that Joseph had his scribes copy Letter VII into his personal history or that Joseph encouraged Benjamin Winchester and Don Carlos Smith to republish the letters in the *Gospel Reflector* and *Times and Seasons*, respectively.]

We may be comfortable applying the name "Cumorah" to both the hill where Mormon buried the large Nephite library and to the hill where Moroni hid up the plates, which he later gave to Joseph Smith.… A "Two-Cumorah" theory is thus the most appropriate, since records were hidden in both Mormon's Cumorah and Moroni's Cumorah. Therefore, it matters little whether it was Joseph Smith or one of his associates who called the hill in New York "Cumorah."

… the prophet Joseph Smith has stated very clearly that the approach to Book of Mormon geography must be primarily of an intellectual nature. In 1842, while serving as editor of the Nauvoo newspaper, "Times and Seasons," he used the paper to educate the people and turn Nauvoo into a cultural center of the west.

One of the books which the prophet publicized was a national bestseller written by John Lloyd Stephens (1841).… In the Times and Seasons articles Joseph Smith apparently gave his opinion that the land southward was north of Panama, in the area of Guatemala or Mexico… The hypothesis was presented as his own personal idea rather than as revelation….

The Stephens articles in the *Times and Seasons* became the foundation for the LDS version of M2C. Proponents claim that because the boilerplate at the end of each issue said the newspaper was "edited by" Joseph Smith, he must have written unsigned articles and articles signed only as "Ed."

However, the boilerplate also said the newspaper was "printed by" Joseph Smith. No one thinks Joseph set type or operated the printing press. He was the "nominal" printer, meaning in name only. Apart from the boilerplate language, there is no evidence that Joseph actually edited or even read anything in the paper before it was printed, apart from material he separately signed or acknowledged.

The authorship of the anonymous editorials that quoted and commented on the Stephens articles remains unclear. I have documented my proposal that the articles were written by Benjamin Winchester.[32] Regardless of who wrote the *Times and Seasons* articles, they don't mention Cumorah. M2C proponents use the articles to reject the New York Cumorah because New York is too far from Mesoamerica.

Palmer proceeded to explain the rationale for relying on scholars to solve the case of Cumorah.

> We will make no attempt to resolve statements of Book of Mormon geography by other Church authorities, but will only try to reconcile the text of the Book of Mormon itself with physical geography and archaeological findings. The statements of Church leaders do not necessarily represent church doctrine. There is no doctrine of infallibility in the Church. If two Church leaders make conflicting statements concerning nondoctrinal matters, it is not a negative reflection on the Church. It is simply a reflection of the open spirit of inquiry and search for knowledge which was preached by Joseph Smith.

Palmer did not point out that there have been no conflicting statements by Church leaders about the New York Cumorah. Any conflicting statements relate to the plausibility of the hemispheric vs. limited theories of geography.

One reason why Palmer's approach remains influential is that he wrote the "Cumorah" entry in the 1992 *Encyclopedia of Mormonism*

---

[32] See my books titled *The Lost City of Zarahemla: From Iowa to Guatemala and Back Again, Brought to Light*, and *The Editors: Joseph, Don Carlos, and William Smith*.

(EoM),[33] in which he cited his own book as well as the work of other M2C scholars such as John L. Sorenson and John Clark.

The next significant book was John L. Sorenson's 1985 book *An Ancient American Setting for the Book of Mormon*, published by Deseret Book Company and the Foundation for Ancient Research and Mormon Studies (FARMS).

FARMS was created in 1979. Regarding Book of Mormon geography, FARMS embraced M2C and adopted a logo that showed Mayan as one of the four languages involved with Mormon studies (along with Hebrew, Greek and Egyptian). All of its publications implicitly or explicitly reject the New York Cumorah in favor of the unknown Mexican location.

Figure 10 - FARMS logo

(I refer to this logo as the "mark of M2C.")

Sorenson's *Ancient American Setting* discussed Cumorah by briefly dismissing the New York setting on page 44.

### Two Cumorahs?

A question many readers will have been asking themselves is a sound and necessary one: how did Joseph Smith obtain the gold plates in upstate New York if the final battleground of the Nephites was in Mesoamerica?

Let's review where the final battle took place. The Book of Mormon makes clear that the demise of both Jaredites and Nephites took place near the narrow neck of land. Yet New York is thousands of miles away from any plausible configuration that could be described as this narrow neck. Thus the scripture itself rules out the idea that the Nephite perished near Palmyra.

That rationale is a good example of the conclusion being the descendant of the assumption. Once you assume the "narrow neck" had to be in Mesoamerica, your conclusion becomes obvious.

On page 29, Sorenson had written,

---

33      http://contentdm.lib.byu.edu/cdm/compoundobject/collection/ EoM/id/4391/show/5649

The only "narrow neck" potentially acceptable in terms of the Book of Mormon requirements is the Isthmus of Tehuantepec in southern Mexico. All LDS students of Book of Mormon geography who have worked systematically with the problem in recent decades have come to agree on this. As we learned above, [where Sorenson discussed the anonymous *Times and Seasons* articles] leading Church members in Joseph Smith's time apparently arrived at a similar view, and he likely did also. This would place the Book of Mormon events within Mesoamerica, the cultural region of central and southern Mexico and northern Central America, where the highest intensity of civilization occurred in ancient America.

Later, in his 2013 book *Mormon's Codex*, Sorenson rejected the New York Cumorah even more dismissively.

There remain Latter-day Saints who insist that the final destruction of the Nephites took place in New York, but any such idea is manifestly absurd. Hundreds of thousands of Nephites traipsing across the Mississippi Valley to New York, pursued (why?) by hundreds of thousands of Lamanites, is a scenario worthy only of a witless sci-fi movie, not of history.[34]

This is a straw man logical fallacy. While there may have been such proposals in the past, few if any current Latter-day Saints find that idea credible.

Those of us who "insist that the final destruction of the Nephites took place in New York" instead see this as a natural continuation of the final wars that began in the land of Zarahemla and progressed as the Nephites retreated to what Mormon knew was a defensive stronghold established by the Jaredites centuries earlier. The abundant archaeological evidence of fortifications in the area corroborate this "scenario."

Nevertheless, the Sorenson view came to be accepted by other

---

[34] John L. Sorenson, *Mormon's Codex* (Neal A. Maxwell Institute and Deseret Book, Salt Lake City, Utah 2013) p. 688.

influential LDS scholars.

## Abstract maps

In July 1938, the *Improvement Era* published an explanation of what may be the first "abstract" map based on the text alone.[35] An editorial sidebar explained:

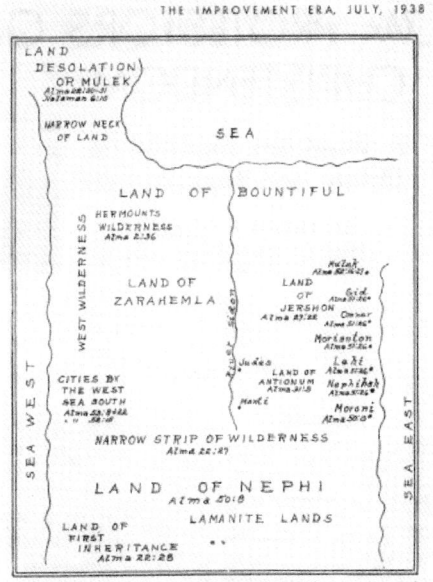

The above diagram shows the relationship of Book of Mormon lands to each other in the first century B. C. as developed in the accompanying article. In fitting this diagram to any map, allowance must be made for the fact that rivers, sea coasts, etc., which deviate several degrees from a meridian may be said to run North or South.

It is suggested that the student try to trace the course of the following journeys or military campaigns on the above diagram.

Alma 43:17-54, 44:22-24, 51:22-37, 52:1-40, 56:9-57, 62:14-38, 63:4-6; Helaman 1:14-33; Mormon 1:6. (Note here that Zarahemla was in the Land Southward.)

Many other lands and cities may be located by using the Book of Mormon index as a guide.

No attempt is made here to suggest the location of any cities in the Land Northward.

Figure 11 - Abstract map from the 1938 *Improvement Era*

MANY individual members of the Church, in private capacity, have expressed their views and their theories concerning Book of Mormon geography. Here is another view-representing merely the personal beliefs of one student of the subject and not necessarily representing the views of the church or its members generally. But this presentation is unique in that it does not attempt to place the scene of action on the present--day map, but merely indicates the relative positions of one place with respect to another, as inferred from a study of the text itself.

The idea deriving a map from the text sounds good in theory, but in practice it requires considerable speculation about vague or uncertain terminology. For example, the article simply assumed that "head of Sidon" meant the "headwaters" and "source" of the river. But the term could also mean a confluence of rivers. There are many examples of each

---

[35] Lynn C. Layton, "An 'Ideal' Book of Mormon Geography, https://archive.org/details/improvementera4107unse/page/n11/mode/2up

connotation.

The assumption that "head of Sidon" means "headwaters" of Sidon leads to the conclusion that the River Sidon flowed north, as depicted on the map accompanying the article.

This assumption in turn has prompted Book of Mormon students to scour the western hemisphere for north-flowing rivers that could qualify as Sidon. This is a nice example of how an assumption has led to a conclusion.[36]

The pursuit of an abstract map did not end in 1938. Many such text-based maps have been proposed over the years, usually as precursors for "finding" a real-world setting. An excellent compilation of such maps is included in John Sorenson's Source Book.

The best-known example today is the abstract map produced by BYU that we'll discuss in the next section.

In my view, the utility of abstract maps is more than offset by the implied endorsement of the interpretative model behind them. These maps are "sticky" ideas that are difficult to forget. Worse, they reflect a particular interpretation of the text based on M2C.

Imprinting M2C interpretations on the minds of believers is a disservice because it forecloses further inquiry. It becomes the "native tongue" for Church members, making it all but impossible for them to consider multiple working hypotheses. These abstract maps create a myside bias that is very difficult to overcome—even with the teachings of the prophets.

## De-correlation of the New York Cumorah

The Cumorah question differs from other questions about Church history because there are no competing quotations or historical facts—no inconsistencies—about the location of Cumorah. From as early as 1827, before Joseph Smith, Jr., even obtained the plates, everyone who knew Joseph and addressed the issue agreed that the hill Cumorah where Joseph found the plates was the same hill Cumorah of Mormon

---

[36] See the discussion of Sidon in Part Five-How Cumorah Fits: Moroni's America.

6:6. Some of these statements are included in Appendix 1.

I have a copy of the 1979 Seminary Manual for Religion 121-122, covering the Book of Mormon. It was published by the Church of Jesus Christ of Latter-day Saints.

On page 461, a paragraph numbered 48-17 reads:

Figure 12 - 1979
Seminary Manual

### Mormon 6:1-6. Where Did the Last Great Nephite-Lamanite Battle Take Place?

It is known that the Hill Cumorah where the Nephites were destroyed is the hill where the Jaredites were also destroyed. This hill was known to the Jaredites as Ramah. It was approximately near to the waters of Ripliancum, which the Book of Ether says, 'by interpretation, is large, or to exceed all.' [Ether 15:8-11] Mormon adds: 'And it came to pass that we did march forth to the land of Cumorah, and we did pitch our tents round about the hill Cumorah; and it was in a land of many waters, rivers, and fountains; and here we had hope to gain advantage over the Lamanites." [Mormon 6:4]

It must be conceded that this description fits perfectly the land of Cumorah in New York, as it has been known since the visitation of Moroni to the Prophet Joseph Smith, for the hill is in the proximity of the Great Lakes and also in the land of many rivers and fountains. Moreover, *the Prophet Joseph Smith himself is on record, definitely declaring the present hill called Cumorah to be the exact hill spoken of in the Book of Mormon.* [italics in original]

Further, the fact that all of his associates from the beginning down have spoken of it as the identical hill where Mormon and Moroni hid the records, must carry some weight. It is difficult for a reasonable person to believe that such men as Oliver Cowdery, Brigham Young, Parley P. Pratt, Orson Pratt, David Whitmer, and many others, could speak frequently of the spot where the Prophet Joseph Smith obtained the plates as the Hill Cumorah, and not be corrected by the Prophet, if that were not the fact. That they did speak of this hill in the days of the Prophet in this definite manner is an established record of history.

(Smith, *Doctrines of Salvation*, 3:233-34.)

Recent discoveries in Church history have corroborated what President Joseph Fielding Smith taught in this quotation. The New York Cumorah was taught even more persistently and clearly than President Smith realized.

In his book, on page 28, Willard Bean wrote about the trends he observed and his consequential fears for the future.

> Though the modern trend in the Book of Mormon geography inclines toward Central America and is anxious to confine most of the pre-Columbian activity to Middle America, surely the time will never come when our guides and missionaries on Hill Cumorah will be instructed to make such an explanation as the following to the many tourists who visit that historic shrine:
>
>> This hill is named in honor of a hill somewhere in Central America or Mexico. It's unfortunate that we do not know just where that other hill was located…
>>
>> That mysterious hill, wherever it was located, was known as Ramah to the Jaredites, and Cumorah to the Nephites…
>>
>> Since the records had been deposited in the Hill Cumorah somewhere in Middle America, this Hill was given the same name, since it was the largest hill nearest Joseph Smith's home. It was unfortunate, indeed, that we do not know the location of that distant Cumorah. If we did we would know the land where these two great nations were swept off the face of the earth. Meantime, we shall be content to consider this hill as a humble replica of that historic and sacred hill far to the south.

Willard Bean's fears have been realized. The North Visitors Center on Temple Square in Salt Lake City, Utah, features a display of Mormon abridging the plates inside a cave decorated with Mayan glyphs. A hundred feet away, a separate exhibit shows Moroni burying the plates in the hill in New York.

Figure 13 - M2C on Temple Square

The long-held teaching about the New York Cumorah has been de-correlated in recent years. The 2017 Book of Mormon Seminary Teacher manual does not relate what the prophets have taught about the location of the Hill Cumorah. Instead, they teach that Cumorah is not in western New York.

Students are presented with a hypothetical map that shows Cumorah north of a "narrow neck" pursuant to the Central American model.[37] in what looks like southern Mexico. BYU students are taught a similar map.[38] An analysis of these maps is included in Appendix 4.

---

[37] See https://www.churchofjesuschrist.org/study/manual/book-of-mormon-seminary-teacher-manual-2017/appendix/possible-book-of-mormon-sites-in-relation-to-each-other?lang=eng and
https://www.churchofjesuschrist.org/bc/content/shared/content/images/gospel-library/manual/14419/book-mormon-land-map_1941052.pdf
[38] https://bom.byu.edu/

## Current Status

As I write this in the year 2020, the teachings of past LDS Church leaders (prophets and apostles) about the New York Cumorah have been relegated to forgotten history through a process I call "de-correlation."

The book *Saints*, volume 1, intentionally omitted historical references to Cumorah.[39] Discussions of Cumorah in Church lesson manuals have been removed in recent editions. Even the Visitors Center at the Hill Cumorah in New York does not explain why the hill has that name. None of the scriptural verses that mention Cumorah are mentioned in the exhibits.

The closest thing to an official Church position on the question of Book of Mormon geography is the Gospel Topics entry on Book of Mormon Geography, but it does not mention Cumorah.

When the entry was first published in January 2019, it quoted this statement from President Ivins:

> Anthony W. Ivins, a Counselor in the First Presidency, stated: "There has never been anything yet set forth that definitely settles that question [of Book of Mormon geography]. So the Church says we are just waiting until we discover the truth.[40]

On my blog[41] I pointed out that the year before, President Ivins had reiterated past teachings about the New York Cumorah as part of the Church's celebration of the purchase of the Hill Cumorah. Shortly thereafter, without notice, the Gospel Topics entry was changed to delete the original reference to President Ivins. I commented on that

---

[39] For more details, see my posts on the Saintsreview blog, such as this one: https://saintsreview.blogspot.com/2018/10/the-historians-explain-censorship-in.html

[40] https://www.lds.org/study/manual/gospel-topics/book-of-mormon-geography?lang=eng#note3

[41] https://presidentnelsonspeaks.blogspot.com/2019/01/

on my blog also.[42]

Appendix 2 shows the original and revised Gospel Topics entry, along with my comments.

Let's review the chronology.

Beginning in 1827, Joseph Smith, Oliver Cowdery, their contemporaries and successors all taught that the Hill Cumorah of Mormon 6:6 is the same hill near Palmyra, New York, where Joseph found the plates.

1842: Anonymous articles (Signed "Ed." for editor) in the *Times and Seasons* claim that ruins in Central America were left by the Nephites. One article claims the ruins of Zarahemla, specifically, have been found. None of the article refer to Cumorah. On September 6, 1842, Joseph Smith writes a letter to the Church that includes this passage:

> And again, what do we hear? Glad tidings from Cumorah! Moroni, an angel from heaven, declaring the fulfilment of the prophets—the book to be revealed.
> (Doctrine and Covenants 128:20)

1879: The LDS Church publishes a new edition of the Book of Mormon that includes footnotes about geography. The notes unequivocally state that the Hill Cumorah is in western New York, but qualifies other identified sites as speculation.

1899: LDS President Joseph F. Smith republishes Letter VII in the *Improvement Era.*, reaffirming the long-accepted teaching that it is a fact that the hill in New York is in fact the Cumorah of Mormon 6:6.

1909: LDS President Joseph F. Smith sends Elder George Albert Smith to Palmyra to purchase the Hill Cumorah. Pliny Sexton refuses to sell.

1910: Former RLDS member Charles Shook writes Cumorah Revisited to refute the hemispheric model and anthropological and

---

[42] https://presidentnelsonspeaks.blogspot.com/2019/02/revisions-to-gospel-topics-essay-on.html

archaeological claims of the Book of Mormon.

1911: RLDS publication *Saints' Herald* publishes an article by RLDS scholar H.A. Stebbins that claims the actual Hill Cumorah of Mormon 6:6 is located in southern Mexico.

1917: RLDS Elder L.E. Hills publishes a map showing the Hill Cumorah of Mormon 6:6 in southern Mexico, based on the 1911 Stebbins article.

1920: LDS leaders delete the footnotes in the 1879 edition, evaluate proposed geography models, and decide not to endorse any geography model.

1924: RLDS Elder Hills publishes *New Light on American Archaeology*, declaring it is a fact that the Hill Cumorah of Mormon 6:6 is in Mexico.

1924: Pliny Sexton dies.

1928: LDS Church President Heber J. Grant purchases the Hill Cumorah in New York and President Anthony W. Ivins reaffirms the fact that this is the Cumorah of Mormon 6:6.

1938: Elder Joseph Fielding Smith, a 20-year member of the Quorum of the Twelve and Church Historian, writes an editorial in the Deseret News about M2C, stating "LOCALE OF CUMORAH, RAMAH, AND RIPLIANCUM. This modernistic theory of necessity, in order to be consistent, must place the waters of Ripliancum and the Hill Cumorah some place within the restricted territory of Central America, notwithstanding the teachings of the Church to the contrary for upwards of 100 years. Because of this theory some members of the Church have become confused and greatly disturbed in their faith in the Book of Mormon. It is for this reason that evidence is here presented to show that it is not only possible that these places could be located as the Church has held during the past century [i.e., in western New York], but that in very deed such is the case."

1950s-1970s: LDS intellectuals write books and articles promoting M2C. President Joseph Fielding Smith, now President of the Quorum of the Twelve, re-publishes his 1938 editorial on Cumorah.

1975: In General Conference, President Marion G. Romney delivers an address titled "America's Destiny" that reaffirms the teaching that the hill in New York is the Hill Cumorah of Mormon 6:6.

1978: In General Conference, Elder Mark E. Petersen reaffirms the New York Cumorah.

1980s: LDS intellectuals, including David Palmer and John Sorenson, publish books promoting M2C. Jack Welch and others start FARMS, which strongly promotes M2C. The academic cycle begins teaching M2C to the youth of the Church.

1990: In response to questions arising about Cumorah, the entire First Presidency (Ezra Taft Benson, Gordon B. Hinckley, and Thomas S. Monson) personally approve a letter that declares "The Church has long maintained, as attested to by reference in the writings of General Authorities, that the Hill Cumorah in western New York state is the same as referenced in the Book of Mormon."

1990s through 2018: LDS intellectuals create the M2C citation cartel that promotes M2C exclusively and censors alternative views. M2C is unambiguously depicted in LDS Church visitors centers, artwork, videos, and CES/BYU curriculum.

2019: Gospel Topics Essay on Book of Mormon Geography released. The first version quotes President Ivins 1929 General Conference talk explaining the Church has no position on Book of Mormon sites other than Cumorah. When it is pointed out that President Ivins also specifically reaffirmed the New York Cumorah in his 1928 General Conference talk, the Gospel Topics Essay is revised to omit the original quotation from President Ivins. The essay provides no references to teachings about the New York Cumorah for readers to consider.

Current Status (2020): Church members are free to believe whatever they want. However, previous teachings by Church leaders about the New York Cumorah cannot be discussed in Church settings, especially not at Church history sites in Palmyra. Only books and organizations that promote M2C can obtain licenses from the Church to use the current official edition of the Book of Mormon. CES and BYU specifically teach M2C as part of the official curriculum.

# Part Four: Book of Mormon people

One of the main criticisms of the Book of Mormon by nonbelievers is the purported lack of evidence of the people and places it describes. Believers who reject the New York Cumorah similarly assert a lack of evidence based on their interpretations of the text.

Of course, there is abundant archaeological and anthropological evidence of ancient people living throughout the Western Hemisphere during Book of Mormon time frames. Connecting such evidence with the descriptions in the text is like solving simultaneous equations in algebra because there are unknown variables on both sides of the equation:

$$X \text{ external evidence} = Y \text{ descriptions in the text?}$$

It is possible to interpret the text to support most theories of Book of Mormon geography based on external evidence from archaeology, anthropology, geology, etc. It is also possible to dispute every theory's interpretation of the text and the evidence. This is why, pending more information, the approach of multiple working hypotheses makes the most sense.

———

Cumorah is an example of simplicity leading through complexity to simplicity on the other side of complexity.

Simplicity: Joseph and Oliver teaching the New York Cumorah.

Complexity: scholars disputing the New York Cumorah for numerous reasons based on external evidence accumulated to confirm their interpretations of the text.

Simplicity: Using external evidence to corroborate and vindicate what Joseph and Oliver taught in the first place.

## Why Cumorahland?

The Hill Cumorah is in western New York state, an area known for

(i) fields of "drumlins," which are long narrow hills, and
(ii) "finger lakes," a series of long, narrow lakes.

These features make the area well suited for military defenses as Willard Bean summarized in his book.

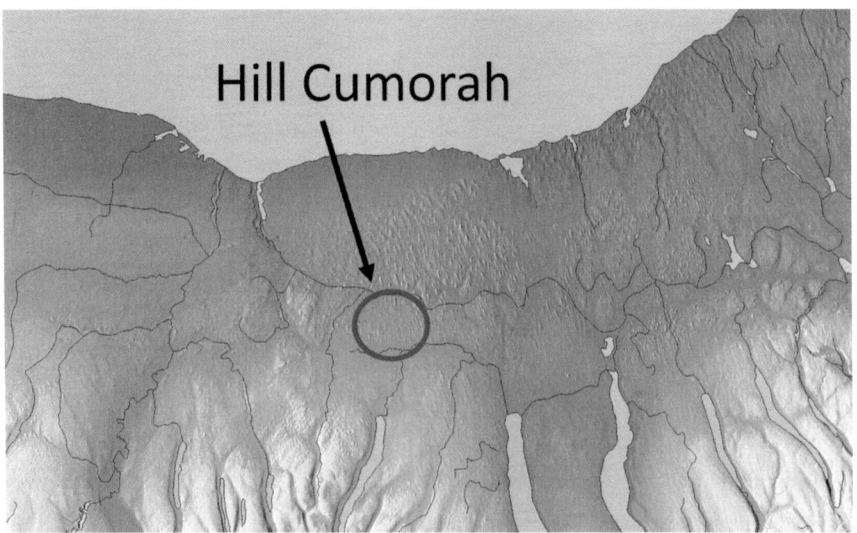

Figure 14 - Map of Cumorahland from https://maps-for-free.com/

> Cumorahland provided the best place in America for a defensive warfare. Interspersed among the few hundred drumlin hills, of which Cumorah is typical, were enough bodies of water to hinder the progress of the invading armies. The Great Lakes to the north protected the Nephites' rear, while the Finger Lakes would narrow the front on which the enemy could approach and would hinder the mobilization of his forces, while at the same time facilitating both the defense and feeding of the defending army.[43]

Early explorers described numerous hilltop forts and burial pits. Heber C. Kimball, a resident of western New York who joined the

---

[43] Bean, pp. 46-7.

Church in 1832 and eventually became a member of the First Presidency under President Brigham Young, described his experience.

> In the towns of Boomfield, Victor, Manchester, and in the regions round about, there were hills upon the tops of which were entrenchments and fortifications, and in them were human bones, axes, tomahawks, points of arrows, beads and pipes, which were frequently found; and it was a common occurrence in the country to plow up axes, which I have done many times myself. I have visited the fortifications on the tops of these hills frequently...
>
> The hill Cumorah is a high hill for that country and had the appearance of a fortification or entrenchment around it. In the State of New York, probably there are hundreds of these fortifications which are now visible, and I have seen them in many other parts of the United States.[44]

Archaeologists continue to work in western New York. The University of Buffalo, for example, has over a million artifacts from this area, most of which have not been studied in detail. Experts have differing interpretations of the evidence. For a more detailed discussion of the archaeology of Cumorahland, see Appendix 6. For more discussion of how the text describes this area, see Part 5, How Cumorah Fits: Moroni's America.

Additional maps are available online at www.mobom.org.

## Language

We have no information about what language the Jaredites used. If, as I propose below, they traveled across Asia and then the Pacific to land in North America, they could have used or assimilated multiple languages. The "non-Jaredite Jaredites," meaning descendants of the "friends" of Jared and his brother who accompanied them to the promised land, could have spread throughout the hemisphere, along with whatever languages they used.

Regarding the Nephites, no pre-Columbian civilizations in the

---

[44] *Life of Heber C. Kimball*, p. 25

Western Hemisphere have been discovered with Hebrew or Egyptian writing. Although a few artifacts have been discovered, their legitimacy is questioned and they are not evidence of widespread use anyway.

Professor Brian D. Stubbs has done important work suggesting links between three Middle-Eastern languages and oral languages of Native Americans, including Algonquin and Uto-Aztecan.[45]

Instead of a problem, the lack of Hebrew or Egyptian per se actually fits the descriptions in the text in two ways.

First, no one knew the Nephite language other than the Nephites.

> But the Lord knoweth the things which we have written, and also that none other people knoweth our language; and because that none other people knoweth our language, therefore he hath prepared means for the interpretation thereof. (Mormon 9:34)

Second, the Book of Mormon describes a numerically dominant illiterate population that sought to destroy the records of the literate population from beginning (Enos) to end (Mormon).

> For at the present our strugglings were vain in restoring them to the true faith. And they swore in their wrath that, if it were possible, **they would destroy our records** and us, and also all the traditions of our fathers. (Enos 1:14)

> And it came to pass that when we had gathered in all our people in one to the land of Cumorah, behold I, Mormon, began to be old; and knowing it to be the last struggle of my people, and having been commanded of the Lord that I should not suffer the records which had been handed down by our fathers, which were sacred, to fall into the hands of the Lamanites, (**for the Lamanites would destroy them**) therefore I made this record out of the plates of Nephi, and hid up in the hill Cumorah all the records which had been entrusted to me by the hand of the Lord, save it were these few plates which I gave unto my son Moroni. (Mormon 6:6)

The people of Zarahemla, who were "exceedingly numerous" when Mosiah discovered them, had no written records. Their leader recited

---

[45] For a useful summary of Stubbs' work and additional resources, see http://bmslr.org/exploring-the-explanatory-power-of-semitic-and-egyptian-in-uto-aztecan/

his genealogy by memory. Mosiah taught them his language and they began writing, but such knowledge was likely limited to the ruling classes. (Omni 1:17-18) The only record of an engraved stone was the one that Coriantumr apparently engraved when he encountered the people of Zarahemla and couldn't communicate.

There were instances of Lamanites interacting with a written language, but they are few and far between.

## Population—DNA

The text does not specifically enumerate the Jaredite and Nephite/Lamanite populations. Estimates based on the text are speculative, ranging from thousands to millions.

Regarding DNA, we do not know for sure what DNA profiles either the Jaredites or Lehi's people would have had, but we have an idea. We will discuss both issues in each section on the different groups.

## Jaredites: Who, What, When and Where

**DNA and Jaredites**. DNA evidence indicates that most indigenous people in the Americas have East Asian ancestry, presumably because they crossed over the frozen Bering Strait thousands of years ago.

That evidence does not contradict the Book of Mormon, however. Instead, it is what we could expect.

The Book of Mormon explains that the Jaredites left "the great tower" (presumably the tower of Babel in modern Iraq or a Sumerian tower, around 2200 B.C.) and spent an unspecified time journeying across land and bodies of water "into the wilderness, yea, into that quarter where there never had man been." (Ether 2:5) They arrived at a seashore where they stayed for four years. (Ether 2:13) Hugh Nibley,[46] among others, inferred that they crossed central Asia and reached the coast of what is now China, which makes sense to me. They could have

---

[46] E.g., see Nibley's *The World of the Jaredites*, p. 190, and his series in the *Improvement Era* in 1951-2, such as the November 1951 issue, online here: https://catalog.churchofjesuschrist.org/assets?id=3df6b264-bacd-4420-a7c6-bb0ef6e0d8ba&crate=0&index=0

traveled in the area that later came to be known as the Silk Road from Iraq to the northeastern coast of China. Although they traversed an uninhabited area, naturally we would expect them to encounter other tribes or civilizations at various points along the way. There would be plenty of opportunity for intermarriage with people having Asian DNA.

The Gospel Topics Essay on Book of Mormon and DNA Studies notes that

> a 2014 study indicates that as much as one-third of Native American DNA may have originated anciently in Europe or West Asia. From this evidence, scientists conclude that some Europeans or West Asians migrated eastward across Asia, mixing with a group that eventually migrated to the Americas millennia before the events described in the Book of Mormon. [47]

That is consistent with the eastward migration of the Jaredites, except for one thing: timing.

The phrase "millennia before" Book of Mormon events refers to the study cited in the essay that focused on the genome of "an approximately 24,000-year-old individual."[48] This is one of several citations in the essay that are based on evolutionary theories that conclude modern humans appeared over 100,000 years ago. That time frame directly contradicts D&C 77:6, which affirms the biblical timeline ("seven thousand years of [earth's] continuance, or its temporal existence"). The Book of Mormon and Pearl of Great Price affirm the creation of Adam as described in the Bible.

The discrepancy has led to discussions of "pre-Adamites" with Adam and Eve being a "special creation." Some people reject the scriptural timeline, while others reject the scientific timeline. Others claim the scientific timeline is an estimate based on erroneous assumptions. A discussion of the discrepancies between scriptural and scientific time frames is beyond the scope of this book. Like the

---

[47] The essay claims that "DNA studies cannot be used decisively to either affirm or reject the historical authenticity of the Book of Mormon." See https://www.churchofjesuschrist.org/study/manual/gospel-topics-essays/book-of-mormon-and-dna-studies?lang=eng.

[48] *Nature* 505 (2014): 87-91, https://www.nature.com/articles/nature12736.

question of Book of Mormon geography, both sides of the equation contain unknown variables that future discoveries and/or revelation may resolve.

My point here is that the narrative in the Book of Ether is congruent with the scientific narrative of the DNA origins of indigenous people in the Western Hemisphere, apart from the time frames.

Jared, his brother, their friends, and all their families embarked in ships (barges) and arrived in the Promised Land after 344 days at sea. (Ether 6:11) By comparison, it took about a year for debris to drift from Japan to Canada after the 2011 tsunami.[49] As I discussed in *Moroni's America*, a First Nations tribe in British Columbia, Canada, has an origin story that relates their ancestors came in tight ships illuminated by shining pearls.

If the Jaredites crossed the North Pacific from China to Canada, we would expect their Asian DNA to show up the way it has.

One researcher has discovered evidence that the people crossed by boat from northern Asia to North America and migrated both northward into what is now northwestern Canada and Alaska and southward into what is now the United States and Latin America.[50]

Assuming as I do that the Jaredites landed in British Columbia, how did Asian DNA expand throughout Latin America?

**Other migrations.** One answer is that the Jaredites were not the only people who migrated from Asia to the Western Hemisphere. They may have come before or after other groups.

Joseph Smith explained it this way:

In this important and interesting book the history of ancient America is unfolded, from its first settlement by a colony that came from the tower of Babel, at the confusion of languages to the beginning of the fifth century of the Christian era. We are informed by these records that America in ancient times has been inhabited by two distinct races of people. The first were called Jaredites and came directly from the tower

[49] See https://www.theguardian.com/world/2012/may/02/motorcycle-japanese-tsunami-reaches-canada#
[50] See https://www.smithsonianmag.com/science-nature/how-humans-came-to-americas-180973739/. This article presents the same dating issues as all DNA/archaeological studies.

of Babel. ... The Jaredites were destroyed about the time that the Israelites came from Jerusalem, who succeeded them in the inheritance of the country.[51]

Notice that Joseph did not define "America" here. Scholars have debated the meaning he intended. Some say he meant the country in which he lived—the United States of America—because that's how people referred to the country in the 1840s. I agree with that view, but I also recognize that some people say Joseph meant to North America, while others claim he meant all of the Western Hemisphere—the continents of North and South America. The last word of the quotation—"country"—corroborates my interpretation, and later in the letter Joseph distinguished between "continent" and "country" when he wrote, "penetrated every **continent**, visited every clime, swept every **country**." But you can reach whatever conclusion you want.

Two important points stand out. First, Joseph did not say these were the *only* two races or groups of people who inhabited America. Others could have come before or after the Jaredites. True, Joseph wrote "from its first settlement by a colony that came from the tower of Babel," but he was describing the Book of Mormon; i.e., the first settlement mentioned in the Book of Mormon, not the first settlement ever.

Second, Joseph said Lehi's people succeeded the Jaredites "in the inheritance of the country." In my view, this limits the scope of the territory occupied by the "Jaredites" and says nothing about the others who crossed the sea with Jared who lived outside "the country." This leads to the second explanation for the spread of Asian DNA throughout the Americas.

**Non-Jaredites.** The Jaredites were not the only people who came with Jared.

The Book of Ether is a record of Ether's ancestors who directly descended from Jared. Ether listed over 30 generations of his ancestors, a direct line back to Jared. The term "Jaredites" (which appears only once in the scriptures, in Moroni 9:23) itself connotes descendants of Jared. Thus, the Book of Ether is explicitly *not* a record of all the people

---

[51] The Wentworth letter. https://www.josephsmithpapers.org/paper-summary/church-history-1-march-1842/2#8180497476075025433

who descended from Jared's brother, or the twenty-two friends who accompanied them on a long overland journey before the sea voyage on the barges.

When the brother of Jared "began to be old," he and Jared gathered the people for a census. (Ether 6:19-21) The report itemizes their children but does not mention their friends, which suggests their friends and their descendants had dispersed.

Moroni explained the limited scope of the Book of Ether. "I, Moroni, proceed to give an account of those ancient inhabitants who were destroyed by the hand of the Lord upon the face of **this north country.**" (Ether 1:1)

The term "this" indicates Moroni was referring to the place where he lived when he engraved the Book of Ether. Recall, Moroni told Joseph that the record was "written and deposited" not far from Joseph's home near Palmyra.

The term "north country" limits the scope of the record; i.e., there were inhabitants elsewhere who were not involved with the destruction.

This leads me to infer that the friends of Jared and his brother likely spread to different areas, primarily south of the land occupied by the Jaredites. Their descendants could have produced or participated in the Olmec civilization, for example.

**Conclusion.** The Book of Ether describes a migration from western Asia to the western hemisphere that could account, at least in part, for the presence of Asian DNA among indigenous people. Moroni's limited the scope of the destruction of the Jaredites to "this north country," suggesting that descendants of non-Jaredites who arrived with Jared inhabited other areas, which is also consistent with the archaeological record.

## Mulekites: Who, What, When and Where

The Book of Mormon tells us little about the Mulekites (a term not used in the text), but we can piece together some information from the Bible and other sources.[52]

---

[52] Garth A. Wilson, "The Mulekites," *Ensign*, March 1987, https://www.churchofjesuschrist.org/study/ensign/1987/03/the-

The people of Zarahemla descended from Mulek, a son of King Zedekiah who escaped the destruction of Jerusalem when his brothers were all slain and Zedekiah was blinded and taken to Babylon around 587 B.C. Some scholars think Mulek had not yet been born; his pregnant mother perhaps escaped to Egypt or Lebanon from whence Phoenician sailors brought them to the New World.

The scriptures say simply that the people of Zarahemla came "out from Jerusalem" and "they journeyed in the wilderness, and were brought by the hand of the Lord across the great waters, into the land where Mosiah discovered them; and they had dwelt there from that time forth." (Omni 1:15-16)

The chronology suggests that the Mulek's group and Lehi's group arrived in the Promised Land about the same time, yet they did not discover one another for hundreds of years until sometime between 279 B.C. and 130 B.C. How was this possible?

If the future city of Zarahemla was located across from Nauvoo, the Mulekites likely sailed up the Mississippi River until they reached the impassable rapids "and dwelt there from that time forth." They had no written language; they kept oral genealogies. This suggests a somewhat more primitive society than the Nephites enjoyed.

They undoubtedly lived along that river, as ancient people did everywhere. Although the people of Zarahemla were more numerous than the people of Mosiah (the Nephites), they had no cities (at least none are mentioned in the text). The first mention of a "city of Zarahemla" is in Alma 2:26 (about 87 B.C.), suggesting that there was no Mulekite city until well after Mosiah encountered them.

If the land of Nephi was in eastern Tennessee (see next section), then it makes sense that the Nephites would not encounter the Mulekites until the Lamanites invaded and forced King Mosiah to lead his people out of the land. The text says "they were led by the power of his arm, through the wilderness until they came down into the land which is called the land of Zarahemla." (Omni 1:13)

I infer they "came down" by descending the Tennessee River, which flows north from Tennessee to Illinois, or the land of Zarahemla. There they discovered the people of Zarahemla as explained in the book of

mulekites?lang=eng

Omni.

This setting leads me to infer as well that Coriantumr left the battlefield in New York and traveled the river systems toward the area Ether prophesied about: the New Jerusalem. If so, Coriantumr would journey down the Ohio River to the Mississippi River toward the Missouri River (which leads to the New Jerusalem). In the Mississippi River, the people of Mulek discovered him. (Omni 1:21) They couldn't communicate, so during the nine months Coriantumr spent with them, he engraved the large stone to tell his story.

There are several Nephite proper nouns that appear to be influenced by Jaredite proper nouns, but these start to appear in the Book of Alma.[53] This suggests Jaredite influence postdated the union of Mosiah's people with Zarahemla's people. This could indicate that

(i) the people of Zarahemla were influenced by Jaredite influence other than Coriantumr's, such as remnants of Jaredite (or non-Jaredite Jaredites) in the area, before they joined Mosiah's people;

(ii) such non-Jaredite Jaredite influence occurred after the Nephites and Mulekites joined together; or

(iii) Jaredite names became popular after Mosiah translated the Jaredite plates.

When Mosiah's people united with Zarahemla's, the people appointed Mosiah to be their king, effectively replacing Zarahemla. From that point on, they were known as Nephites.

## Nephites: Who, What, When and Where

**DNA and Nephites/Lamanites.** Although the Book of Ether offers an explanation for Asian DNA among ancient people in the western hemisphere, critics also focus on the lack of Israelite DNA among indigenous people on the theory that both Mulek's group and Lehi's group would have brought such DNA to the New World.

In the Wentworth letter, Joseph made two key points.

---

[53] Robert F. Smith, "Reuse of Jaredite Names Among the Mulekites, Lamanites and Nephites," https://onoma.lib.byu.edu/index.php/Reuse_of_Jaredite_Names_Among_the_Mulekites,_Lamanites_and_Nephites

I was also informed concerning the aboriginal inhabitants of this **country**, and shown who they were, and from whence they came... The second race came directly from the city of Jerusalem, about six hundred years before Christ. They were principally Israelites, of the descendants of Joseph. The Jaredites were destroyed about the time that the Israelites came from Jerusalem, [around 586 B.C.] who succeeded them in the inheritance of the **country**. The principal nation of the second race fell in battle towards the close of the fourth century. The remnant are the Indians that now inhabit this **country**.

Three times in this passage Joseph refers to "country." When Moroni first visited Joseph Smith, he

gave a general account of the promises made to the fathers, and also **gave a history of the aborigenes of this country**, and said they were literal descendants of Abraham. He represented them as once being an enlightned and intelligent people, possessing a correct knowledge of the gospel, and the plan of restoration and redemption. He said this history was written and deposited not far from that place, and that it was our brother's privilege, if obedient to the commandments of the Lord, to obtain and translate the same by the means of the Urim and Thummim, which were deposited for that purpose with the record.[54]

This direct link between what Moroni told Joseph and what Joseph told Mr. Wentworth suggests our identification of the "remnant" of the "descendants of Joseph" should focus on "this country."

Historians have recognized that much of the Wentworth letter "echoes some wording from Orson Pratt's *A[n] Interesting Account of Several Remarkable Visions, and of the Late Discovery of Ancient American Records*."[55] Pratt spent several pages discussing his theory that the Book of Mormon setting extended from Lehi's purported landing in Chile to the extinction events in New York at Cumorah.

In my book *Brought to Light*, I compared the two documents in detail, thereby revealing an important insight into Joseph's claim that "the remnant are the Indians that now inhabit this country." That claim

---

[54] https://www.josephsmithpapers.org/paper-summary/history-1834-1836/68
[55] https://www.josephsmithpapers.org/paper-summary/church-history-1-march-1842/2#historical-intro

completely replaced Pratt's hemispheric theory.

In other words, Joseph specifically deleted Pratt's discussion of South and Central America and specified that Lehi's remnant are the Indians in the United States, circa 1842.

The essence of that comparison is included in Appendix 5.

### Identification in the Doctrine and Covenants.

Four revelations in the Doctrine and Covenants corroborate what Joseph wrote in the Wentworth letter. The Lord identified tribes living in New York, Ohio, and Missouri as Lamanites. Joseph Smith personally told the Sac and Fox tribal leaders that the Book of Mormon told about their fathers.[56] The tribes lived in Michigan and Ohio until they were moved to Illinois and then west of the Mississippi across from Nauvoo.

D&C 28, a "Revelation given through Joseph Smith the Prophet to Oliver Cowdery, at Fayette, New York, September 1830."

> 8 And now, behold, I say unto you that you shall go unto the Lamanites and preach my gospel unto them; and inasmuch as they receive thy teachings thou shalt cause my church to be established among them; and thou shalt have revelations, but write them not by way of commandment.
> 9 And now, behold, I say unto you that it is not revealed, and no man knoweth where the city Zion shall be built, but it shall be given hereafter. Behold, I say unto you that **it shall be on the borders by the Lamanites.**
> 14 And thou shalt assist to settle all these things, according to the covenants of the church, before **thou shalt take thy journey among the Lamanites.**
> 15 And it shall be given thee from the time thou shalt go, until the time thou shalt return, what thou shalt do.
> 16 And thou must open thy mouth at all times, declaring my gospel with the sound of rejoicing. Amen.

D&C 30, a "Revelation given through Joseph Smith the Prophet to David Whitmer, Peter Whitmer Jr., and John Whitmer, at Fayette, New

---

[56]  https://www.josephsmithpapers.org/paper-summary/account-of-meeting-23-may-1844/2

York, September 1830."

> 5 Behold, I say unto you, Peter, that you shall take your journey with your brother Oliver; for the time has come that it is expedient in me that you shall open your mouth to declare my gospel; therefore, fear not, but give heed unto the words and advice of your brother, which he shall give you. 6 And be you afflicted in all his afflictions, ever lifting up your heart unto me in prayer and faith, for his and your deliverance; for I have given unto him power to build up my church among the **Lamanites**;

D&C 32, a "Revelation given through Joseph Smith the Prophet to Parley P. Pratt and Ziba Peterson, in Manchester, New York, early October 1830. Great interest and desires were felt by the elders respecting the Lamanites, of whose predicted blessings the Church had learned from the Book of Mormon. In consequence, supplication was made that the Lord would indicate His will as to whether elders should be sent at that time to the Indian tribes in the West."

> 1 And now concerning my servant Parley P. Pratt, behold, I say unto him that as I live I will that he shall declare my gospel and learn of me, and be meek and lowly of heart.
> 2 And that which I have appointed unto him is that he shall go with my servants, Oliver Cowdery and Peter Whitmer, Jun., **into the wilderness among the Lamanites.**
> 3 And Ziba Peterson also shall go with them; and I myself will go with them and be in their midst; and I am their advocate with the Father, and nothing shall prevail against them.

D&C 54, a "Revelation given through Joseph Smith the Prophet to Newel Knight, at Kirtland, Ohio, June 10, 1831."

> 7 Wherefore, go to now and flee the land, lest your enemies come upon you; and take your journey, and appoint whom you will to be your leader, and to pay moneys for you.
> 8 And thus you shall take your journey into the regions westward, unto the land of Missouri, unto the borders of the Lamanites.

These tribes were genetically distinct from the indigenous people

88

further west and south in North America and Central and South America. Those people have predominantly Haplogroups A, B, C, and D, while the tribes from the northeastern U.S. and Canada have a relatively high incidence of Haplogroup X2.

This map of X Haplogroup shows that X is mostly concentrated in the Middle-East and the Northeastern parts of the U.S. and Canada. The genetic connection between these two regions remains unclear.

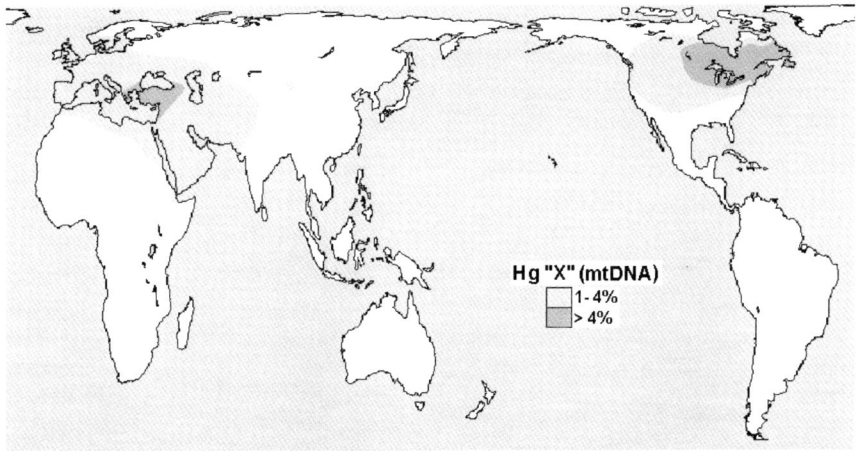
Figure 15 - X Haplogroup from Wikipedia

There are numerous papers on this topic, some of which are referenced in the Gospel Topics Essay on DNA, discussed above.

The Wikipedia article explains that

> ...no presence of mt-DNA ancestral to X2a has been found in Europe or the Near East. New World lineages X2a and X2g are not derived from the Old World lineages X2b, X2c, X2d, X2e, and X2f, indicating an early origin of the New World lineages "likely at the very beginning of their expansion and spread from the Near East". A 2008 study came to the conclusion that the presence of haplogroup X in the Americas does not support migration from Solutrean-period Europe.

> The lineage of haplogroup X in the Americas is not derived from a European subclade, but rather represents an independent subclade, labelled X2a. The X2a subclade has not been found in Eurasia, and has

most likely arisen within the early Paleo-Indian population, at roughly 13,000 years ago.[57]

The X2a subclade raises dating issues similar to those I mentioned in connection with the Jaredites. Consequently, the DNA evidence neither proves nor disproves the claims of the Book of Mormon. This is another area in which we await additional information, but the areas where X2a is found raise a question about where the Nephites lived.

### Where did the Nephites live?

We can accept the teachings of the prophets about the New York Cumorah, but that does not explain how the Nephites and Lamanites ended up there.

Proponents of M2C and other settings that reject the New York Cumorah make a good point when they say New York is too far away for the Nephites to travel there only to fight a battle of extinction. Whether they would have traveled from Baja, Mesoamerica, Panama, Chile, or any other site in Latin America, such a journey would be improbable but not impossible.

Recognizing this, several people have proposed settings in and around New York, the eastern United States, and the Heartland area (Illinois, Indiana and Ohio).

All these scenarios depend on a theory about Lehi's voyage.

The Book of Mormon explains that Lehi's group left Jerusalem and traveled south until they traveled "nearly eastward" until they arrived at the seashore, which we assume was the coast of the Arabian peninsula. (1 Nephi 17) From there they sailed to the Promised Land.

There are two ways to sail to the western hemisphere: east or west. Those believers who think Lehi sailed east think Lehi landed along the western coast of Central or South America, such as in Chile, Panama, Guatemala, or Baja. Their models are based on such landing sites.

An undated cryptic note written by Frederick G. Williams said Lehi "landed on the continent of South America in Chile thirty degrees south Lattitude," but any link to Joseph Smith is speculative.[58] One of the

---

[57] https://en.wikipedia.org/wiki/Haplogroup_X_(mtDNA)

[58] Frederick G. Williams, "Did Lehi Land in Chile?"

anonymous 1842 *Times and Seasons* articles claimed Lehi "landed a little south of the isthmus of Darien" which is modern Panama, and again any link to Joseph Smith is speculative.[59]

For Lehi, the alternative to sailing east is sailing west, then south along the coast of Africa, around Cape Horn, then north and west across the Atlantic. Prevailing winds and currents would take a sailing ship toward North America, similar to the route Columbus took to the Caribbean and Gulf of Mexico.

The practicality of such a voyage was demonstrated in 2008-2010 and in 2019 by a sailing ship constructed to replicate a Phoenician ship found in the Mediterranean and dated to around 600 B.C.[60]

There are other reasons to infer Lehi sailed west, including the prevailing winds during the time of year he presumably departed from the Arabian peninsula and an interpretation of Isaiah 18:1 that places the latter-day promised land beyond Africa.[61]

The Williams statement mentioned "thirty degrees south latitude." If that statement was based on something Williams heard, the speaker (whether Joseph or someone else) might have said Lehi landed at thirty degrees latitude and Williams inferred the rest. Coincidentally, Jerusalem is at about 30 degrees latitude (31.7 degrees north latitude). In North America, modern Tallahassee is at 30 degrees north latitude. This raises a possibility that Lehi landed somewhere along the panhandle of Florida.

When I embarked on the investigation that led to *Moroni's America*, I took the New York Cumorah as a "pin in the map" given to us by prophets. Then I made a hypothesis that Zarahemla was across from Nauvoo, pursuant to D&C 125. Next I put myself in the position of an earthbound society trying to describe geography.

I was surprised at how well the text described the land, assuming Lehi landed in the panhandle of Florida.

---

https://scholarsarchive.byu.edu/cgi/viewcontent.cgi?filename=14&article=1065&context=mi&type=additional

[59] *Times and Seasons*, Vol. 3, No. 22 (15 September 1842): 922, online at http://www.latterdaytruth.org/pdf/100148.pdf

[60] https://www.phoeniciansbeforecolumbus.com/

[61] "Reproducing Lehi's and Mulek's Voyages," https://www.mobom.org/lehi-cross-ocean

Using *Moroni's America* as a framework for discussion,[62] it's easy to see why the New York Cumorah makes sense.

Figure 16 - Overview of Nephite lands

Lehi landed in Florida, probably along the west coast or panhandle. Nephi and his family and others fled from Laman and Lemuel and went to the highlands of eastern Tennessee, around Chattanooga. The Nephites lived there until the Lamanites invaded and the Lord led them "down into" the land of Zarahemla, where they joined with the Mulekites as we discussed in the previous section.

The Book of Mormon describes the Nephite expansion from the land of Zarahemla (along the Upper Mississippi River in what is now Illinois) to the land Bountiful, which I consider to be the area north of the Ohio River in what is now Indiana and Ohio. The Ohio River was a natural border between the Lamanites in the land southward and the Nephites in the land northward.

---

[62] See Part Five-How Cumorah fits: *Moroni's America.*

Mormon explained it this way:

> Now the land south was called Lehi, and the land north was called Mulek, which was after the son of Zedekiah; for the Lord did bring Mulek into the land north, and Lehi into the land south.
> (Helaman 6:10)

Mulek landed in Iowa, across from Nauvoo, and the Nephites spread throughout the Midwest north of the Ohio River, while Lehi landed in Florida and the Lamanites spread throughout the south, bordered on the north by the Ohio River.

When the final wars started at Zarahemla, the Nephites retreated further and further north and east. The Lamanites destroyed the Nephite cities along the way.

Mormon knew the history of the Jaredites and gathered the remainder of his people to the "land of Cumorah" because he "had hope to gain advantage over the Lamanites" there. (Mormon 6:4)

This made sense because the Jaredites had four years to prepare for their final battles. They had built defensive structures on hill tops and, presumably a bunker in the Hill Cumorah. It was this bunker that Mormon used to secure the Nephite records

———

As I've said throughout this book, my concept of *Moroni's America* is only one of several working hypotheses. I include this map and explanation here because I think it works. Others have suggested variations here and there which are entirely plausible.

In other words, the *Moroni's America* setting works well for me. I think it is consistent with every known statement by the prophets as well as the descriptions of geography in the Book of Mormon itself. It fits with the prophecies and promises made in the text. External evidence corroborates this setting, as we'll see in Part Five.

And yet, I'm entirely open to better ideas. If you have ideas, I'd be happy to consider them as well. Over the years, people have suggested lots of alternatives to me. I only ask that you do enough research to understand the issues and make sure your ideas have not been previously proposed, because if they have, I've probably already considered them.

With the overall framework of Moroni's America as a working hypothesis, we can look at the extrinsic evidence and see whether it corroborates the hypothesis.

## Population—Numbers

The Book of Mormon describes Jaredites, Nephites, Lamanites, and the people of Zarahemla, but never gives a specific number of people in their respective populations. Some aspects of their societies are mentioned, but as Mormon explained, he could not relate "a hundredth part of the proceedings of this people." (Helaman 3:14)

We cannot locate something if we don't know what we're looking for. Does the Book of Mormon describe huge populations of people who inhabited the entire western hemisphere? Large, sophisticated populations who lived in densely populated urban environments? Small populations spread out in communities along rivers?

Proponents of M2C favor large Nephite populations because that fits the archaeology of Mesoamerica, and the text does not exclude such a working hypothesis. However, in my view the text describes a much smaller population, which is consistent with the archaeology in North America.

The limitations of the abridged text leave us with few definitive answers, but we can make reasonable inferences, consider the teachings of the prophets, and evaluate the external evidence to see what these populations may have looked like.

**Jaredites**. The Jaredites conducted a census but only listed the children of Jared and his brother. (Ether 6:19-21) Jared had four sons and eight daughters. His brother had twenty-two sons and daughters. Beyond that, we have no population counts until chapter 15, when Coriantumr remembered what Ether had told him.

> And it came to pass when Coriantumr had recovered of his wounds, he began to remember the words which Ether had spoken unto him.

He saw that there had been slain by the sword already nearly two millions of his people, and he began to sorrow in his heart; yea, there had been slain two millions of mighty men, and also their wives and their children. (Ether 15:1–2)

This passage has apparently led many people—both believers and unbelievers—to infer that two million Jaredites were killed at the final battle of Cumorah.

*BYU Studies* offers a comparison of "The Two Final Battles" involving the Jaredites and the Nephites.[63] The chart claims 2 million or more Jaredites died at the hill Ramah and around 230,000 Nephites died at the same location, which they called Cumorah.

# The Two Final Battles

|  | Jaredites | Nephites |
|---|---|---|
| when | ca. 300 B.C. | 385 A.D. |
| where | hill Ramah | hill Cumorah (hill Ramah) |
| who | Coriantumr and Shiz | Nephites and Lamanites |
| how many | 2 million or more | around 230,000 Nephites |
| who gathered | men, wives, children | men, wives, children |
| outcome | both sides destroyed | Nephites destroyed |
| Spirit | ceased to strive with | ceased to strive with |
| prophet | Ether | Mormon |
| account | Ether 13–15 | Mormon 6–7 |
| record | 24 gold plates | plates of Mormon |
| survivor | Coriantumr | Moroni |

Figure 17 - Two Final Battles - *BYU Studies*

---

[63] See https://byustudies.byu.edu/further-study-chart/138-the-two-final-battles/. We will discuss the Nephites separately below.

Supporters of M2C use these large numbers to justify their rejection of the New York Cumorah, claiming there is no evidence in western New York of battles of this size.[64] Critics of the Book of Mormon also point to these numbers as both unrealistic and unauthenticated by external evidence. In both cases, their assumptions about what the text says leads to their respective conclusions.

But what do the scriptures say?

When Coriantumr remembered what Ether had told him and saw that two millions of his people had been slain, this was more than four years before the final battle at the hill Ramah.

After his reminiscence, Coriantumr wrote to Shiz, hoping to spare his people. Instead, the people on both sides became angry and found another battle. Coriantumr fled to the waters of Ripliancum. There "they fought an exceedingly sore battle" and Coriantumr was wounded again, but his armies prevailed and the armies of Shiz fled southward. Only after that did the army of Coriantumr pitch his tents by the hill Ramah.

Then they spent four years gathering their people. (Ether 15:14)

The text supports two inferences regarding the millions of people.

(i) Coriantumr could have been reflecting on the death of "two millions" of his people during the conflicts during his lifetime leading up to the time of his reflection.

(ii) Alternatively, Coriantumr could have been thinking of the accumulated deaths of his people during their recorded history.

The latter inference makes more sense to me because the record of the Jaredites consists of a series of civil wars. For example, in Chapter 8, Jared rebelled against his father, gave battle and imprisoned his father, only to have Jared's siblings kill Jared's army. (Ether 8:2-6)

Ether listed over 30 generations from the original Jared. Three times he wrote someone was "a descendant" of an ancestor, suggesting there could have been more generations involved.

---

[64] E.g., see a compilation of reasons to reject the New York Cumorah here: https://www.fairmormon.org/answers/Book_of_Mormon/Geography/New_Worl d/Hill_Cumorah#Question:_Are_the_large_population_counts_described_in_the_ Book_of_Mormon_during_the_final_battle_at_the_Hill_Cumorah_accurate.3F

A generation is normally 30-40 years, but any given generation could be shorter or longer in time. The common interpretation of Enos, for example, is that Jacob was his father, making Enos Lehi's grandson. Enos wrote around 420 B.C.—about 180 years after Lehi left Jerusalem.

Regardless of how much time elapsed during the 30+ generations of the Jaredites, the death of two million people (or more, if wives and children were counted separately) is not surprising. It amounts to around 67,000 per generation. If a generation is around 35 years on average, that means about 2,000 people/year dying in conflicts. Such a number would leave little, if any, evidence beyond the burial mounds we find throughout the midwestern and eastern U.S.

What about the final Jaredite battle at Cumorah?

The 8-day Jaredite battle at Cumorah could not have involved more than a few thousand, as we see from the count of the actual number killed on the last two days. (Ether 15:15-32)

Even after four years, Coriantumr could gather only a relatively few people to Cumorah. They fought for five days without enumerating the casualties, but at the end of the sixth day, there were only 121 people left. The next day, there were only 59 left. Over the next two days, everyone was killed except Coriantumr and Shiz.

If we assume, based on the numbers Ether gave us, that half the people were killed each day, that calculates to about 7,744 on the first day of battle—total, including both sides.

It turns out that Oliver Cowdery addressed this point in 1835 and came to the same conclusion.

In Letter VII, Oliver explained that Mormon foresaw the approaching destruction and its parallel to the Jaredite destruction in the same place. Speaking from Mormon's perspective, and after describing the mile-wide valley west of the Hill Cumorah, Oliver wrote:

"In this vale lie commingled, in one mass of ruin **the ashes of thousands**, and in this vale was destined to consume the fair forms and vigerous systems of tens of thousands of the human race—blood mixed with blood, flesh with flesh, bones with bones and dust with dust!"[65]

---

[65] http://www.josephsmithpapers.org/paper-summary/history-1834-1836/92

Oliver, writing from the perspective of Mormon's prophetic understanding, described the remains of the Jaredites as "the ashes of thousands." Not millions, but thousands. Not even tens of thousands, which was the number to be killed in the yet future final battle of the Nephites.

Just thousands.

In the early 1800s, students were taught to count in ones, tens, hundreds, thousands, tens of thousands, and hundreds of thousands. This correlates to the Roman Numeral system. Both the Book of Mormon and the Doctrine and Covenants use the phrase "tens of thousands," even though the phrase does not appear in the Bible.

For Oliver to write "thousands" instead of "tens of thousands" suggests the number was lower than ten thousand, and certainly lower than twenty thousand.

An interpretation of the text that has fewer than ten thousand Jaredites being killed at Ramah, and other deaths in the thousands (but not millions) over the course of Jaredite history, is easily compatible with the archaeological evidence in western New York.

**Nephites**. In the quotation above, Oliver wrote that "tens of thousands" would die in the final battle of the Nephites at Cumorah. That would include both Nephites and Lamanites killed there.

Is that compatible with the scriptures?

The text never reports a Nephite census number. Populations estimates for Book of Mormon people vary widely, with some estimates in the millions, but the text describes a relatively small population.

When Lachoneus assembled the Nephites in the center of the land to defend against the robbers, they "did march forth by thousands and tens of thousands," another application of the Roman Numeral counting system. (3 Ne. 3:22) No "hundreds of thousands" are mentioned.

However large the number was, "they did dwell in one land, and in one body," beginning in the latter end of the 17th year. They had "reserved for themselves provisions... that they might subsist for the space of seven years." We wonder, how many people using A.D. 17 technology could the Nephites assemble in one place, together with enough provisions to last for seven years?

A million? Highly unlikely. Even today's modern cities could survive at most for a few weeks without fresh supplies.

Because Mormon never used the term "hundreds of thousands," I infer the Nephite population was usually in the tens of thousands, possibly up to two hundred thousand, but probably lower than that.

Early in his own life history, Mormon described a war with the Lamanites.

> And it came to pass that the Nephites had gathered together a great number of men, even to exceed the number of thirty thousand. (Mormon 1:11)

If a "great number of men" was a little over 30,000, Mormon was not dealing with a population in the millions. In fact, the largest enumerated Nephite army in the entire Book of Mormon was only 42,000 men (Morm. 2:9), assembled after gathering in their people (2:7). That army faced a Lamanite force of 44,000.

A few years later a Nephite army 30,000 faced a Lamanite army of 50,000 men, the largest enumerated army in the text (2:25). This was around 346 AD, only about 40 years before the final conflict at Cumorah. I infer that the decrease in the Nephite army from 42,000 to 30,000 was due to casualties in the wars.

From 346 until 388, Mormon describes a continual retreat from the Lamanites, with occasional victories but mostly slaughter—an "exceedingly great slaughter." There is nothing in the account to support a significant increase in numbers for the army, apart from whatever population growth could be possible in such conditions.

At some point—the text does not say when—Mormon makes an agreement with the Lamanite king for a last stand at Cumorah. He was optimistic; "here we had hope to gain advantage over the Lamanites." But by 384, after Mormon "had gathered in all our people in one to the land of Cumorah," he realizes there is no hope. His forces were inadequate, and "knowing it to be the last struggle of my people," he hides up the records and awaits the onslaught of the overwhelming Lamanite force.

Nevertheless, the *BYU Studies* table showed 230,000 Nephites killed at Cumorah, not including Lamanite deaths. That is the traditional interpretation of Mormon 6.

But is it accurate?

If Mormon actually had a force of 230,000 men, in a favorable location that gave an advantage to the defense, it does not seem likely he would have lost his hope even before the Lamanites arrived. He had withstood 50,000 Lamanites with an army of 30,000. His warriors would be more desperate at Cumorah than before.

My reading of the text has Mormon hopeful—until he actually gathers in all the people and sees how few remain.

Mormon said he could behold (see), from the top of the hill Cumorah, those who had fallen in the battle, consisting of "the ten thousand of my people" and "the ten thousand of my people who were led by my son Moroni." (Mormon 6:11-12).

One interpretation of this passage is the phrase "ten thousand" represents a military unit, not a specific number. For example, a "tumen" is a unit of ten thousand households and soldiers, as used by Mongol and Turkic people.[66] The "ten thousand" was also a military group of mostly Greeks that Xenophon wrote about in the *Anabasis.*[67]

It's possible that Mormon used a similar term to designate a military unit and Joseph translated it literally as "ten thousand," whether the actual number was really ten thousand.

The other 210,000 listed in the *BYU Studies* chart come from verses 13-15.

It's easy to misunderstand these verses because in verses 11 and 12, Mormon said "we did **behold** [my 10,000]… and we also **beheld** [Moroni's 10,000]. In both cases, behold is a synonym for "see" and "saw," respectively.

But starting in verse 13, Mormon did not say he saw the other groups of ten thousand.

Instead, Mormon starts verse 13 with the phrase "And behold."

It is a quirk of English that "behold" has dual meanings. As a transitive verb, it means to observe or see, as Mormon used it in verses 11 and 12. But as an intransitive verb, it is "used in the imperative,

---

[66] https://en.wikipedia.org/wiki/Tumen_(unit)

[67] https://en.wikipedia.org/wiki/Ten_Thousand

especially to call attention."[68] The phrase "and behold" is used 286 times in the Book of Mormon. It is used to call attention, not to describe what the writer is actually seeing.

Mormon used the word in the imperative several times in his own book.

**And behold,** ye shall take the plates of Nephi unto yourself (Mormon 1:4)

**And behold,** I withstood him with forty and two thousand. And it came to pass that I beat him with my army that he fled before me. **And behold,** all this was done, and three hundred and thirty years had passed away. (Mormon 2:9)

**And behold,** I had employed my people, the Nephites, in preparing their lands and their arms against the time of battle. (Mormon 3:1)

**And behold** they did harden their hearts against the Lord their God. (Mormon 3:3)

**and behold,** they shall come forth according to the commandment of the Lord, when he shall see fit, in his wisdom. **And behold,** they shall go unto the unbelieving of the Jews; (Mormon 5:13–14)

**And behold,** the Lord hath reserved their blessings, which they might have received in the land, for the Gentiles who shall possess the land. (Mormon 5:19)

**And behold,** the ten thousand of Gidgiddonah had fallen, and he also in the midst. (Mormon 6:13)

Verses 13 and 14 also use the past perfect "had fallen," indicating they had died previously. We cannot tell when, exactly, these other leaders fell with their respective "ten thousand" but there are two possibilities, similar to the situation we have with Coriantumr.

(i) Mormon was listing the other military units who died during the

---

[68] https://www.merriam-webster.com/dictionary/behold. See also http://webstersdictionary1828.com/Dictionary/behold

final wars leading up to Cumorah; or

(ii) Mormon was reminiscing about all the leaders and their units that he commanded from the time he became the general of the Nephites in his sixteenth year. (Mormon 2:2)

Considering the number of battles Mormon participated in during his career, it does not seem unreasonable that, at the end of his life, he would recognize these earlier military leaders and their armies who sacrificed for their people.

You might wonder, why would Mormon write about his previous leaders and their people who had fallen?

First, he was with his son on top of the Hill Cumorah in New York looking back on everything that had happened. In verses 17-22, he reflected on the loss of his entire nation, the people who had refused his call to repent all the way back to the time when he was 15 and saw their wickedness and wanted to preach, but was prevented (Mormon 1:15).

That happened around 325 A.D.. In Chapter 6, he was writing around the year 385 A.D. He was looking back at 60 years of his life. In Chapter 5, he recounted how he agreed to lead the Nephite armies again in 379 A.D. He described the conflict, the Lamanites burning towns, villages and cities, treading the Nephites under their feet, and sweeping down and destroying all the Nephites who were not fast enough to flee, even after the Nephites "did stand against them boldly."

After 380, Mormon stopped writing about the "awful scene of blood and carnage" until he wrote the letter in 384 and gathered "all the remainder of our people unto the land of Cumorah." It is possible they gathered more than 20,000 to the *land* of Cumorah, but by the time they retreated to the *hill* Cumorah, there were only the 20,000 left. That explains why Oliver wrote that there were only *tens of thousands* of bodies left, which presumably included dead Lamanites.

If this is the case, then the rest of his people, the ones Mormon listed in verses 13-15, had died long before the final battle at Cumorah. Mormon does not say he could see those dead people from Cumorah.

This means that, at the Hill Cumorah, two units of 10,000 Nephites were killed. If an equivalent number of Lamanites were killed, that totals 40,000. This fits the "tens of thousands" Oliver mentioned.

Moroni referred to "the great and tremendous battle at Cumorah."

The Book of Mormon mentions another "tremendous battle" around 77-76 B.C. that resulted in a "tremendous slaughter among the people of Nephi." It was "such an one as never had been known among all the people of the land from the time Lehi left Jerusalem." (Alma 28:2-3)

How many people were killed?

"Tens of thousands of the Lamanites were slain and scattered abroad."

Again, not hundreds of thousands. Only "tens of thousands," and they were not all slain; the record does not specify how many were merely scattered.

This war to protect the people of Ammon in the land of Jershon led to "a great mourning and lamentation." How many were the people of Ammon?

About 64-63 B.C., thirteen years after the "tremendous battle" that saved the people of Ammon, the people of Ammon wanted to join the Nephites in another defensive war. Because of their oath, they could not do so themselves, but they had "many sons" who hadn't entered the oath and now covenanted to fight for the liberty of the Nephites (Alma 53:16-17)

They could come up with only 2,000 young men to fight (the stripling warriors, presumably teenagers). Assuming an equivalent number of girls, that makes 4,000 teenagers. If we assume there are about the same number of pre-teens as teens, that makes 8-10,000 pre-adults. In some societies, including some modern societies, half the population is under the age of 20. That seems plausible here because the Lamanites had killed 1,005 adults before ceasing the slaughter (Alma 24:22)

We could realistically assume there were only around 20,000 people of Ammon. If so, describing as a "tremendous" a battle that involved only tens of thousands of warriors makes good sense, just as it did when Moroni described the final battle at Cumorah.

### What evidence should we expect to find at Cumorah?

Our assumptions determine our conclusions. The smaller numbers I propose, consistent with what Oliver explained, are consistent with the archaeology of the New York hill Cumorah. We don't need a massive mountain somewhere upon which 2 million people could fight and die. We don't even need a place where hundreds of thousands of people could fight and die. And we wouldn't expect to find evidence of such mass destruction.

By comparison, the famous Battle of Hastings, which was relatively recent (1066), changed the course of British history. 10,000 men were said to have died there, in a specific spot of England that was well documented and known ever since. Nevertheless, the exact location is uncertain.[69] Only one skeleton that might be related to the battle has ever been found.

> No bones have previously been discovered of anyone who fought and died during the historic event.... The Norman invaders were thought to have buried their dead in a mass grave. Although no grave pits of the Normans have been found, it is believed that this is due to the high acidity of the soil, which means all the remains have long deteriorated."[70]

The uncertainty about the setting for the Battle of Hastings and the lack of recovered skeletons should inform our expectations for Cumorah. If, as I propose here, mere thousands of Jaredites died over 2,000 years ago, and only tens of thousands of Lamanites and Nephites died 1600 years ago, what evidence would we expect to find?

Mormon made the point that "their flesh, and bones, and blood lay upon the face of the earth, being left by the hands of those who slew them to molder upon the land, and to crumble and to return to their mother earth." (Mormon 6:15) Unburied bodies don't last long. All traces would be gone within a few years at most.

Useful articles such as weapons would be salvaged by survivors, either immediately after the battle or over ensuing years as various tribes passed through the area.

What we do have in western New York is a series of small forts and defensive positions, mass graves containing hundreds, but not

---

[69] http://anglosaxon.archeurope.info/index.php?page=the-location-of-the-battle
[70]     https://www.ancient-origins.net/news-history-archaeology/archaeologists-believe-they-have-found-skeleton-battle-hastings-07459

thousands, of bodies, and in the vicinity of the hill Cumorah itself, decades of farmers plowing up arrowheads, ax heads, and similar stone weapons which they gave away or sold to tourists. Just a few years ago a Jaredite era arrowhead was found on top of the Hill Cumorah, not far from the parking area.

This evidence is not *proof* of the New York Cumorah, of course. It is merely evidence to consider. But this evidence is consistent with the text and it corroborates what the prophets have said.

In my view, this framework establishes the New York Cumorah as a viable working hypothesis. It's also nice that it corroborates the teachings of the prophets.

# Part Five: Making Sense

The case for Cumorah involves the teachings of Joseph Smith, Oliver Cowdery, their contemporaries and their successors in Church leadership. It involves external evidence about Cumorahland, including archaeology, anthropology, geography, and geology. It involves an understanding of the who, what, when and where of the Book of Mormon people that corroborates the teachings of the prophets.

But it also involves making sense of how Cumorah fits in the larger picture.

- What type of society does the Book of Mormon describe?
- How do Book of Mormon people fit within the context of anthropology and archaeology beyond Cumorahland?
- How does Cumorah fit with Church history?
- And how does the text of the Book of Mormon describe a geographical setting in which the New York Cumorah makes sense?

## Type of Society

What kind of society does the Book of Mormon describe?

Some of the early Saints believed the Book of Mormon described great cities and monuments, such as those found in Central and South America as documented by Alexander von Humboldt and Stephens and Catherwood. The anonymous 1842 *Times and Seasons* articles made the connection explicitly, as did the writings of Benjamin Winchester, Orson and Parley P. Pratt, and others.

Many modern scholars agree with this interpretation. M2C scholars and their followers, for example, find many "correspondences" between ancient Mayan civilization and the Nephite record. They view the Nephite society as a large population organized as an advanced civilization, a "state level" society as opposed to a chiefdom or tribal society.[71]

In the Wentworth letter, Joseph wrote:

> I was also informed concerning the aboriginal inhabitants of this country, and shown who they were, and from whence they came; a brief sketch of their origin, progress, civilization, laws, governments, of their righteousness and iniquity, and the blessings of God being finally withdrawn from them as a people was made known unto me: I was also told where there was deposited some plates on which were engraven an abridgement of the records of the ancient prophets that had existed on this continent.[72]

The text explains that the Nephites observed the law of Moses. They had kings and, for a few generations, a government of judges. Around 30 A.D. they divided into tribes with "a chief or leader over them: and thus they became tribes and leaders of tribes." (3 Nephi 7:3)

Nephites and Lamanites had military organizations. Nephites had lawyers and "officers" who enforced the law. They had churches and different denominations. They had a "chief market," although other markets are never mentioned.

> For there were many merchants in the land, and also many lawyers, and many officers.
> And the people began to be distinguished by ranks, according to their riches and their chances for learning; yea, some were ignorant because of their poverty, and others did receive great learning because of their riches. (3 Nephi 6:11–12)

All of these are biblical terms that I assume Joseph used to approximate what the ancient text said. The text can be interpreted to describe multiple working hypotheses, including, but not limited to, (i) a sophisticated "state-level" society that required a large population, or

---

[71] For an overview of the distinction, see
https://www2.palomar.edu/anthro/political/pol_3.htm
[72] https://www.josephsmithpapers.org/paper-summary/church-history-1-march-1842/2

(ii) a network of modest city-states linked by common language and traditions.

For example, when we think of "great learning" we might think of a formal education at a prestigious university. An ancient society would consider "great learning" to be an apprenticeship with the priestly or ruling class, such as the education received by the sons of King Benjamin in Mosiah 1.

Modern lawyers are trained professionals who focus on secular law. In the Bible, "lawyers" were scholars in the Mosiac law, equivalent to "scribes" who taught the law of Moses. Because the Nephites observed the law of Moses, the presence of "lawyers" does not constitute a state-level society. Likewise, "officers" are people who enforce the law, a necessity in every society, including tribal societies.

Joseph's mother, Lucy Mack Smith, recalled what Joseph told them before he translated the plates.

> During our evening conversations, Joseph would occasionally give us some of the most amusing recitals that could be imagined: he would describe the ancient inhabitants of this continent; their dress, mode of travelling, and the animals upon which they rode; their cities, and their buildings, with every particular; he would describe their <mode of> warfare, as also their religious worship. This he would do with as much ease, seemingly, as if he had spent his whole life with them.[73]

Joseph never expounded on these topics publicly. Apart from identifying the mounds in the midwestern United States as evidence of the divine authenticity of the Book of Mormon, he did not describe Nephite buildings or cities. We are left with interpreting the text.

The Nephites had small villages, villages, towns, cities, large cities, and great cities (e.g., Mosiah 27:6; Alma 8:7), but no population numbers are provided for any of these.

The King James Version (KJV) uses the same terms, so comparing to the Bible may give us insights into what Joseph meant by the terms.

---

[73]  https://www.josephsmithpapers.org/paper-summary/lucy-mack-smith-history-1845/94

The Old Testament uses two words for "city" (*eer* and *kiriah*) and one for "village" (*chatsair*). The Old Testament differentiation seems to be based not on size primarily, but on the presence or absence of a defense wall. Cities had walls, while villages were unwalled. Villages, being unwalled, were usually smaller than cities, but that was not always the case....

Recent population projections based on the density of cities from cultures similar to those of biblical times along with a count of the number of house units found in excavations suggest that most cities could support 160-200 persons per acre. Thus **Shechem might have had a population of 2,000 to 2,500** during the Old Testament period; Jerusalem in Solomon's time could have supported 5,000 to 6,500. Even when Jerusalem expanded in Josiah's time, it would have had no more than 25,000 inhabitants.[74]

Shechem was described as a "city" despite its small population of 2,000 to 2,500 people. (Judges 9:41-49)

Another source of possible definitions is the 1828 Webster's dictionary, which defines "city" as "In a general sense, a large town; a large number of houses and inhabitants, established in one place."[75] A "village" is "A small assemblage of houses, less than a town or city, and inhabited chiefly by farmers and other laboring people."[76] A "town" is "Any collection of houses, larger than a village. In this use the word is very indefinite, and a town may consist of twenty houses, or of twenty thousand."[77]

In New York, a "village" is part of a town, but can be part of more than one town. Joseph Smith would have been familiar with this terminology because he lived in the village of Palmyra, in the town of Palmyra, before his parents moved to the farm. The Smith farm straddled the towns of Manchester and Palmyra. Cumorah is in the town of Manchester, but outside any village. A "city" differs from a

---

[74] https://www.studylight.org/dictionaries/hbd/c/cities-and-urban-life.html.
[75] http://webstersdictionary1828.com/Dictionary/city.
[76] http://webstersdictionary1828.com/Dictionary/village.
[77] http://webstersdictionary1828.com/Dictionary/town.

village because cities are not part of a town and have their own charters but villages are subject to uniform village laws and exist within towns. [78]

The Book of Mormon refers to "cities" 78 times and refers to a "city" 312 times. One of these is "the great city Jerusalem." At the time Lehi left Jerusalem, the population was about 25,000 people. [79]

Six cities in the Book of Mormon were also described as "great," including Ammonihah (Alma 9:4, 16:9), the Lamanite Jerusalem (Alma 21:2), Zarahemla (Hel. 1:18) and the cities that were destroyed prior to the coming of Christ (3 Nephi 9:3-9): Moronihah, Moroni, and Jacobugath.

The five Nephite cities, assuming a population comparable to Jerusalem in Israel, may have had a total population of 125,000.

Another comparison to consider are the Greek city-states (*poleis*) in the B.C. era. "A recent reconstruction based on estimated household sizes and city areas suggests around half of all *poleis* had total populations below 5,000."[80] Athens and Sparta could have had much larger populations, around 150,000-200,000 and 125,000 respectively.

Based on these references, I infer that a Nephite "city" would range from around 2,000 to 5,000 people, a large city could range from around 5,000 to 20,000 people, and a great city would have around 25,000 people. Villages and towns would be smaller in population than a city.

The Nephite population naturally varied over time. When they arrived in the Promised Land, Lehi's party consisted of his family, Ishmael's family, and possibly unmentioned servants and others added during the journey from Jerusalem to the coast.

While they did not encounter any "nation" in the promised land

The first cities mentioned in the promised land were the city of Lehi-

---

[78] https://en.wikipedia.org/wiki/Administrative_divisions_of_New_York_(state)

[79] Seely, Jo Ann H.; Seely, David Rolph; and Welch, John W., "Glimpses of Lehi's Jerusalem" (2004). Maxwell Institute Publications. 39 *Glimpses of Lehi's Jerusalem*, p. 5, https://scholarsarchive.byu.edu/cgi/viewcontent.cgi?article=1038&context=mi

[80] Duncan Keenan-Jones and Mark Hebblewhite, "The Pitfalls of Using Ancient Population, Army and Casualty Data without Expert Curation," *Cliodynamics: The Journal of Quantitative History and Cultural Evolution* (2019), https://escholarship.org/uc/item/3x5411p8

Nephi (Mosiah 7:1) and the city of Shilom (Mosiah 7:21). Alma's converts built the city of Helam. (Mosiah 23:20) The city of Zarahemla is first mentioned in Alma 2:26 but is not referred to as a "great" city until Helaman 1:18. All of this suggests population growth and territorial expansion. The text doesn't provide enough information to assess relative population at any given time, however.

If the "great" Nephite cities had a total population of around 125,000 people, the unknown number of other cities could have had a similar total population, making a total population of 250,000. Add in villages and towns, and presumably more rural areas, and we could have a total Nephite population, well after the integration of the people of Zarahemla, of as many as 500,000 people.

We could estimate larger or smaller populations than these—again, we have evidence for multiple working hypotheses.

We have better data for biblical populations—although scholars dispute these numbers, too.[81] 600,000 able-bodied men reportedly left Egypt during the exodus (Numbers 2:32), giving a total population of around 2.5-3 million. That is 15 times as large as the enumerated armies in the Book of Mormon, which is another way to approximate a Nephite population of a few hundred thousand.

These estimates are quite general and speculative, but they fall within a reasonable range, based on the text.

Now, let's see how they fit the external evidence.

## Moundbuilders: Hopewell (Nephites) and Adena (Jaredites)

When the Europeans arrived in North America, they discovered ancient earthworks, or mounds, that predated the Indians (Native

---

[81] For a dispute about the Exodus, see http://www.noble-minded.org/exodus.html One peer-reviewed article, paywall protected article suggests the total population during the Exodus was only 20,000, based on a conclusion that the Hebrew word translated as "thousand" should read "leader." Colin J. Humphreys, " The Number of People in the Exodus from Egypt: Decoding Mathematically the Very Large Numbers in Numbers I and XXVI," *Vetus Testamentum*, Vol. 48, Fasc. 2 (Apr., 1998), pp. 196-213 (18 pages).

Americans) they encountered. Europeans assumed the "Mound Builders" were an ancient civilization, possibly from Asia or possibly some of the lost tribes of Israel from the Bible, that was destroyed by Native Americans who came later.[82]

Some have proposed that the Book of Mormon was composed by Joseph Smith and/or Sidney Rigdon as a Christian retelling of the Mound Builder myth.[83]

However, the Book of Mormon explains that the indigenous people in America are the descendants of the people who built the mounds, a conclusion reached decades after the Book of Mormon was published.

> During the last 100 years, extensive archaeological research has changed our understanding of the mounds. They are no longer viewed as isolated monuments created by a mysterious race. Instead, the mounds of North America have been proven to be constructions by Native American peoples for a variety of purposes.[84]

Unlike the Mound Builder myth, the Book of Mormon describes two separate groups of people, one more ancient than the other. Decades after the Book of Mormon was published, archaeologists identified two distinct cultures in the Midwestern United States that date to Book of Mormon time frames.

The earlier group, named the *Adena* in 1902 after the location of the plantation where distinctive cultural attributes were identified, have been dated in the Ohio River Valley from about 1,000 to 200 B.C.[85]

---

[82] For an overview with references, see https://en.wikipedia.org/wiki/Mound_Builders, but realize this site reflects the views of its authors and is subject to change.

[83] E.g., Dan Vogel, *Indian Origins and the Book of Mormon* (Signature Books, Inc., 1986), online at http://signaturebookslibrary.org/scripture-test/

[84] https://www.smithsonianmag.com/history/white-settlers-buried-truth-about-midwests-mysterious-mound-cities-180968246/

[85] Archaeologists provide varying estimates of the dating of the Adena. E.g., see https://openvirtualworlds.org/omeka/exhibits/show/moundbuildersart/moundbuilders/earlywoodland, https://en.wikipedia.org/wiki/Adena_culture and https://www.in.gov/dnr/parklake/8614.htm.

Adena mounds and artifacts have been found throughout the midwestern U.S. through western New York and Pennsylvania.

The second group was named the *Hopewell* in 1892 after the owner of certain earthworks in Ohio.[86] Hopewell have traditionally been dated from 100 B.C. to 500 A.D. Updated dating on Hopewell in Scioto, Oho, gave The median calibrated dates range from BC 220 to 340 AD.[87]

The Hopewell had an exchange system from Florida to Lake Ontario that extended as far west as Kansas.

An in-depth analysis of the Adena and Hopewell civilizations is beyond the scope of this book, although I will discuss some scientific peer-reviewed papers below. When assessing similarities (so-called "correspondences"), it's important to remember that the Book of Mormon does not contain "even a hundredth part" of Nephite history and culture. (Jacob 3:13; Words of Mormon 1:5; Helaman 3:14; 3 Nephi 5:8, 26:6; Ether 15:33).

What we look for is a society that could be described the way it is described in the Book of Mormon.

———

Charles Shook, whose book *Cumorah Revisited* prompted Stebbins to develop M2C, discussed the Mound Builders as well. He made the same argument discussed above, but separately claimed the Nephites could not have been Mound Builders because they came from Central and South America—a claim Stebbins had made before he developed M2C.

> Instead of coming by way of Behring Strait, they entered our continent at two different points, the Nephites landing somewhere on the west coast of south America and the Mulokites [sic] near the Isthmus of Panama.[88]

---

[86] There are many websites, academic papers, textbooks, and other references about the Hopewell. See a summary: https://en.wikipedia.org/wiki/Hopewell_tradition.

[87] Nolan, et al., "New Dates on Scioto Hopewell Sites: A SCHoN Project," *Current Research in Ohio Archaeology 2017*.

[88] Shook, *Cumorah Revisited*, p. 178.

Shook cites a series of authorities which he summarizes this way:

> We have three lines of evidence, then, which refute the Book of Mormon claim that the ancient inhabitants of Central America and Mexico came from over the sea and from South America. First, the traditions; second, the languages, and, third, the architectural features. These evidences strongly declare that the ancient Mayas and Nahuas came from the north.[89]

His argument falls apart if Lehi landed in Florida and had nothing to do with Central or South America.

Shook also claimed the Mound Builders were one civilization consisting of numerous tribes. He apparently did not know about the distinction between Hopewell and Adena; he did not mention either group in his book, likely because the distinction was not well established in 1910.

All of this means that Stebbins, followed by Hills and then LDS scholars, developed M2C to respond to the Shook arguments that were based on outdated anthropology and Orson Pratt's speculation about where Lehi and Mulek landed—even though Joseph Smith rejected Pratt's speculation in the Wentworth letter.

―――――

During his lifetime, Joseph Smith identified Hopewell mounds as Nephite/Lamanite and an Adena burial as Jaredite.

As Zion's Camp journeyed from Kirtland to Missouri in 1834, Joseph Smith and his companions crossed the plains of Ohio, Indiana, and Illinois. From the banks of the Mississippi River, Joseph wrote a letter to his wife Emma. He told her that they had been

> wandering over the plains of the Nephites, recounting occasionally the history of the Book of Mormon, roving over the mounds of that once

―――――

[89] Shook, *Cumorah Revisited*, p. 235.

beloved people of the Lord, picking up their skulls and their bones, as a proof of its divine authenticity.[90]

The connection between the Book of Mormon and the mounds in the midwestern United States was widely recognized among both members and nonmembers. The 1834 book *Mormonism Unvailed* included the first published account of Zelph, the warrior whose bones were dug up in Illinois by members of Zion's Camp.

> A large mound was one day discovered, upon which Gen. Smith ordered an excavation to be made into it ; and about one foot from the top of the ground, the bones of a human skeleton were found, which were carefully laid out upon a board, when Smith made a speech, prophesying or declaring that they were the remains of a celebrated General among the Nephites, mentioning his name and the battle in which he was slain, some 1500 years ago.[91]

Wilford Woodruff and others who were present described the event in their journals.[92] Woodruff wrote,

> While on our travels **we visited many of the mounds which were flung up by the ancient inhabitants of this continent probably by the Nephites & Lamanites.** We visited one of those Mounds and several of the brethren dug into it and took from it the bones of a man. **We visited one of those Mounds:** considered to be 300 feet above the level of the Illinois River. Three persons dug into the mound & found a body. Elder Milton Holmes took the arrow out of the back bones that killed Zelph & brought it with some of the bones in to the camp. I visited the same mound with Jesse J. Smith. Who the other persons were that dug in to the mound & found the body I am undecided. **Brother Joseph had a vision respecting the person.** He said he was a white Lamanite. The curse was

---

[90]   https://www.josephsmithpapers.org/paper-summary/letter-to-emma-smith-4-june-1834/2
[91] https://archive.org/details/mormonismunvaile00howe/page/158/mode/2up
[92] One brief version is in the Joseph Smith Papers here:
https://www.josephsmithpapers.org/paper-summary/history-1838-1856-volume-a-1-23-december-1805-30-august-1834/489 . Other accounts are here:
https://josephsmithfoundation.org/account-of-zelph/

taken from him or at least in part. He was killed in battle with an arrow. The arrow was found among his ribs. One of his thigh bones was broken. This was done by a stone flung from a sling in battle years before his death. His name was Zelph.

Some of his bones were brought into the Camp and the thigh bone which was broken was put into my wagon and I carried it to Missouri. Zelph was a large thick set man and a man of God. **He was a warrior under the great prophet Onandagus that was known from the hill Cumorah or east sea to the Rocky mountains.** The above knowledge Joseph received in a vision.[93]

In the late 1800s, an archaeologist assigned the name Naples Mound #8 to the mound. The mound was scientifically excavated in 1990. "The artifacts found during the excavation confirmed the mound to be a Hopewell burial mound, dating from 100 B.C. to 500 A.D."[94]

In 1844, a Church member who owned a farm east of Nauvoo in Illinois noticed that his pigs had dug into a mound of earth and uncovered some bones. One was a human skull that was much larger than his face, similar to many other reports from Adena burials. He showed it to his family, including his daughter who reported the incident.

Her father dug up the mound and found twelve giant bodies buried like spokes of a wheel. While he was excavating, Joseph Smith rode by on his horse and said, "Jacob, those were Jaredites. Cover them up and let them rest—fence them in so nothing can disturb them further."

The distinction Joseph made between Jaredite and Nephite mounds and skeletons parallels the distinctions made now between Adena and Hopewell mounds. Archaeologists believe the Hopewell succeeded the Adena with some amount of overlap that is not well understood.

Likewise, linguistic evidence in the Book of Mormon indicates some overlap between the Jaredites and the people of Zarahemla. But

---

[93] Wilford Woodruff Journal, digitized and online at https://catalog.churchofjesuschrist.org/assets?id=14079217-b2a7-4eff-8b53-1be6c1e9bea5&crate=0&index=23
[94] https://en.wikipedia.org/wiki/Naples_Mound_8.

Coriantumr was the last surviving Jaredite (other than Ether) and he lived with the people of Zarahemla only "nine moons." They couldn't communicate. How could there be any cross-cultural influence?

Likely, it was not contact with the Jaredites that led to the borrowed names. Instead, it was contact with the non-Jaredite Jaredites, meaning the descendants of those who came with Jared.

The non-Jaredite Jaredites spread throughout the continent, not confined to what Moroni called "this north country." Naturally, the people of Zarahemla would have interacted with these people.

Joseph Smith said Zelph was known from the Rocky Mountains to Cumorah, and modern archaeologists have corroborated this claim with the artifacts found in the mound. There is abundant evidence that people were living throughout this region during Book of Mormon times.

What do archaeologists say about these people?

A survey of the scientific literature about Hopewell archaeology was published in 2009 by Elliot Abrams.[95] The Introduction notes:

> There are few archaeological cultures in the United States that have garnered national and international recognition as much as those societies collectively termed "Hopewellian." These societies were responsible for designing and building some of the largest indigenous earthen architecture in the country and for manufacturing artifacts from imported, long-distance materials that attest to a considerable artistic and aesthetic tradition. The geographic scale of Hopewellian remains further heightens the accomplishments of these various societies, with associated earthen mounds dispersed, albeit unevenly, throughout much of the eastern half of the country, and especially within the Mississippi and Ohio River valleys.

The article discusses the changing connotation of the term "Hopewell."

---

[95] Elliot M. Abrams, "Hopewell Archaeology: A View from the Northern Woodlands," *J Archaeol Res* (2009) 17:169–204. Additional references to articles on the Hopewell and Adena can be found on mobom.org.

The meaning of the terms "Hopewell" and "Hopewellian" has changed over time, from a single unified society to a diverse set of specific Middle Woodland societies, each internally bound through several diverse spheres of alliances. More specifically, Hopewell connotes those Middle Woodland societies participating in some expansive form of riverine-specific regional integration materially reflected through large-scale earthworks and/or earthwork centers and exotic artifacts principally deposited in funerary contexts. Hopewell is "… not a shared belief system or formally organized trade network" (Charles et al. 2004, p. 43) but rather refers to an "… increased intensity of negotiation and contestation…" (Charles et al. 2004, p. 49) within and among these societies.

Does this description match the Book of Mormon societies?

One of the ramifications of Mormon's inability to discuss even "a hundredth part" of Nephite society and history is the unexplained appearance in the narrative of outsiders.

Many references in the text demonstrate that believers lived among unbelievers. The case Alma presented before Mosiah, which we discussed at the beginning of this book, involved such religious differences. Nephite society, like Hopewell society, was not one united by a "shared belief system."

Jacob, for example, confronted Sherem. The text says only "there came a man among the people of Nephi whose name was Sherem." He was not identified as a Lamanite. He preached against Christ, claiming the Nephites had converted the law of Moses into a false tradition, because the law of Moses was "the right way." (Jacob 7:12)

Alma went on a mission to the people of Ammonihah, who had a different belief system. The chief judge of that land apparently approved the burning of people who shared Alma's beliefs, along their records which contained the scriptures. (Alma 14:5)

Zoram "was leading the hearts of the people to bow down to dumb idols," (Alma 31:1), perhaps including the animal effigies found in Hopewell burial sites and earthworks.

When Alma brought his people to the land of Zarahemla, "king Mosiah granted unto Alma that he might establish churches throughout all the land of Zarahemla." (Mosiah 25:19) Alma established seven churches—not very many for a large population, but sufficient for "whosoever were desirous to take upon them the name of Christ." (Mosiah 25:23)

The Book of Mormon mentions hunting animals for food (Enos 1:3; Ether 10:19), as well as crops and flocks, such as in Alma 34:24-5: "Cry unto him over the crops of your fields, that ye may prosper in them. Cry over the flocks of your fields, that they may increase."

At one point, the people planted seeds, including unknown species.

> And we began to till the ground, yea, even with all manner of seeds, with seeds of corn, and of wheat, and of barley, and with neas, and with sheum, and with seeds of all manner of fruits; and we did begin to multiply and prosper in the land.
> (Mosiah 9:9)

Scholars have debated the meaning of these passages. Did the plates refer to seed-bearing plants that Joseph translated using English equivalents he was familiar with, or did the plates refer to specific species that were the same ones Joseph knew? The terms "neas" and "sheum" suggest the Nephites used species Joseph didn't recognize, but it's also possible, for example, that when the plates referred to "maygrass" Joseph translated that as "wheat."

Archaeologists have mixed ideas about Hopewell agriculture.

> Scholars have suggested diverse models ranging from a true agricultural economy based on local seed-bearing plants (Smith 1992; Steinhilper and Wymer 2006; Wymer 1997) to a more nomadic hunting and gathering economy essentially devoid of domesticates (Yerkes 2005, 2006). The collective data from various Middle Woodland sites (Wymer 1996, 1997) clearly indicate an increased commitment to obtaining and consuming local seed-bearing plants.

> The presence of maygrass, a species whose growth may have required human intent, further adds to the argument for intentional gardening, as does the various metric measures of thresholds of human modification on seeds (Smith 1992). As a cautionary note, however, it is possible that

early sedentary communities in resource-rich environments consumed both domesticated garden species as well as intensively collected wild plants.[96]

The Book of Mormon describes a series of cities that had loose affiliation with one another under the broad umbrella of "Nephite" and "Lamanite" jurisdiction.

When Alma led his followers into the wilderness, they promptly built a city named after the first person he baptized, Helam. (Mosiah 23:19) The city was independent of any outside government. They didn't seek anyone's permission. When the Lamanite army discovered the city, they asserted authority over it because of their superior numbers, not by any appeal to authority. The Lamanite king promptly gave Amulon autonomous power over the people of Helam, making him "a king and a ruler" as if this was the normal practice. (Mosiah 23:37-39)

When Alma visited Ammonihah as a missionary, he was subject to a different "chief judge" than the "chief judge" in Zarahemla. Burning books and people would be unthinkable in Zarahemla, but it was officially authorized in Ammonihah.

Studies of the Hopewell have also discussed the sociopolitical organization of the culture.

> The initial conceptualization of Hopewellian populations involved a unified political entity based on shared ideological foundations. It is no surprise that the notion of local communities being allied, forming some type of wider sociopolitical corporate entity such as lineages and clans, appeared early in Hopewell studies (Prufer 1964, p. 72).

> The first statements of supralocal organization were predicated on the presence of nonlocal artifacts and the scale of earthwork construction, the latter association being quite common in archaeology (Abrams 1989). The hypothesis of regional polities was given strong empirical support by Brown's (1979) pioneering research identifying charnel houses with group leadership and through Struever and Houart's (1972) contribution to the study of high-status artifacts in mound centers.

---

[96] Abrams, p. 179.

The recognition of local sites being spatially associated with mounded architecture added to the notion of **spatially dispersed yet allied communities** (Buikstra 1976; Charles and Buikstra 1983, 2002). Contemporary research and models continue this legacy of linking local communities within broad and diverse types of sociopolitical corporate units, variously termed "peer polities" (Braun 1986; Fig. 3), "local symbolic communities" (Ruby et al. 2005), the "corporate ceremonial sphere" (Smith 1992), the "sustainable community" (Ruby et al. 2005), or more anthropologically based terms such as lineages, clans, and moieties (Thomas et al. 2005). (Abrams, page 180)

"Spatially dispersed yet allied communities" is a good description for the way Mosiah "made a proclamation throughout all the land, that the people gathered themselves together." (Mosiah 2:1) A Lamanite king also "sent a proclamation throughout all the land, amongst all his people who were in all his land, who were in the regions round about." (Alma 22:27) Pahoran also "sent a proclamation throughout this part of the land; and behold, they are flocking to us daily, to their arms, in the defence of their country and their freedom, and to avenge our wrongs." (Alma 61:6) The usurper king of Zarahemla even "joined an alliance with" the king of the Lamanites. (Alma 61:8)

Carr and Case (2005c) allude to the presence of a council of leaders, a valuable concept in furthering our understanding of leadership (and subsequent burial) within Hopewellian polities. Again, variability exists in terms of both metrics and scales of societal distinctions among Hopewellian polities…. Seeman's (1988) study of possible trophy skulls suggested that warfare may have episodically characterized political relations. Alternatively, relations within Hopewellian society have been portrayed as generally nonviolent (Carr 2006), owing to the relative absence of trauma on Hopewellian skeletons, a hypothesis supported by skeletal analysis (Johnston 2002; Milner 1995). (Abrams, page 183.)

A "council of leaders" compares with the Nephite system of lower and higher judges, as well as the council of war held by Moroni and Teancum. (Alma 52:19) Episodic warfare and periods of peace are common to the Hopewell and the Book of Mormon societies.

The scientific literature recognizes that the Hopewellian societies ended abruptly, but the cause is unclear.

The Book of Mormon relates a period of peace following the appearance of Jesus Christ for about 200 years. At that point, the people "began to be divided into classes." Persecution ensued until "there was a great division among the people" in the 231ˢᵗ year. (4 Nephi 1:35) They divided themselves into Nephites and Lamanites again, not based on genealogy but on their acceptance or rejection of the gospel.

Eventually both groups became wicked.

Around 327 A.D. a war commenced between the Nephites and Lamanites. From then until the final battle at Cumorah about 385, the record shows Nephites abandoning their homes and cities. They were "hunted and driven." (Mormon 2:20) Mormon wrote that "whatsoever lands we had passed by, and the inhabitants thereof were not gathered in, were destroyed by the Lamanites, and their towns, and villages, and cities were burned with fire; and thus three hundred and seventy and nine years passed away." (Mormon 5:5)

Mormon's observation that lands where the people were not "gathered in" were destroyed implies that people joined together for defensive purposes.

When they discuss the end of the Hopewell societies, archaeologists remark that "the archaeological expectations of a collapse do not appear." Cities appear abandoned and earthwork construction stopped, but not due to environmental decline or widespread disease. Evidence of "heightened death rates" has not been found in Ohio—exactly what we would expect if people were fleeing toward the land of Cumorah.

> As a direct counterpoint to its origins, Hopewellian societies "end," in a strict material sense, when earthwork construction was discontinued and long-distance artifacts were no longer obtained. This pattern occurred in the lower Illinois River Valley c. A.D. 200 and in the Scioto River Valley c. A.D. 350–400 (Dancey 2005, p. 131)… **The archaeological expectations of a collapse do not appear for Hopewellian societies**. Neither evidence of widespread diseases nor heightened death rates have been recovered (Dunnell and Greenlee 1999)…
>
> This does not preclude cultural disruption and cognitive dissonance, but it does preclude large-scale death. In this categoric sense, Hopewellian societies end but do not collapse. Although settlement data and chronology are painfully limited, **a physical restructuring of Ohio**

**communities on a local level following c. A.D. 300–400 appears to have occurred.** Evidence from sites such as the Water Plant site (Dancey 1988, 1992) and the Swinehart Village site (Schweikart 2005) indicates **the aggregation of smaller Hopewellian/Middle Woodland residential sites into defensive, often enclosed, communities.** Importantly, these sites tend to be away from the Hopewellian heartland, formed instead on the margins of the lands used by earlier generations (Burks 2005; Seeman 1996). **In other areas, a large-scale abandonment of the valley is evidenced** (Abrams and Freter 2005b). These patterns imply that some type of economic readjustment necessitated the abandonment of prime resource-rich areas. (Abrams, page 186.)

These observations about the end of Hopewellian society fit my understanding of the text; i.e., from AD 350-400, the Nephites were in retreat, abandoning their earthworks on the way toward Cumorah. In a situation of mass retreat and fleeing we would not expect evidence of disease or high death rates within communities. The bodies of people slain on battlefields are not buried to be found centuries later by archaeologists; they are left in the open to be consumed like the bodies of any other animals.

Mormon noted that some communities gathered together, presumably where they were out of the way. As the article says, archaeologists have observed "the aggregation of smaller Hopewellian/Middle Woodland residential sites into defensive, often enclosed, communities. Importantly, these sites tend to be away from the Hopewellian heartland, formed instead on the margins of the lands used by earlier generations."

The articles corroborate my view that Nephite society was much smaller than many have supposed in the past. The archaeologists have found evidence of small horticulture, but not large-scale agriculture.

———

In Part One I quoted Alice Beck Kehoe's observations about the Hopewell earthworks. Drawings from the Squier and Davis book, *Ancient Monuments of the Mississippi Valley*, are widely available online.[97]

---

[97] The book with its illustrations is available here:
https://archive.org/details/ancientmonuments00squi

The National Park Service (NPS) maintains some of the sites as part of the Hopewell Culture National Historical Park, where NPS operates a visitors' center near Chillicothe, Ohio.

> The most striking Hopewell sites contain earthworks in the form of circles, squares, and other geometric shapes. Many of these sites were built to a monumental scale, with earthen walls up to 12 feet high outlining geometric figures more than 1,000 feet across. Conical and loaf-shaped earthen mounds up to 30 feet high are often found in association with the geometric earthworks. Hopewell Culture National Historical Park preserves six earthwork complexes: High Bank Works, Hopeton Earthworks, Hopewell Mound Group, Mound City Group, Seip Earthworks and Spruce Hill Earthworks[98]

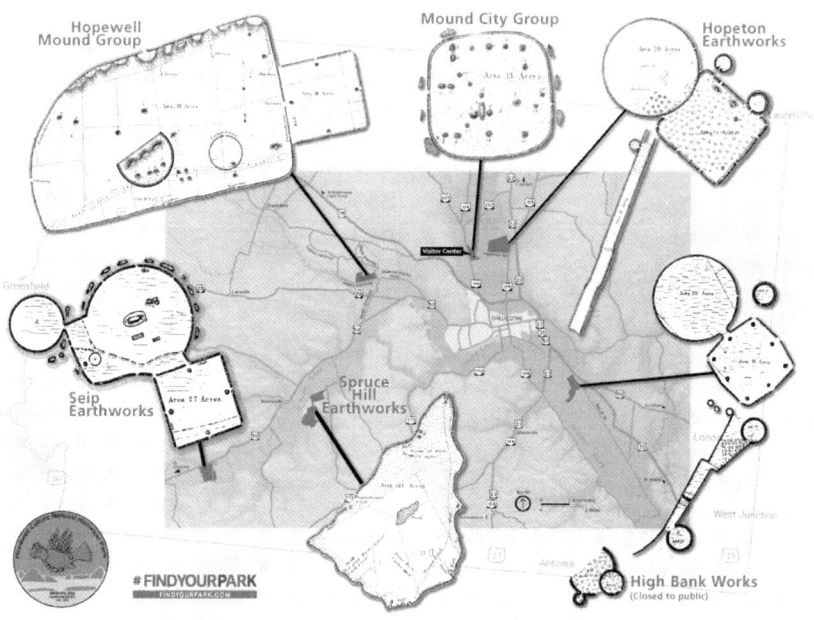

Figure 18 - Ohio earthworks preserved by the National Park Service

Kehoe pointed out that "the Middle Woodland period climaxed

---

98 https://www.nps.gov/hocu/learn/historyculture/places.htm. The web page includes explanations and additional graphics to explain the Hopewell earthworks.

trends in population growth and increasing social complexity. Trans-America routes brought beautiful manufactures, sophisticated decorative styles, and exotic materials to an aristocratic class... Hopewell geometric embankments remain unique, embodying mathematical knowledge as no other civilization envisaged."[99]

One of the most impressive earthworks is the Great Circle Earthwork in Newark, Ohio. Squier and Davis said "These works are so complicated that it is impossible to give anything like a comprehensive description of them."[100]

Archaeologists continue to make new discoveries about the Hopewell and Adena cultures that may provide insights into the Book of Mormon cultures.

For example, Alma 50:1 says that Moroni "cause that his armies... should commence in digging up heaps of earth round about all the cities." A 2006 paper about the excavation of a Hopewell site in Ohio found that "the embankment wall and ditch were likely built after mound building was well established at this site."[101]

Another paper reports the discovery of Appalachian copper at Hopewell sites in Ohio.[102] It had been assumed that Hopewell copper came from western Lake Superior, over 600 miles to the northwest. This link to eastern Tennessee corroborates the geography proposed in *Moroni's America*.

I could cite many more examples from the scientific literature, but this book is merely an overview. Later in this book we'll look at the question of Sidon as an example of the number of details involved with sorting through the simultaneous equation of text and evidence.

There is a lot of opportunity for further research in this area.

---

[99] Kehoe, p. 76.

[100] The quotation and overview at http://www.jqjacobs.net/archaeo/newark.html. Some LDS authors have proposed interpretations related to the Book of Mormon. See https://bookofmormonevidence.org/his-plan-of-salvation/.

[101] Mark J. Lynott, "Excavation of the East Embankment Wall, Hopewell Mound Group: A Preliminary Report," *The Newsletter of Hopewell Archaeology in the Ohio River Valley*, Volume 7, Number 1, December 2006.

[102] Kevin C. Nolan, et al., "Scale and Community in Hopewell Networks (SCHoN), Chapter 5 in *Encountering Hopewell in the Twenty-first Century, Ohio and Beyond. Volume Two: Settlements, Foodways, and Interaction* (2020).

Although there is no single source for papers about the archaeology of North America, I have dozens of them because I subscribe to Academia.edu which curates academic papers on the topics of your choice. That's a good place to start if you're interested in more details. The Bibliography includes a few web pages that focus on the archaeology and anthropology of ancient North America.

I also have a collection of books on the topics, both new and old, some of which are included in the Bibliography. Wayne May, publisher of *Ancient American* magazine, incorporates academic papers in his articles and books, which I recommend.

## Cumorah and the Two Sets of Plates

Thus far, we have discussed Cumorah primarily in terms of the final battles of the Jaredites and Nephites. Mormon 6:6 relates another important aspect of the New York Cumorah—the repository of Nephite records.

> 6 And it came to pass that when we had gathered in all our people in one to the land of Cumorah, behold I, Mormon, began to be old; and knowing it to be the last struggle of my people, and having been commanded of the Lord that I should not suffer the records which had been handed down by our fathers, which were sacred, to fall into the hands of the Lamanites, (for the Lamanites would destroy them) therefore I made this record out of the plates of Nephi, and **hid up in the hill Cumorah all the records which had been entrusted to me by the hand of the Lord**, save it were these few plates which I gave unto my son Moroni. (Mormon 6:6)

Many older Church members are familiar with the teaching that this repository of records was in the same hill in New York where Joseph found the plates. There were two separate storage places for plates in that hill.

1. Moroni's stone box, in which he deposited the abridged plates with the Urim and Thummim and breastplate.

2. Mormon's repository of all the Nephite records he used to write the abridgment.

New and younger Church members probably don't know about this repository in the New York Cumorah because it has been de-correlated, but it is a critical element of the case for Cumorah.

Shortly before he died in August, Brigham Young gave the most extensive public comment about the repository on June 17, 1877 at a conference in Farmington. He said

> I lived right in the country where the plates were found from which the Book of Mormon was translated, and I know a great many things pertaining to that country.

> I believe I will take the liberty to tell you of another circumstance that will be as marvelous as anything can be. **This is an incident in the life of Oliver Cowdery, but he did not take the liberty of telling such things in meeting as I take.**

> I tell these things to you, and I have a motive for doing so. **I want to carry them to the ears of my brethren and sisters, and to the children also, that they may grow to an understanding of some things that seem to be entirely hidden from the human family.**

> **Oliver Cowdery went with the Prophet Joseph when he deposited these plates.** Joseph did not translate all of the plates; there was a portion of them sealed, which you can learn from the Book of Doctrine and Covenants.

> **When Joseph got the plates, the angel instructed him to carry them back to the hill Cumorah,** which he did. Oliver says that when Joseph and Oliver went there, the hill opened, and they walked into a cave, **in which there was a large and spacious room.** He says he did not think, at the time, whether they had the light of the sun or artificial light; but that it was just as light as day.

**They laid the plates on a table; it was a large table that stood in the room.** Under this table there was a pile of plates as much as two feet high, and there were altogether in this room **more plates than probably many wagon loads**; they were piled up in the corners and along the walls.

The first time they went there the sword of Laban hung upon the wall; but when they went again it had been taken down and laid upon the table across the gold plates; it was unsheathed, and on it was written these words: "This sword will never be sheathed again until the kingdoms of this world become the kingdom of our God and his Christ."

**I tell you this as coming not only from Oliver Cowdery, but others who were familiar with it, and who understood it just as well as we understand coming to this meeting,** enjoying the day, and by and by we separate and go away, forgetting most of what is said, but remembering some things.

So is it with other circumstances in life. **I relate this to you, and I want you to understand it.** I take this liberty of referring to those things **so that they will not be forgotten and lost.**

Carlos Smith was a young man of as much veracity as any young man we had, and **he was a witness to these things.** Samuel Smith saw some things, Hyrum saw a good many things, but Joseph was the leader.

Now, you may think I am unwise in publicly telling these things, thinking perhaps I should preserve them in my own breast; but such is not my mind. **I would like the people called Latter-day Saints to understand some little things with regard to the workings and dealings of the Lord with his people here upon the earth.** I could relate to you a great many more, all of which are familiar to many of our brethren and sisters (emphasis added).[103]

Brigham Young had discussed this repository on previous occasions, but by July 1877 he knew he was about to die. He had been ill most of the year and was declining. He also knew that the knowledge of the repository would be forgotten and lost, so he had it put on record in

---

[103] Available online at http://jod.mrm.org/19/36.

the *Journal of Discourses.*

David Whitmer said Oliver had told him about visiting the repository in Cumorah.

Several others related the account, with varying details. They are included in Appendix 1, Cumorah Teachings.

―――――

Those who reject the New York Cumorah claim that Brigham Young, David Whitmer, Heber C. Kimball, Wilford Woodruff, etc., were either mistaken or were describing a spiritual vision Oliver Cowdery had. The vision, they claim, involved the actual repository in the "real" hill Cumorah somewhere else, most likely in southern Mexico.

Everyone can read the accounts and decide for themselves what to believe.

However, another little-known incident in Church history, related on several occasions by David Whitmer, plays a significant role in understanding the repository of records in the New York Cumorah. It also adds insight into the translation of the plates.

―――――

In May, 1829, Joseph and Oliver finished translating the abridged plates in Harmony, Pennsylvania. They translated the Title Page—the last leaf of the plates—and then considered starting over at the beginning to re-translate the Book of Lehi that had been lost as part of the 116 pages.

They inquired, and the Lord told them not to retranslate those plates. Instead, they would have to translate the plates of Nephi.

> 30 Behold, I say unto you, that **you shall not translate again those words which have gone forth out of your hands**...
> 38 And now, verily I say unto you, that an account of those things that you have written, which have gone out of your hands, is engraven upon the plates of Nephi;

39 Yea, and you remember it was said in those writings that a more particular account was given of these things upon the plates of Nephi.

40 And now, because the account which is engraven upon the plates of Nephi is more particular concerning the things which, in my wisdom, I would bring to the knowledge of the people in this account—

41 Therefore, **you shall translate the engravings which are on the plates of Nephi**, down even till you come to the reign of king Benjamin, or until you come to that which you have translated, which you have retained;

42 And behold, you shall publish it as the record of Nephi; and thus I will confound those who have altered my words.
(Doctrine and Covenants 10:30, 38–42)

One problem: they did not have the plates of Nephi.

Yet.

Moroni had deposited the abridged plates, which Joseph later called the "original Book of Mormon," in the stone box. Those were the plates Joseph had obtained and translated.

Not any original plates of Nephi.

Through the Urim and Thummim, the Lord commanded Joseph to leave Harmony and travel to the Whitmer farm in Fayette, New York, to complete the translation. He needed to write to David Whitmer, asking him to pick up Joseph and Oliver. Before he left Harmony, Joseph had to give the abridged plates to a divine messenger.

This he did.

David Whitmer drove his horse and wagon to Harmony. Joseph and Oliver loaded the wagon and they proceeded toward Fayette. Along the way, they passed the messenger who had the plates.

David Whitmer repeated this account multiple times. Edward Stevenson recorded one version in his journal:

He also relates an little very interesting incident that occurred in June 1829, David, Oliver, & Joseph were riding from Harmony Pa.—the 2 former in front & Joseph back sitting in the bed on hay or straw David had been down with his team over 100 miles to fetch Joseph up to his mothers to translate the Book of Mormon about 2 ½ days drive.

While thus riding an aged looking old man came walking along putting his hand on the wagon bed, he had on his back a knapsack & the strap crossed on his breast he took his handkerchief and wiped his face to remove the sweat as it seemed to them

David who was driving his team said to the man will you get up and ride **No said he I am only going over to Comorah** & suddenly disappeared they stopped the team at the sudden disappearance of the fine looking stranger he says that they all felt so strangely—that they asked the Prophet to enquire of the Lord who this stranger was.
Soon David said they turned around & Joseph looked pale almost transparent & said that was one of the Nephites and he had the plates of the Book of Mormon in the knapsack—[104]

In 1878, Orson Pratt and Joseph F. Smith visited David in Richmond, Missouri. He related the event to them and they recorded it in their journals and reported it to President Taylor of the Quorum of the Twelve.

"When I was returning to Fayette, with Joseph and Oliver, all of us riding in the wagon. Oliver and I on an old-fashioned wooden spring seat and Joseph behind us-while traveling along in a clear open space, a very pleasant, nice-looking old man suddenly appeared by the side of our wagon and saluted us with, 'Good morning, it is very warm,' at the same time wiping his face or forehead with his hand.

We returned the salutation, and, by a sign from Joseph, I invited him to ride if he was going our way; but he said very pleasantly, **'No, I am going to Cumorah.'**

This name was something new to me; **I did not know what Cumorah meant.** We all gazed at him and at each other, and as I looked around

---

[104] Edward Stevenson, Diary, 9 February 1886, LDS Church Archives, cited in Lyndon W. Cook, Editor, *David Whitmer Interviews*, p. 181

inquiringly of Joseph, the old man instantly disappeared, so that I did not see him again."

Joseph F. Smith asked: "Did you notice his appearance?"

David Whitmer: "I should think I did. He was, I should think, about five feet eight or nine inches tall and heavy set.... His hair and beard were white, like Brother Pratt's, but his beard was not so heavy. I also remember that he had on his back a sort of knapsack with something in, shaped like a book."[105]

Although these interviews took place long after the event, they are credible because David remembered it as the first time he heard the name *Cumorah*. It was a name that became important once he read the Book of Mormon and understood what happened at Cumorah.

Another indicia of credibility and reliability is the explanation by Edward Stevenson that before he left Salt Lake City to travel back east, Zina Young asked him to ask David Whitmer about this account. Whitmer and his missionary companion, Hyrum Smith, had converted Zina's family in 1832 when she was a young girl. Apparently David had told the family about this messenger all those years previously.[106]

David's focus on the name *Cumorah* is important because it raises the important question: why would a divine messenger carrying the plates be heading for Cumorah if he was supposed to be transporting the plates to Fayette?

———

When they got to Fayette, Joseph met the messenger, who gave him the plates of Nephi to translate pursuant to D&C 10.

Question: Where did the messenger get the plates of Nephi?

Answer: From Mormon's repository in the Hill Cumorah.

The repository contained all the original Nephite records that

---

[105] *Millennial Star*, vol. 40, p. 772

[106] See my explanation here: http://www.lettervii.com/2019/09/david-whitmer-and-cumorah-messenger.html

Mormon had brought from the hill Shim. (Mormon 4:23) This included the original 24 plates of Ether as well. Recall what Brigham Young said.

> [There] was a large table that stood in the room. Under this table there was a pile of plates as much as two feet high, and there were altogether in this room more plates than probably many wagon loads; they were piled up in the corners and along the walls.

These were original, unabridged plates. Among them were the plates of Nephi, commonly referred to as the "small plates of Nephi." These were the plates Joseph was commanded to translate in D&C 10.

It's easy to follow the sequence of events.[107]

1. Joseph obtained the abridged plates from Moroni's stone box.

2. Joseph and Oliver completed the translation of the abridged plates. The Lord commanded them not to re-translate the portion that was lost (the 116 pages), but instead they would have to translate the original—not abridged—plates of Nephi.

3. Before leaving Harmony, Joseph gave the abridged plates to the messenger.

4. The messenger took the abridged plates to the repository in the Hill Cumorah.

5. The messenger picked up the small plates of Nephi and took them to Fayette, where he gave them to Joseph.

6. Joseph and Oliver translated the small plates and published them as 1 Nephi through Words of Mormon.

Those unfamiliar with the geography should refer to this map.

---

[107] A color schematic is available here: http://www.lettervii.com/p/the-two-sets-of-plates-schematic.html

Areas where Joseph, Oliver, and David lived and worked during 1828-1830.
From https://www.lds.org/scriptures/bc/images/03990_000_history-map-1.pdf .

The two-sets-of-plates explanation helps answer several questions in Church history. For example, Joseph said

> by the wisdom of God, they [the plates] remained safe in my hands, until I had accomplished by them what was required at my hand. When, according to arrangements, the messenger called for them, I delivered them up to him; and he has them in his charge until this day, being the second day of May, one thousand eight hundred and thirty-eight. (Joseph Smith—History 1:60)

However, Brigham Young said that "When Joseph got the plates, the angel instructed him to carry them back to the hill Cumorah, which he did." This statement could not refer to the Harmony plates because Joseph gave those to a messenger before he left Harmony. It was the messenger on the road to Fayette who took those plates to Cumorah. Both statements would be true if Joseph delivered the abridged plates to the messenger before leaving Harmony, but returned the plates of Nephi to the repository.

In the Wentworth letter, Joseph wrote that "The volume was something near six inches in thickness, a part of which was sealed." However, none of the Eight Witnesses said anything about a sealed portion. That indicates they saw the plates of Nephi.

Witnesses provided different estimates of the weight and size of the plates. This could be explained by them hefting the plates of Nephi instead of the abridged plates.

————

The case for Cumorah starts and ends with the credibility of Joseph Smith and Oliver Cowdery. Their credibility is also on the line with respect to the translation of the Book of Mormon.

My proposal that Joseph translated two sets of plates relies on the critical assumption that Joseph actually used the plates during the translation. Otherwise—if all he did was read words that appeared on a stone in a hat—it wouldn't matter whether he possessed the plates of Nephi at all. This is an important aspect of the debated over the translation process.

D&C 10:41, for example, says "you shall translate the engravings which are on the plates of Nephi." This tells us Joseph was translating *engravings*, or characters, on specific plates. If he never consulted the plates, this revelation would be meaningless to him.

No other explanation makes sense in the totality of the circumstances. If Joseph never used the plates to translate, what was the point of having a portion of them sealed? If all he did was read from the stone, or the interpreters, without referring to the actual plates, the stone would have prevented him from reading any forbidden material in the sealed portion anyway.

In my book *A Man that Can Translate*, I offer an explanation that reconciles the various accounts about the translation. I believe Joseph and Oliver told the truth when they said Joseph translated the plates with the Urim and Thummim. Others who said Joseph used a stone in a hat related what they observed during a demonstration. They repeated that story for what they thought was a good reason, as I explain in that book.

But Joseph and Oliver were correct about the translation, and understanding that Joseph translated two separate sets of plates corroborates their testimonies.

Those who reject the New York Cumorah claim that neither Joseph nor Oliver claimed revelation about the hill. That's a red herring fallacy. Neither Joseph nor Oliver would have any need for revelation about the location of Cumorah because they actually visited Mormon's repository in the hill.

Orson Pratt made this point when he stated,

> When Moroni, about thirty-six years after, made the deposit of the book entrusted to him, he was, without doubt, inspired to select **a department of the hill separate from the great sacred depository of the numerous volumes** hid up by his father.

> The particular place in the hill, where Moroni secreted the book, was revealed, by the angel, to the Prophet Joseph Smith, to whom the volume was delivered in September, A.D. 1827. **But the grand repository of all the numerous records of the ancient nations of the western continent, was located in another department of the hill,** and its contents under the charge of holy angels, until the day should come for them to be transferred to the sacred temple of Zion.

> The hill Cumorah, with the surrounding vicinity, is distinguished as the great battle-field on which, and near which, two powerful nations were concentrated with all their forces, men, women, and children, and fought till hundreds of thousands on both sides were hewn down, and left to moulder upon the ground.[108]

Cameron Packer wrote an article[109] on the topic that includes ten references to the room of records. Recall that Brigham Young said there

---

[108] Orson Pratt, "The Hill Cumorah; or the sacred depository of wisdom and understanding," *The Latter-Day Saints' Millennial Star*, July 7, 1866. Online at
http://www.lettervii.com/2016/08/the-hill-cumorah-sacred-depository.html.
[109] Cameron J. Packer, "Cumorah's Cave," Journal of Book of Mormon Studies 13/1-2 (2004): 50-57, 170-71. Online at
http://publications.mi.byu.edu/publications/jbms/13/1/S00006-50be6ae14ef1b5Packer.pdf

were "more plates than probably many wagon loads." Heber C. Kimball (Item 2) said Joseph and others "saw more records than ten men could carry." Item 6 relates that Brigham Young "said there was great wealth in the room in sacred implements, vestments, arms, precious metals and precious stones, more than a six-mule team could draw."

These comments suggest that Joseph, Oliver and others may have moved the plates from the repository in Cumorah.

When asked where the plates are now, David Whitmer said they were in New York, not in Cumorah, "but not far away from that place."

Mormon moved the records to Cumorah from the hill Shim. Perhaps Joseph and the others moved them back to the hill Shim to protect them. David said, "when they [the plates] are translated much useful information will be brought to light. But till that day arrives, no Rochester adventurers shall ever see them or the treasures."[110]

President Anthony W. Ivins spoke about Cumorah in the April 1928 General Conference to commemorate the acquisition of the Hill Cumorah. He said these records

> and the other sacred records which were deposited in the hill Cumorah **still lie in their repository**, awaiting the time when the Lord shall see fit to bring them forth, that they may be published to the world.
>
> **Whether they have been removed from the spot where Mormon deposited them we cannot tell**, but this we know, that they are safe under the guardianship of the Lord, and that they will be brought forth at the proper time, as the Lord has declared they should be, for the benefit and blessing of the people of the world, for his word never fails....
>
> **Without doubt, these treasures lie concealed today, some of them, at least, to be brought forth in the not-distant future.** How soon this will be we do not know, but this is certain, we are more than a century nearer that time than we were at the time when Joseph Smith took from their resting place, in the hill Cumorah, the plates from which he translated the contents of the Book of Mormon.

---

[110] Edward Stevenson, *Reminiscences of Joseph the Prophet and the Coming Forth of the Book of Mormon* (1877), page 14, online at https://archive.org/stream/reminiscencesofj00stev#page/n17/mode/2up.

**All of these incidents to which I have referred, my brethren and sisters, are very closely associated with this particular spot in the state of New York.** Therefore I feel, as I said in the beginning of my remarks, that **the acquisition of that spot of ground is more than an incident in the history of the Church;** it is an epoch—**an epoch which in my opinion is fraught with that which may become of greater interest to the Latter-day Saints than that which has already occurred.** We know that all of these records, all the sacred records of the Nephite people, were deposited by Mormon in that hill. That incident alone is sufficient to make it the sacred and hallowed spot that it is to us....

I bear witness to you that the words which I have read here, quoted from the Book of Mormon, which refer to the future will be fulfilled. **Those additional records will come forth, they will be published to the world, that the children of our Father may be converted to faith in Christ, our Lord and Redeemer, through obedience to the doctrines which he taught.** May God our Father hasten that day, is my humble prayer, and I ask it through Jesus Christ. Amen.

## How Cumorah fits: Moroni's America

In Part One we discussed the way we experience shifts in perception that can lead to greater understanding. One example of that is that when I interpret the text, I use basic assumptions that others may not use.

1. Terms such as "land northward" and "land southward" are relative terms, not proper nouns. For example, if you are in Washington, D.C., New York City is the "land *northward.*" But if you are in Boston, New York City is the "land *southward.*"

2. Different terms usually mean different things. A "small neck of land" is not the same as a "narrow neck of land," which in turn is not the same thing as a "narrow neck," which is not the same thing as a "narrow pass." In geography, a "neck of land" is an *isthmus* and a "neck of water" is a *strait.* Both an isthmus and a strait can lead to other places.

3. Ancient people traveled by water whenever possible. Mormon mentioned that his abridgment could not contain "a hundredth part of

the proceedings of this people... their shipping and their building of ships." (Helaman 3:14) Water travel opens the possibility of much different distances mentioned in the text than the assumption of only travel by land.

4. Directions (north, south, east, west) are the same as we use today.

5. Joseph translated the ancient plates in his own language, using terms familiar to him in his environment. The only thing he said was a "literal translation" was the Title Page. That means the rest of the text may be something other than a "literal translation," which allows a more fluid interpretation than a literal translation would.

These assumptions may require a shift in perception for those who have been taught to think according to an M2C interpretation of the text, but I suggest this new perception leads to specific interpretations of the text that align well with external evidence.

Here's the overview of what I call Moroni's America.

Lehi landed along the panhandle of Florida. Nephi and his family and followers (among whom were local hunter/gatherer people) escaped Laman and his followers by fleeing north on a river through Georgia and then north to eastern Tennessee in the Chattanooga area. From there, Mosiah fled down the Tennessee River north to the Ohio River and southern Illinois (the land of Zarahemla). From there, Mosiah traveled to the "first landing" of Mulek, what would become the city of Zarahemla, across from Nauvoo. The Nephites expanded into Ohio (Bountiful) and then further east and north into Pennsylvania and New York. When the final wars started in Zarahemla, the Nephites gradually retreated to Cumorah, where Mormon knew the Jaredites had fortifications.

———

I briefly discussed the issue of Sidon in Part Three—Abstract Maps. Here we will consider the issue in more detail as an example of how to analyze the issues to avoid logical and factual thinking errors.

———

## Example: What does "head of the river" mean?

One key to understanding the geography of the Book of Mormon is to understand the meaning of the phrase, "head of the river Sidon." It can mean either (i) *headwaters* (source) or (ii) *confluence* (where rivers meet).

The definition you choose determines which way the river flows. The reason: the city of Zarahemla is on the west bank of the River Sidon. The text does not say whether the river flows north or south, but it does explain that the "head of the river Sidon" is south of Zarahemla.

Therefore, if the "head of the river" means the "headwaters, or source," then the river must flow north.

If the "head of the river" means a confluence, the river may flow north or south.

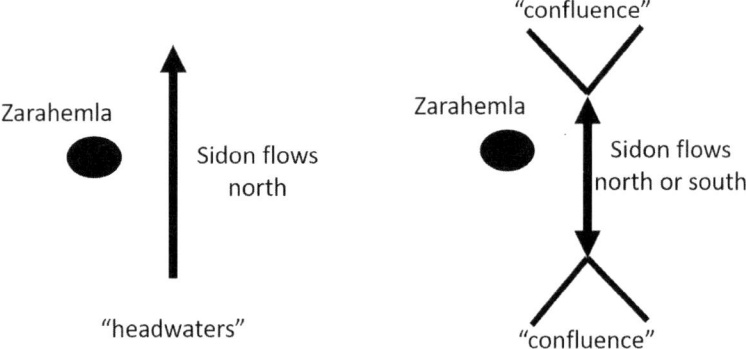

The direction of flow leads eventually to the real-world identity of the river. There are only so many north-flowing and south-flowing rivers in the western hemisphere.

Those who believe that Sidon flows north think there are only two possibilities: the Usumacinta and the Grijalva in Mesoamerica. (Orson Pratt and others thought Sidon was the Magdalena river in Colombia, which also flows north.) No one thought of the Tennessee River in the United States, which also flows north into the Ohio River, or the numerous small rivers that flow north into the Great Lakes, but that's a separate topic.

Those who believe the Sidon flows south focus primarily on the Mississippi River.

The text seems to explain that the land of Nephi is both (i) south of the land of Zarahemla and (ii) higher in elevation. That implies that a river from Nephi to Zarahemla would be north-flowing. But such a river is not necessarily Sidon.

In *Moroni's America*, for example, I propose the north-flowing river is the Tennessee River, which flows north from Tennessee (the land of Nephi) to Illinois (the land of Zarahemla) on the Ohio River. Nephites traveling to the City of Zarahemla could continue west on the Ohio River to the Mississippi (Sidon) and then north on the Mississippi.

———

There are three key passages in the text. The first two occur when Mormon explained the overall geography by referring to "the head of the river."

> 27 And it came to pass that the king sent a proclamation throughout all the land, amongst all his people who were in all his land, who were in all the regions round about, which was bordering even to the sea, on the east and on the west, and which was divided from the land of Zarahemla by a narrow strip of wilderness, which ran from the sea east even to the sea west, and round about on the borders of the seashore, and the borders of the wilderness which was on the north by the land of Zarahemla, through the borders of Manti, by **the head of the river Sidon**, running from the east towards the west—and thus were the Lamanites and the Nephites divided.

> 29 And also there were many Lamanites on the east by the seashore, whither the Nephites had driven them. And thus the Nephites were nearly surrounded by the Lamanites; nevertheless the Nephites had taken possession of all the northern parts of the land bordering on the wilderness, at **the head of the river Sidon**, from the east to the west, round about on the wilderness side; on the north, even until they came to the land which they called Bountiful.

(Alma 22:27–29)

Neither of these passages explain which direction the river flows.

The first question is, if Joseph was translating a Nephite term that meant "headwaters," why didn't he dictate "headwaters" in these passages? Or "source" or another synonym?

Presumably Joseph didn't intend to use an ambiguous term, but from our vantage point, it does look ambiguous. In this situation, we normally consult the dictionary to interpret the text.

The favorite dictionary for Book of Mormon terminology is either a Bible dictionary or the 1828 Webster's dictionary, on the theory that Joseph was using contemporary meanings. It is available online at http://webstersdictionary1828.com/Dictionary/Head

That dictionary gives these possibly relevant alternatives:

11. The top of a thing, especially when larger than the rest of the thing; as the head of a spear; the head of a cabbage; the head of a nail; the head of a mast.

12. The forepart of a thing, as the head of a ship, which includes the bows on both sides; also, the ornamental figure or image erected on or before the stem of a ship.

18. The principal source of a stream; as the head of the Nile.

23. Body; conflux.

30. The part most remote from the mouth or opening into the sea; as the head of a bay, gulf or creek.

HEAD, verb intransitive hed. To originate; to spring; to have its source, as a river.

A broad river that heads in the great Blue Ridge of mountains.

The majority of those definitions support the "headwaters" connotation. If you are predisposed toward M2C, your bias is confirmed. You don't have to look any further. You've proven your point and anyone who doesn't agree is simply wrong.

But if you don't have your mind made up, or if you reject M2C for other reasons, you don't stop yet. You notice that number 23 offers an alternative.

The dictionary defines "conflux" this way:

CONFLUX, noun [Latin See Confluence.]

1. A flowing together; a meeting of two or more currents of a fluid.

Not surprisingly, the dictionary supports both connotations.

At this point, we can simply choose to believe whatever we want. Usually this is what we do. We have found our answer, and it confirms our bias. But if we haven't convinced everyone else, and we feel compelled to do so, we may seek more ways to confirm our bias.

The alternative is to recognize that we now have multiple working hypotheses. We can pursue both and see where they lead. We can allow others to believe whatever they want and work together to build Zion anyway.

After consulting the dictionary, we can look at other similar passages in the scriptures for guidance. In this case, when Lehi described his dream, he used the phrase "the head of the river."

13 And as I cast my eyes round about, that perhaps I might discover my family also, I beheld **a river of water**; and it ran along, and it was near the tree of which I was partaking the fruit.

14 And I looked to behold **from whence it came**; and I saw **the head thereof** a little way off; and at **the head thereof** I beheld your mother Sariah, and Sam, and Nephi; and they stood as if they knew not whither they should go.

15 And it came to pass that I beckoned unto them; and I also did say unto them with a loud voice that they should come unto me, and partake of the fruit, which was desirable above all other fruit.

16 And it came to pass that they did come unto me and partake of the fruit also.

17 And it came to pass that I was desirous that Laman and Lemuel should come and partake of the fruit also; wherefore, I cast mine eyes **towards the head of the river**, that perhaps I might see them.

(1 Nephi 8:13–17)

Those who claim the term means *headwaters* point out that Lehi looked to behold "from whence it came" and saw the "head" of the river. They think that means Lehi was looking at the source.

It's easy to see how this is a fallacy. Rivers come "from" both the headwaters (original source) and the confluences of tributaries.

In fact, most rivers are a series of confluences. Anyone who looks upriver will see confluences as tributaries flow into the river. Rivers become larger as they flow downstream because of these confluences.

Consequently, the passage in Lehi is just as ambiguous as the dictionary definition. We're back to believing whatever we want.

If the dictionary and other scriptural references are ambiguous, what next?

The next step depends on your assumption about the translation.

Believers agree that Joseph Smith "translated" the Book of Mormon, but they don't agree on what the word "translated" means. Again, we face two alternatives.

(i) Some scholars and historians say Joseph never translated anything in the ordinary sense of the word. They say Joseph merely read words that appeared on the stone in a hat (or in vision), and he didn't even use the plates. They say the words were provided by an unknown supernatural translator who used vocabulary and syntax from Early Modern English, not the 1800s.

(ii) Others say Joseph actually translated the characters engraved on the plates, after studying the characters with the Urim and Thummim. They say he translated the plates "after the manner of [his] language" (D&C 1:24), using his own vocabulary, syntax, etc.

If you agree with assumption (i), you might research the use of the phrase "head of the river" in Early Modern English. You might consult databases of published work from the 1500s. If you find references, they will likely confirm your bias, whatever your bias is, just like the dictionary and scriptural references.

If you agree with assumption (ii), you might research other uses contemporary with Joseph Smith. You will probably find examples that confirm your bias, whatever your bias is, just like the dictionary and scriptural references.

Here's what I found.

———

Joseph Smith translated the abridged plates (including Alma 22) in Harmony, Pennsylvania. He also translated the Book of Lehi (the lost 116 pages) in Harmony. We don't know what those pages included, but it seems likely Lehi would have recorded his dream there because it played such an important role in the lives of his family as they left Jerusalem to find the promised land. If so, Joseph would have translated the dream roughly the same way he did when he translated Nephi's original plates. After all, Nephi quoted his father in Chapter 8:2-28.

Harmony is located near the Great Bend of the Susquehanna River, about twenty miles upstream from Binghamton, Broome County, New York. In the early 19th century, this was a busy transportation corridor. Hundreds of boats and rafts could pass by Harmony in a single day.

Binghamton was located at the confluence of the Susquehanna and Chenango Rivers. Today, the site of the confluence is a public park, named, appropriately "Confluence Park."[111]

The river flows south from near Cooperstown, New York, into Pennsylvania toward Harmony. At the Great Bend, the river turns north and west to Binghamton and through New York until it turns south again back into Pennsylvania toward Philadelphia.

---

[111]    https://www.binghamton.edu/programs/cap/tours/binghamton/confluence-park.html

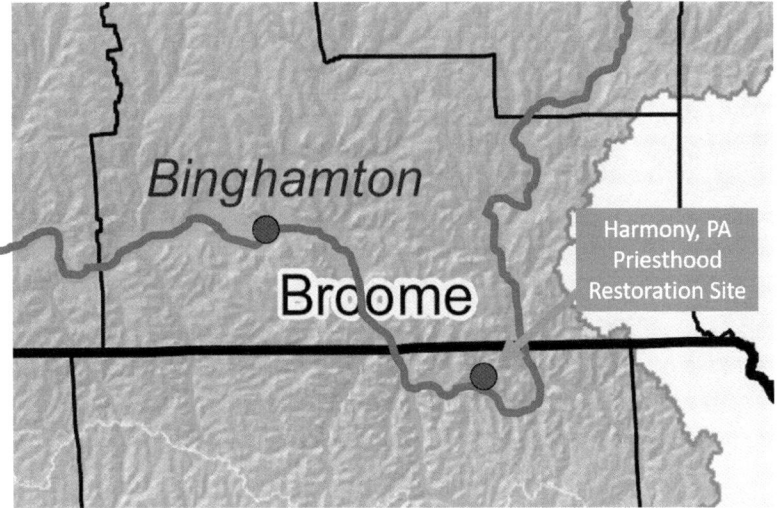

Figure 19 - Map of Susquehanna near Harmony

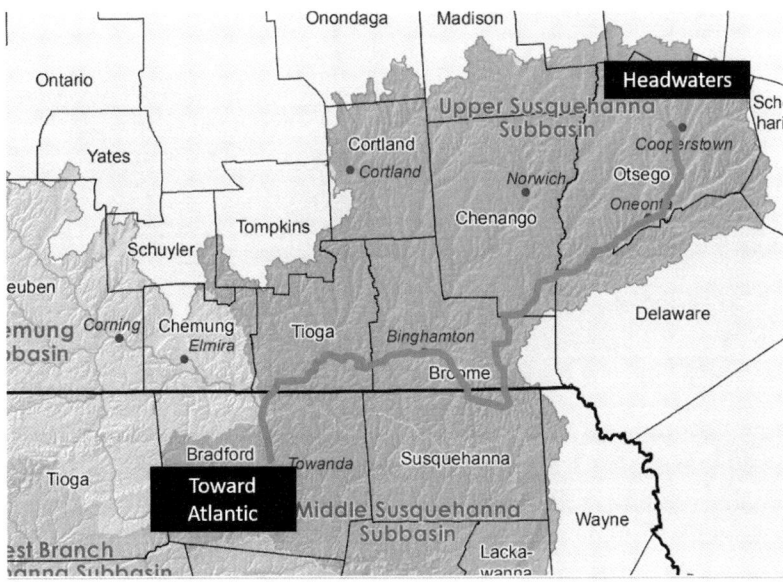

Figure 20 - Map of Susquehanna from Cooperstown

It turns out that Binghamton was known as "the head of the river."

If you've read my book *Infinite Goodness* or seen my presentations, you're familiar with Jonathan Edwards, the famous author and preacher in the First Awakening in New England in the 1700s. I've proposed that the nonbiblical language (and much of the biblical language, too) in the Book of Mormon echoes the writings of Jonathan Edwards. I infer that Joseph Smith was familiar with Edwards' works, whether from reading them or hearing them preached. An eight-volume collection of Edwards' writings was on sale in the Palmyra bookstore that Joseph visited weekly to get the newspaper for his father. Edwards' letters and sermons were published in religious newspapers and magazines. Ministers quoted Edwards frequently.

The echoes of Edwards' writings appear not only in the Book of Mormon, but in the Doctrine and Covenants and Joseph's personal writings. In my view, as part of God's preparation of Joseph to become a prophet, Joseph had internalized Edwards' words, phrases and concepts.

Edwards spent much of his career as a missionary to the Stockbridge Indians in western Massachusetts. In 1751, Jonathan Edwards wrote a letter to British supporters of the mission.

> There had been here the last summer a man whose name was Jonah from Onohquaga, a town of the Oneidas situated on Susquehanna River **near the head of the river** about 200 miles southwest from Albany. He was one of the principal inhabitants of the town, who, having heard of the things which were doing here for the instruction of the Indians, came to visit this place and make report to his people.

In another letter, he wrote

> Mr. Spencer went the last Fall, far into the western wilderness; to the Oneidaes, one of the Tribes of Indians called the six Nations, living on Suscohannah River, **towards the Head of the River**, to a Place called by the Indians Onohouhquauga, about 180 miles southwest from Albany on Hudsons River. where He continued almost through the winter;

Onohguaga doesn't appear on modern maps, but you can find it if you do historical research. The editors of Edwards' works explained the background.

After mid-April 1755, Gideon Hawley returned to Onohquaga, the Indian settlement **near modern Binghamton, New York**, taking with him Edwards' son Jonathan, Jr. The lad was not quite ten but was already speaking Mahican with his friends at school and play.

Edwards referred to this in a 1755 letter to his son.

> … this is a comfort to us, that the same God that is here, is also at Onohquaga; and that though you are out of our sight and out of our reach, you are always in God's hands, who is infinitely gracious; and we can go to him, and commit you to his care and mercy.

This is a lot of detail, but it shows that Jonathan Edwards, whose influence is apparent throughout Joseph's writings, referred to a confluence of the Susquehanna River with the Chenango River as the "head of the river." It strikes me as not a coincidence to see this phrase used to describe an important site just twenty miles from Harmony, where Joseph translated the plates.

A placard at Confluence Park in Binghamton explains that

> Confluence Park is located at the confluence of the Susquehanna and Chenango Rivers. It has been a gathering place for peoples from prehistory to the present… Extensive archaeological work by Binghamton University has verified our Native American forbears settled, fished, hunted and traded along these banks. The Iroquois considered the confluence sacred for its position where the rivers met.

Because the "head of the river" Susquehanna was a confluence of two rivers that Native Americans considered sacred, it seems plausible to me that the "head of the river" in the Book of Mormon would also be a confluence of two rivers that Nephites considered significant.

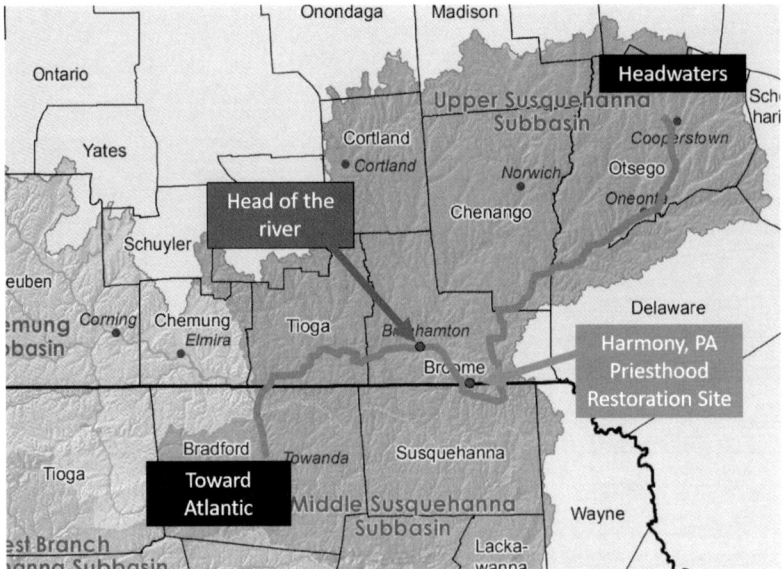

Figure 21 - Map of Susquehanna "head of the river"

There are other reasons to interpret "head of the river" to mean a confluence. I've written elsewhere about two examples from Church history.[112]

In Letter VIII, Oliver Cowdery wrote

> This gentleman, whose name is Stowel, resided in the town of Bainbridge, **on or near the head waters of the Susquehannah river**. Some forty miles south, or down the river, in the town of Harmony, Susquehannah county, Pa....[113]

Bainbridge is located at a bend in the Susquehanna River where several streams or brooks flow into the river, making it a convergence. Bainbridge is hundreds of miles downstream from the source of the Susquehanna.

---

[112] https://www.lettervii.com/2015/12/head-of-sidon-in-church-history.html
[113] https://www.josephsmithpapers.org/paper-summary/history-1834-1836/105

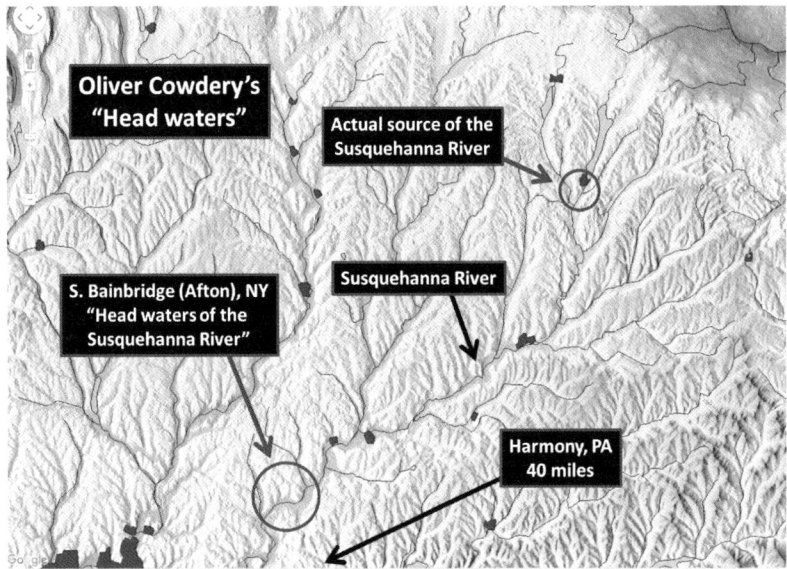

Figure 22 - Map of "head waters" of the Susquehanna

Consequently, Harmony is located 40 miles downriver from the "head waters" of the Susquehanna and 20 miles upriver from the "head of the river." In these examples, both proximate to Joseph Smith when he translated the Book of Mormon, neither term refers to the actual source of the river.

———

I think the details in this analysis help understand the text of the Book of Mormon and the geography it describes. You may agree or disagree. Everyone who accepts M2C disagrees with my conclusions, although the facts I presented here are easy to verify.

Regardless of your conclusions, at least now you can make an informed decision.

———

If you're curious about how the New York Cumorah fits within the overall setting of the Book of Mormon in the new world, my book

*Moroni's America* offers a detailed explanation based on the text of the Book of Mormon.

## Conclusion

The historical record regarding the Hill Cumorah includes statements by Joseph Smith, Oliver Cowdery, David Whitmer, Martin Harris, Brigham Young, Heber C. Kimball, Wilford Woodruff, and many others who knew Joseph and Oliver.

In this book I've explained why I conclude that the New York Cumorah is the most plausible explanation for the testimonies of these witnesses, based on my assessment of credibility, reliability, opportunity, bias, motive—all the normal factors that bear on the believability of someone's testimony. I've introduced some extrinsic and scientific evidence that corroborates the New York Cumorah, including archaeology, anthropology, geography, and geology.

But I fully recognize and accept that others have different opinions, interpretations, supporting facts, etc. Unity through diversity.

You will reach your own conclusions.

———

In all our discussions of these issues, I like to think of something Joseph Smith wrote in a letter to Oliver Granger in July 1840.

> In order to conduct the affairs of the kingdom in righteousness it is all important that the most perfect harmony, kind feeling, good understanding, and confidence should exist in the hearts of all the brethren, and that true Charity—love one towards another, should characterize all their proceedings. If there are any uncharitable feelings, any lack of confidence, then pride, arrogancy and envy will soon be manifested and confusion must inevitably prevail and the authorities of the Church set at naught.[114]

---

[114]   https://www.josephsmithpapers.org/paper-summary/letter-to-oliver-granger-between-circa-22-and-circa-28-july-1840/1#source-note

# Appendix 1: Cumorah teachings

This Appendix contains, as far as could be found, all statements issued by Joseph Smith, Jr., Oliver Cowdery, David Whitmer, Martin Harris, and members of the First Presidency and Quorum of the Twelve, plus official publications of the Church of Jesus Christ of Latter-day Saints on the subject of the hill Cumorah and the geography of the Book of Mormon.

Many other leaders of the Church have re-affirmed the New York Cumorah. Their teachings are added at the end of this Appendix.

These statements evince a sharp distinction between two separate but related teachings by Church leaders that have often been commingled or conflated; i.e.,

1. The Hill Cumorah of Mormon 6:6 is in western New York, near Palmyra.

2. We don't know where the other events of the Book of Mormon took place, but there are many possibilities.

———

**1. Early 1827** – Joseph Smith (quoted by his mother Lucy Mack Smith)

[In January 1827, Joseph] returned with his wife, in good health and fine spirits. Not long after this his father had occasion to send him to Manchester on business. <And,> as he started quite early in the morning, we expected him home, at the outside, by 6. o clock in the evening. But when 6. came he did not arrive.— we always had a peculiar anxiety about him whenever he was absent from us; for, it seemed as if something was always taking place to jeopardize his life. But to return, he did not get home till the night was far spent. On coming in, threw himself into a chair, apparently much exhausted. My husband did not observe his appearance, and immediately exclaimed, "Joseph, why have you staid so late? has anything happened you? we have been much distressed about you these three hours. As Joseph made no reply, he continued his interrogations until I finally said: now, father, (as that was the manner in which I commonly addressed him) let him rest a moment— dont touble him now— you see he is home safe, and he is very tired; so pray wait a little.

The fact is, I had learned to be a little cautious about matters with regard to Joseph; for I was accostomed to see him look as he did on that occasion, and could not easily mistake the cause thereof. Presently he smiled, and said in a very calm tone, "I have taken the severest chastisement, that I have ever had in my life". My husband, supposing it was from some of the neighbors, was quite angry; and observed, "I would like to know what business any body has to find fault with you."

"Stop, father, Stop." said Joseph, "it was the angel of the Lord— **as I passed by the hill of Cumorah, where the plates are**, the angel of the Lord met me and said, that I had not been engaged enough in the work of the Lord; that the time had come for the record to <be> brought forth; and, that I must be up and doing, and set myself about the things which God had commanded me to do: but, Father,' continued he, 'give yourself no uneasiness concerning the reprimand that I have received; for I now know the course that I am to pursue; so all will be well."

It was also made known to him at this interview, that he should make another effort to obtain the plates on the 22d. of the following September; But this he did not mention to us at that time.

https://www.josephsmithpapers.org/paper-summary/lucy-mack-smith-history-1845/111

## 2. 1827 – Moroni (related by David Whitmer in 1881)

In 1881, David Whitmer gave an interview to the *Kansas City Journal* in which he explained what Joseph told him.

"Did Joseph Smith ever relate to you the circumstances of his finding the plates?"

"Yes, he told me that he first found the plates in the year 1823; that during the fall of 1823 he had a vision, an angel appearing to him three times in one night and telling him that there was a record of an ancient people deposited in a hill near his father's house, **called by the ancients `Cumorah,'** situated in the township of Manchester, Ontario County, N. Y. The angel pointed out the exact spot, and, sometime after, he went and found the records or plates deposited in a stone box in the hill, just as had been described to him by the angel. It was some little time, however, before the angel would allow Smith to remove the plates from their place of deposit."

https://whitmercollege.com/interviews/kansas-city-journal-1881/

**3. 1829** – Martin Harris (quoted by Stephen S. Harding, the fourth territorial Governor of Utah). Harding met Martin Harris in Palmyra at the printing shop. In 1882, he wrote a letter about his experience.

"About two weeks after this I met Martin Harris. He was glad to see me; inquired how I felt since my dream. He told me that since he saw me at Mr. Smith's he had seen fearful signs in the heavens. That he was standing alone one night, and saw a fiery sword let down out of heaven, and pointing to the east, west, north, and south, then **to the hill of Cumorah**, where the plates of Nephi were found."

https://archive.org/details/GR_1666/page/n65/mode/2up

**4. 1830** – Oliver Cowdery (quoted by Parley P. Pratt) during the mission to the Lamanites (D&C 28, 30 and 32).

"This Book, which contained these things, **was hid in the earth by Moroni, in a hill called by him, Cumorah, which hill is now in the State of New York, near the village of Palmyra, in Ontario County**.

"In that neighborhood there lived a young man named Joseph Smith, who prayed to the Great Spirit much, in order that he might know the truth; and the Great Spirit sent an angel to him, and told him where this Book was hid by Moroni; and commanded him to go and get it. He accordingly went to the place, and dug in the earth, and found the Book written on golden plates.

"But it was written in the language of the forefathers of the red man; therefore this young man, being a pale face, could not understand it; but the angel told him and showed him, and gave him knowledge of the language, and how to interpret the Book. So he interpreted it into the language of the pale faces, and wrote it on paper, and caused it to be printed, and published thousands of copies of among them; and then sent us to the red men to bring some copies of it to them, and to tell them this news. So we have now come from him, and here is a copy of the Book, which we now present to our red friend, the chief of the Delawares, and which we hope he will cause to be read and known among his tribe; it will do them good."

We then presented him with a Book of Mormon.

There was a pause in the council, and some conversation in their own tongue, after which the chief made the following reply: "We feel truly thankful to our white friends who have come so far, and been at such pains to tell us good news, and especially this new news concerning the Book of our forefathers; it makes us glad in here"— placing his hand on his heart.

*Autobiography of Parley P. Pratt,*
http://www.gutenberg.org/files/44896/44896-h/44896-h.htm

**5. First formal Church History, 1835** – Oliver Cowdery and Joseph Smith wrote a series of essays, published as letters, about early Church history, including the restoration of the Priesthood, the visit of Moroni, and Joseph's recovery of the plates. Letters I and II were published in ***The Messenger and Advocate*** in Kirtland, Ohio, in October and November 1834. An excerpt from Letter I was canonized in the Pearl of Great Price as a note to Joseph Smith-History.

In December 1835, Joseph Smith ordained Oliver Cowdery as Assistant President of the Church. In 1835, when Letters IV through VIII were published, the First Presidency consisted of Joseph Smith,

Jr., President; Oliver Cowdery, Assistant President; Sidney Rigdon, First Counselor; and Frederick G. Williams, Second Counselor.

President Williams began copying the letters into President Smith's personal history before another scribe completed the work, as Joseph noted in his journal. This history can be seen in the Joseph Smith Papers and is the source of the quotations below.

In 1840, Joseph Smith and Sidney Rigdon specifically approved of the republication of all eight letters in the *Gospel Reflector*, a newspaper in Philadelphia published by Benjamin Winchester. Also in 1840, Joseph Smith gave the letters to his brother, Don Carlos Smith, with instructions to republish them in the *Times and Seasons* in Nauvoo. Don Carlos published them in 1840-1841. Parley P. Pratt republished all eight letters in the *Millennial Star*.

**Excerpt from Letter IV.**

He [Moroni] then proceeded and gave a general account of the promises made to the fathers, and also gave a history of the aborigenes of this country, and said they were literal descendants of Abraham. He represented them as once being an enlightned and intelligent people, possessing a correct knowledge of the gospel, and the plan of restoration and redemption. **He said this history was written and deposited not far from that place**, and that it was our brother's privilege, if obedient to the commandments of the Lord, to obtain and translate the same by the means of the Urim and Thummim, which were deposited for that purpose with the record.

"Yet," said he, "the scriptures must be fulfilled before it is translated, which says that the words of a book, which were sealed, were presented to the learned; for thus has God determined to leave men without excuse, and show to the meek that his arm is <not> shortned that it cannot save."

A part of the book was sealed, and was not to be opened yet. The sealed part, said he, contains the same revelation which was given to John upon the isles of Patmos, and when the people of the Lord are prepared, and found worthy, then it will be unfolded unto them.

On the subject of bringing to light the unsealed part of this record, it may be proper to say, that our brother was expressly informed, that it must be done with an eye single to the glory of God; if this consideration did not wholly characterize all his procedings in relation to it, the adversary of truth would overcome him, or at least prevent his making that proficiency in this glorious work which he otherwise would.

While describing the place where the record was deposited, he gave a minute relation of it, and the vision of his mind being opened at the same time, he was permitted to view it critically; and previously being acquainted with the place, he was able to follow the direction of the vision, afterward, according to the voice of the angel, and obtain the book.

https://www.josephsmithpapers.org/paper-summary/history-1834-1836/68

### Excerpt from Letter VII.

I must now give you some description of the place where, and the manner in which these records were deposited.

You are acquainted with the mail road from Palmyra, Wayne Co. to Canandaigua, Ontario Co. N.Y. and also, as you pass from the former to the latter place, before arriving at the little village of Manchester, say from three to four, or about four miles from Palmyra, you pass a large hill on the east side of the road. Why I say large, is because it is as large perhaps, as any in that country. To a person acquainted with this road, a description would be unnecessary, as it is the largest and rises the highest of any on that route. The north end rises quite sudden until it assumes a level with the more southerly extremity, and I think I may say an elevation higher than at the south a short distance, say half or three fourths of a mile. As you pass toward [C]anandaigua it lessens gradually until the surface assumes its common level, or is broken by other smaller hills or ridges, water courses and ravines. I think I am justified in saying that this is the highest hill for some distance round, and I am certain that its appearance, as it rises so suddenly from a plain on the north, must attract the notice of the traveller as he passes by.

At about one mile west rises another ridge of less height, running parallel with the former, leaving a beautiful vale between. The soil is of the first quality for the country, and under a state of cultivation, which gives a prospect at once imposing, **when one reflects on the fact, that here, between these hills, the entire power and national strength of both the Jaredites and Nephites were destroyed.**

By turning to the 529th and 530th pages of the book of Mormon you will read Mormon's account of the last great struggle of his people, **as they were encamped round this hill Cumorah**. (it is printed Camorah, which is an error.) In this vally [sic] fell the remaining strength and pride of a once powerful people, the Nephites—once so highly favored of the Lord, but at that time in darkness, doomed to suffer extermination by the hand of their barbarous and uncivilized brethren. From the top of this hill, Mormon, with a few others, after the battle, gazed with horror upon the mangled remains of those who, the day before, were filled with anxiety, hope or doubt. A few had fled to the South, who were hunted down by the victorious party, and all who would not deny the Saviour and his religion, were put to death. Mormon himself, according to the record of his son Moroni, was also slain.

But a long time previous to this disaster it appears from his own account, he foresaw approaching destruction. In fact, if he perused the records of his fathers, which were in his possession, he could have learned that such would be the case. Alma, who lived before the coming of the Messiah, prophesies this. He, however, by divine appointment, abridged from those records, in his own style and language, a short account of the more important and prominent items, from the days of Lehi to his own time, **after which he deposited, as he says, on the 529th page, all the records in this same hill, Cumorah and after gave his small record to his son Moroni**, who, as appears from the same, finished, after witnessing the extinction of his people as a nation. …

**This hill, by the Jaredites, was called Ramah: by it, or around it pitched the famous army of Coriantumr their tents.** Coriantumr was the last king of the Jaredites The opposing army were to the west, and in this same vally [sic], and near by, from day to day, did that mighty race spill their blood, in wrath, contending, as it were, brother against brother, and father, against son. In this same spot, in full view from the top of this same hill, one may gaze with astonishment upon the ground which was twice covered with the dead and dying of our fellow men. Here may be seen where once sunk to nought the pride and strength of two mighty nations; and here may be contemplated, in solitude, while nothing but the faithful record of Mormon and Moroni is now extant to inform us of the fact…

**In this vale lie commingled,** in one mass of ruin the ashes of thousands, and in this vale was destined to consume the fair forms and vigerous systems of tens of thousands of the human race—blood mixed with blood, flesh with flesh, bones with bones and dust with dust!

### Excerpt from Letter VIII

I have now given suffcient on the subject of the hill Cumorah—it has a singular and imposing appearance for that country, and must ex[c]ite the curiosity curious enquiry of every lover of the book of Mormon: though I hope never like Jerusalem and the sepulcher of our Lord, the pilgrims. In my estimation, certain places are dearer to me for what they now contain than for what they have contained. For the satisfaction of such as believe I have been thus particular, and to avoid the question being a thousand times asked, more than any other cause, shall procede and be as particular as heretofore.

### 6. 1836 "An Angel Came Down from the Mansions of Glory"

**Hymn 16**, Collection of Sacred Hymns, 1835 (published in 1836)

Pursuant to D&C 25, Emma Smith selected hymns for the first Church hymnal, published in Kirtland, Ohio, in 1836. Hymn 16 mentions Cumorah.

An angel came down from the mansions of glory,
**And told that a record was hid in Cumorah,**
Containing the fulness of Jesus's gospel;
And also the cov'nant to gather his people.

Attributed to W.W. Phelps

From the Historical Introduction in the Joseph Smith Papers: "At a meeting of the church's presidency on 14 September 1835, it was "decided that Sister Emma Smith proceed to make a selection of sacred hymns, according to the revilation, and that President W. W. Phelps be appointed to revise and arrange them for printing." (Minute Book 1, 14 Sept. 1835)"

https://www.josephsmithpapers.org/paper-summary/collection-of-sacred-hymns-1835/24

Emma retained this hymn in the hymnal she produced in Nauvoo in 1841 as Hymn 262.

### 7. 1840 An Angel from on High

Elder Parley P. Pratt wrote the lyrics of this hymn, which he included in the hymnal he, Brigham Young and John Taylor published in Manchester, England in 1840 as hymn #197.

https://archive.org/stream/collectionofsacr00youn#page/218/mo

de/2up

Emma Smith added this hymn to her 1841 Nauvoo collection as hymn #275.

https://archive.org/stream/collectionofsacr01smit#page/302/mode/2up

These are the lyrics of the first verse.
An angel from on high
The long, long silence broke;
Descending from the sky,
These gracious words he spoke:
**Lo! in Cumorah's lonely hill**
A sacred record lies concealed.
Lo! in Cumorah's lonely hill
A sacred record lies concealed.
Lyrics by Parley P. Pratt

In the 1985 Hymnal (current) this hymn appears as #13

https://www.lds.org/music/library/hymns/an-angel-from-on-high-13?lang=eng&_r=1

## 8. 1842 *Times and Seasons* (D&C 128)

Eighteen months after Don Carlos Smith republished the eight historical letters in the *Times and Seasons*, Joseph Smith wrote a letter that he sent to the Editor of the *Times and Seasons* for publication. This letter has since been canonized as D&C 128.

20 And again, what do we hear? **Glad tidings from Cumorah! Moroni, an angel from heaven, declaring the fulfilment of the prophets—the book to be revealed.** A voice of the Lord in the wilderness of Fayette, Seneca county, declaring the three witnesses to bear record of the book! The voice of Michael on the banks of the Susquehanna, detecting the devil when he appeared as an angel of light! The voice of Peter, James, and John in the wilderness between

Harmony, Susquehanna county, and Colesville, Broome county, on the Susquehanna river, declaring themselves as possessing the keys of the kingdom, and of the dispensation of the fulness of times!

### 9. 1844 *The Prophet* in New York City.
In 1844, Joseph's brother (and Apostle) William Smith republished the eight historical letters in a Church newspaper in New York City titled *The Prophet*. Also in 1844, the eight letters were republished in England as a separate pamphlet that sold thousands of copies.

### 10. 1853 Heber C. Kimball.
Special conference in the Tabernacle, Salt Lake City, August 13, 1853 (JD 2:110)

I have lived in the State of New York, town of Bloomfield, Monroe County, right in the heart of the country where the ancient Lamanites, and other veterans, destroyed each other, root and branch; where the Book of Mormon was discovered in the hill of **Cumorah**.

### 11. 1853 Heber C. Kimball.
Discourse in the Bowery, Salt Lake City, September 28, 1856 ( JD 4:105–JD 4:106)

Brother Mills mentioned in his song, that crossing the Plains with handcarts was one of the greatest events that ever transpired in this Church. I will admit that it is an important event, successfully testing another method for gathering Israel, but its importance is small in comparison with the visitation of the angel of God to the Prophet Joseph, and with the reception of the sacred records from the hand of Moroni at the hill **Cumorah**.

How does it compare with the vision that Joseph and others had, when they went into a cave in the hill **Cumorah**, and saw more records than ten men could carry? There were books piled up on tables, book upon book. Those records this people will yet have, if they accept of the Book of Mormon and observe its precepts, and keep the commandments.

Again, how does it contrast with Joseph's being sent forth with his brethren to search out a location in Jackson County, where the New Jerusalem will be built, where our Father and our God planted the first garden on this earth, and where the New Jerusalem will come to when it comes down from heaven?

I mention these few things by way of contrast with the handcart operation; they are events that I have heard Joseph speak of, time and time again.

## 12. 1853 Brigham Young.

Discourse in the Bowery, Salt Lake City, November 6, 1864 (JD 10:364)

I defy any man on earth to point out the path a Prophet of God should walk in, or point out his duty, and just how far he must go, in dictating temporal or spiritual things. Temporal and spiritual things are inseparably connected, and ever will be. The first act that Joseph Smith was called to do by the angel of God, was, to get the plates from the hill **Cumorah**, and then translate them, and he got Martin Harris and Oliver Cowdery to write for him. **He would read the plates**, by the aid of the Urim and Thummim, and they would write. They had to either raise their bread from the ground, or buy it, and they had to eat and drink, and sleep, and toil, and rest, while they were engaged in bringing forth the great Work of the last days. All these were temporal acts, directed by the spirit of revelation.

Remarks by President Heber C. Kimball, delivered in the Tabernacle, Bountiful, Sunday, April 12, 1868.

(1860s, 1868, HCK Forbearance • JD 12:188)

I have been, as I have already told you, to where Adam offered sacrifices and blessed his sons, and I felt as though there were hundreds of angels there, and there were angels there like unto the three Nephites. I have also been over the hill Cumorah, and I understand all about it.

(1860s, 1868, HCK Forbearance ¶8 • JD 12:191)

Discourse by President Brigham Young, delivered in the Third Ward Meetinghouse, Salt Lake City, Sunday Evening, June 21, 1874

(1870s, 1874, BY Secret of • JD 18:235)

When Joseph first received the knowledge of the plates that were in the hill Cumorah, he did not then receive the keys of the Aaronic Priesthood, he merely received the knowledge that the plates were there, and that the Lord would bring them forth, and that they contained the history of the aborigines of this country. He received the knowledge that they were once in possession of the Gospel, and from that time he went on, step by step, until he obtained the plates, and the Urim and Thummim, and had power to translate them.

(1870s, 1874, BY Secret of ¶10 • JD 18:239)

## 13. 1877 President Brigham Young

Just two months before he died, as he was travelling through Utah reorganizing the Priesthood and setting in order the Temple ordinances, Brigham Young spoke to a Special Conference in Farmington. As recorded in the Journal of Discourses, President Young said this:

**"I lived right in the country where the plates were found from which the Book of Mormon was translated, and I know a great many things pertaining to that country. I believe I will take the liberty to tell you of another circumstance that will be as marvelous as anything can be.** This is an incident in the life of Oliver Cowdery, but he did not take the liberty of telling such things in meeting as I take. I tell these things to you, and **I have a motive for doing so.** I want to carry them to the ears of my brethren and sisters, and to the children also, that they may grow to an understanding of some things that seem to be entirely hidden from the human family.

Oliver Cowdery went with the Prophet Joseph when he deposited these plates. Joseph did not translate all of the plates; there was a portion of them sealed, which you can learn from the Book of Doctrine and Covenants. **When Joseph got the plates, the angel instructed him to carry them back to the hill Cumorah, which he did.** Oliver says that when Joseph and Oliver went there, the hill opened, and they walked into a cave, in which there was a large and spacious room. He says he did not think, at the time, whether they had the light of the sun or artificial light; but that it was just as light as day. **They laid the plates on a table; it was a large table that stood in the room. Under this table there was a pile of plates as much as two feet high, and there were altogether in this room more plates than probably many wagon loads;** they were piled up in the corners and along the walls. The first time they went there the sword of Laban hung upon the wall; but when they went again it had been taken down and laid upon the table across the gold plates; it was unsheathed, and on it was written these words: "This sword will never be sheathed again until the kingdoms of this world become the kingdom of our God and his Christ."

**I tell you this as coming not only from Oliver Cowdery, but others who were familiar with it,** and who understood it just as well as we understand coming to this meeting, enjoying the day, and by and by we separate and go away, forgetting most of what is said, but remembering some things. So is it with other circumstances in life. **I relate this to you, and I want you to understand it. I take this liberty of referring to those things so that they will not be forgotten and lost.** Carlos Smith was a young man of as much veracity as any young man we had, and he was a witness to these things. Samuel Smith saw some things, Hyrum saw a good many things, but Joseph was the leader.

**Now, you may think I am unwise in publicly telling these things, thinking perhaps I should preserve them in my own breast; but such is not my mind.** I would like the people called Latter-day Saints to understand some little things with regard to the workings and dealings of the Lord with his people here upon the earth."

http://jod.mrm.org/19/36

**14. 1899,** *Improvement Era.*

President Joseph F. Smith, as counselor in the First Presidency and Editor of the *Improvement Era*, republished the eight historical letters again in Salt Lake City in 1899.

We visited the **Hill Cumorah** and were accorded the courtesy of going thereon by the wife of Mr. George Sampson, a brother of Admiral Wm. Sampson, who before his death owned the property. When we went up there and looked around, we felt that we were standing on holy ground. The brethren located, as near as they thought was possible, the place from which the plates of the Book of Mormon were taken by the Prophet. We were delighted to be there. **Looking over the surrounding country we remembered that two great races of people had wound up their existence in the vicinity, had fought their last fight,** and that hundreds of thousands had been slain within sight of that hill. **Evidence of the great battles that have been fought there in days gone by are manifest in the numerous spear and arrow-heads that have been found by farmers while plowing in that neighborhood. We were fortunate enough to obtain a few of the arrowheads.**

(1900s, 1906, April, 5th Session, Elder George Albert Smith., ¶17 • CR)

I had the pleasure of standing upon the summit of the Hill Cumorah in company with President Grant. Being there upon that height of land, which so splendidly commands a view of the whole surrounding country, I could not refrain from recalling the time when Moroni stood upon the crown of that hill with the evidence of the ruins of the civilization of his people about him. And this warning, written in the Book of Ether, let me say, in closing, comes from the prophet of God who was also the historian of the great Jaredite nation, by abridging and translating their history into the Nephite language. This warning comes, then, from the historian of one civilization that had perished about the Hill Cumorah; it came also from the same man who was a witness of the destruction of the civilization of his own people at the same place.

(1920s, 1927, October, 1st Session, Elder Brigham H. Roberts, ¶35 • CR)

### 15. 1928, President Anthony W. Ivins in General Conference
On April 6, 1928, President Anthony W. Ivins of the First Presidency spoke in General Conference about the Hill Cumorah in New York, which had recently been purchased by the Church.

"Reference has been made by the President of the acquisition by the Church **of the spot of ground in the state of New York known as the hill Cumorah.** It appears to me to be an event of such importance that I desire to devote the short time which is at my disposal this morning to a discussion of that subject. There have been some differences of opinion in regard to it, and in order that I might be correct in the statements which I make I have this morning finished a short manuscript which I would like to read—the first time, I believe, in my experience, that I have ever addressed a congregation in this manner, and I do it for the purpose stated....

This sealed portion of the record which came into the hands of Joseph Smith but was not translated by him so far as we are aware, with the abridgment made by Mormon, the record of Ether, **and the other sacred records which were deposited in the hill Cumorah still lie in their repository**, awaiting the time when the Lord shall see fit to bring them forth, that they may be published to the world.

Whether they have been removed from the spot where Mormon deposited them we cannot tell, but this we know, that they are safe under the guardianship of the Lord, and that they will be brought forth at the proper time, as the Lord has declared they should be, for the benefit and blessing of the people of the world, for his word never fails....

"All of these incidents to which I have referred, my brethren and sisters, **are very closely associated with this particular spot in the state of New York.** Therefore I feel, as I said in the beginning of my remarks, that the acquisition of that spot of ground is more than an incident in the history of the Church; it is an epoch—an epoch which in my opinion is fraught with that which may become of greater interest to the Latter-day Saints than that which has already occurred. **We know that all of these records, all the sacred records of the Nephite people, were deposited by Mormon in that hill.** That incident alone is sufficient to make it the sacred and hallowed spot that it is to us.... Those additional records will come forth, they will be published to the world, that the children of our Father may be converted to faith in Christ, our Lord and Redeemer, through obedience to the doctrines which he taught."

### 16. 1975 President Marion G. Romney.

In the October 1975 General Conference, President Romney, then First Counselor in the First Presidency, gave a talk titled "America's Destiny" that included these statements:

**In the western part of the state of New York near Palmyra is a prominent hill known as the "hill Cumorah."** (Morm. 6:6.) On July twenty-fifth of this year, as I stood on the crest of that hill admiring with awe the breathtaking panorama which stretched out before me on every hand, **my mind reverted to the events which occurred in that vicinity some twenty-five centuries ago—events which brought to an end the great Jaredite nation.**

You who are acquainted with the Book of Mormon will recall that during the final campaign of the fratricidal war between the armies led by Shiz and those led by Coriantumr "nearly two millions" of Coriantumr's people had been slain by the sword; "two millions of mighty men, and also their wives and their children." (Ether 15:2.)

[Notice, he does not say two million died at Cumorah, but instead "during the final campaign of the fratricidal war."]

As the conflict intensified, all the people who had not been slain—men "with their wives and their children" (Ether 15:15)—**gathered about that hill Cumorah** (see Ether 15:11)....

Thus perished at the foot of Cumorah the remnant of the once mighty Jaredite nation, of whom the Lord had said, "There shall be none greater ... upon all the face of the earth." (Ether 1:43.)

As I contemplated this tragic scene from the crest of Cumorah and viewed the beautiful land of the Restoration as it appears today, I cried in my soul, "How could it have happened?"

...

"The tragic fate of the Jaredite and the Nephite civilizations is proof positive that the Lord meant it when he said that this "is a land of promise; and whatsoever nation shall possess it shall serve God, or they shall be swept off when the fulness of his wrath shall come upon them. And the fulness of his wrath cometh upon them when they are ripened in iniquity." (Ether 2:9.)"

https://www.lds.org/general-conference/1975/10/americas-destiny?lang=eng

## 17. 1978. Elder Mark E. Peterson.

In the October 1978 General Conference, Elder Mark E. Peterson of the Quorum of the Twelve said:

Moroni's father was commander of the armies of this ancient people, known as Nephites. His name was Mormon. The war of which we speak took place **here in America** some four hundred years after Christ. (See Morm. 6.)

As the fighting neared its end, **Mormon gathered the remnant of his forces about a hill which they called Cumorah, located in what is now the western part of the state of New York.**

Their enemies, known as Lamanites, came against them on this hill….

When finished with the record, **Moroni was to hide it up in that same Hill Cumorah which was their battlefield.** It would come forth in modern times as the Book of Mormon, named after Moroni's father, the historian who compiled it.

https://www.lds.org/general-conference/1978/10/the-last-words-of-moroni?lang=eng

**18.** *Articles of Faith*, **by James E. Talmage, published by the Church**

**The final struggles between Nephites and Lamanites were waged in the vicinity of the Hill Cumorah, in what is now the State of New York**, resulting in the destruction of the Nephites as a nation, about 400 A.D. The last Nephite representative was Moroni, who, wandering for safety from place to place, daily expecting death from the victorious Lamanites, wrote the concluding parts of the Book of Mormon, and hid the record in Cumorah. It was this same Moroni who, as a resurrected being, gave the records into the hands of Joseph Smith in the present dispensation. …

Here they [the Jaredites] became a flourishing nation; but, giving way in time to internal dissensions, they divided into factions, which warred with one another until the people were totally destroyed. **This destruction, which occurred near the Hill Ramah, afterward known among the Nephites as Cumorah**…

19. 1990 – Letter from the Office of the First Presidency (President Ezra Taft Benson, Gordon B. Hinckley and Thomas S. Monson).

"The Church has long maintained, as attested to by references in the writings of General Authorities, that the Hill Cumorah in western New York state is the same as referenced in the Book of Mormon."

# Appendix 2. Gospel Topics Entry on Book of Mormon Geography

This Appendix consists of my comments on the anonymous Gospel Topics entry on Book of Mormon Geography found at this web page:

https://www.churchofjesuschrist.org/study/manual/gospel-topics/book-of-mormon-geography?lang=eng

Two versions of this entry have been published so far. The first was published in January 2019. I posted a critique of the entry on my blogs within a few days. Subsequently, in February 2019, a second version of the entry was published that addressed some of my observations but left several significant errors.

In this Appendix, we will look at:

1. My proposed revisions for the first version of the entry.

2. A comparison between the first and second versions of the entry.

3. My proposed revisions for the second (current) version of the entry.

## 1. My proposed revisions for the first (original) version of the Gospel Topics entry on Book of Mormon Geography

Here are the revisions I proposed for the entry for clarification and accuracy. Proposed changes are indicated in **bold** typeface.

| Original | Proposed Revisions |
|---|---|
| Book of Mormon Geography Overview | Book of Mormon Geography Overview |
| *The Church takes no position on the specific geographic location of Book of Mormon events in the ancient Americas.* | ***Apart from the Hill Cumorah in western New York,*** *the Church takes no position on the specific geographic* |

| | |
|---|---|
| *Church members are asked not to teach theories about Book of Mormon geography in Church settings but to focus instead on the Book of Mormon's teachings and testimony of Jesus Christ and His gospel.* | *location of Book of Mormon events in the ancient Americas. Church members are asked not to teach theories about Book of Mormon geography in Church settings but to focus instead on the Book of Mormon's teachings and testimony of Jesus Christ and His gospel.* |
| | **Explanation**: Church leaders, including members of the First Presidency and Quorum of the Twelve, have consistently and persistently taught that the Hill Cumorah referred to in Mormon 6 is the same hill in western New York from which Joseph Smith, Jr., obtained the ancient Nephite records that he translated into the Book of Mormon. To date, no member of either of these quorums has ever officially questioned or repudiated the teachings of his predecessors. |
| The Book of Mormon includes a history of an ancient people who migrated from the Near East to the Americas. This history contains information about the places they lived, including descriptions of landforms, natural features, and the distances and cardinal directions between important points. The internal consistency of these descriptions is one of the striking features of the Book of Mormon. | The Book of Mormon includes a history of an ancient people who migrated from the Near East to the Americas. This history contains information about the places they lived, including descriptions of landforms, natural features, and the distances and cardinal directions between important points. The internal consistency of these descriptions is one of the striking features of the Book of Mormon.<br><br>**Explanation**: No change suggested. Although the term "Americas" was never used during Joseph Smith's lifetime, and instead was invented to obscure early Church history sources, neither Joseph Smith nor Oliver Cowdery left a clear statement about where Lehi landed. |
| Since the publication of the Book of Mormon in 1830, members and leaders | Since **before** the publication of the Book of Mormon in 1830, members |

| | |
|---|---|
| of The Church of Jesus Christ of Latter-day Saints have expressed numerous opinions about the specific locations of the events discussed in the book. | and leaders of The Church of Jesus Christ of Latter-day Saints have consistently taught that the Hill Cumorah referred to in Mormon 6 is in western New York.<br><br>The New York Cumorah was declared to be a fact in an important essay about Church history written by Oliver Cowdery with the assistance of Joseph Smith. Published in 1835 as "Letter VII" in the *Messenger and Advocate* and republished in many other Church newspapers, at least twice at the direction of Joseph Smith, Letter VII was also copied into Joseph's personal history, where it can be read today in the Joseph Smith Papers. https://www.josephsmithpapers.org/paper-summary/history-1834-1836/90<br><br>Regarding the specific locations of other events discussed in the book, however, members and leaders have expressed numerous opinions.<br><br>**Explanation**: There is a clear distinction between formal, published teachings about the New York Cumorah, which have never varied, and expressions about other locations, which have been private and/or speculative. |
| Some believe that the history depicted in the Book of Mormon occurred in North America, while others believe that it occurred in Central America or South America. Although Church members continue to discuss such theories today, the Church takes no position on the geography of the Book of Mormon except that the events it describes took place in the Americas. | Some believe that the history depicted in the Book of Mormon occurred in North America, while others believe that it occurred in Central America or South America. Although Church members continue to discuss such theories today, the Church takes no position on the geography of the Book of Mormon except that the events it describes took place in the Americas **and that the Hill Cumorah** |

| | is in western New York. |
|---|---|
| | **Explanation**: It is critical to keep the two separate elements distinct. |
| The Prophet Joseph Smith himself accepted what he felt was evidence of Book of Mormon civilizations in both North America and Central America. While traveling with Zion's Camp in 1834, Joseph wrote to his wife Emma that they were "wandering over the plains of the Nephites, recounting occasionally the history of the Book of Mormon, roving over the mounds of that once beloved people of the Lord, picking up their skulls and their bones, as a proof of its divine authenticity."1 In 1842, the Church newspaper *Times and Seasons* published articles under Joseph Smith's editorship that identified the ruins of ancient native civilizations in Mexico and Central America as further evidence of the Book of Mormon's historicity.2<br><br>Note 2: "Traits of the Mosaic History, Found among the Azteca Nation," *Times and Seasons*, June 15, 1842, 818–20; see also "American Antiquities," *Times and Seasons*, July 15, 1842, 858–60. Although it is not clear how involved Joseph Smith was in writing these editorials, he never refuted them. | The Prophet Joseph Smith himself personally linked locations in North America with the Book of Mormon. While traveling with Zion's Camp in 1834, Joseph wrote to his wife Emma that they were "wandering over the plains of the Nephites, recounting occasionally the history of the Book of Mormon, roving over the mounds of that once beloved people of the Lord, picking up their skulls and their bones, as a proof of its divine authenticity."1<br><br>**Others, contemporary with Joseph Smith, suggested other locations.** In 1842, the Church newspaper *Times and Seasons* published anonymous articles that identified the ruins of ancient native civilizations in Mexico and Central America as further evidence of the Book of Mormon's historicity.2<br><br>**Unlike the anonymous editorials, Joseph Smith signed an article titled "Church History," published in the March 1842 *Times and Seasons*, commonly referred to as the Wentworth letter. In this article, Joseph adapted the contents of a pamphlet written by Elder Orson Pratt, a member of the Quorum of the Twelve. Pratt had speculated at length about evidence for the Book of Mormon in Central America. Joseph replaced Pratt's speculation with the simple statement that "The remnant are the Indians that live in this country."3**<br><br>**In October 1842, the *Times and** |

| | |
|---|---|
| | *Seasons* published a letter written and signed by Joseph Smith and sent to the editor for publication. Now canonized as D&C 128:20, the letter included this statement: "And again, what do we hear? Glad tidings from Cumorah! Moroni, an angel from heaven, declaring the fulfilment of the prophets—the book to be revealed."<br><br>Note 2: "Traits of the Mosaic History, Found among the Azteca Nation," *Times and Seasons*, June 15, 1842, 818–20; see also "American Antiquities," *Times and Seasons*, July 15, 1842, 858–60. **Although Joseph Smith was listed as the nominal editor of the *Times and Seasons* at the time, he never explicitly approved of or rejected these editorials.**<br><br>**Note 3: "Church History," *Times and Seasons*, March 1, 1842, republished in the Joseph Smith Papers with Historical Background notes here:** https://www.josephsmithpap ers.org/paper-summary/church-history-1-march-1842/1<br><br>Explanation: The proposed changes are necessary to clarify the historical facts and distinguish between fact and inference. |
| Anthony W. Ivins, a Counselor in the First Presidency, stated: "There has never been anything yet set forth that definitely settles that question [of Book of Mormon geography]. So the Church says we are just waiting until we discover the truth."3 | **President Anthony W. Ivins, a Counselor in the First Presidency, made clear the distinction between the known location of Cumorah in New York and the uncertain locations of other Book of Mormon geography in two General Conference addresses. In April 1928,** |

| | shortly after the Church purchased the hill Cumorah in New York, President Ivins described that hill and stated: "We know that all of these records, all the sacred records of the Nephite people, were deposited by Mormon in that hill." 4 |
|---|---|
| | The following year, President Ivins stated: "There has never been anything yet set forth that definitely settles that question [of the location of Zarahemla and other sites]. So the Church says we are just waiting until we discover the truth."5 |
| | Note 4. Anthony W. Ivins, in Conference Report, Apr. 1928, 16. |
| | Note 5. (same as original note 3) |
| | Explanation: The original version of the essay omitted the context of President Ivins' statements. The revisions provide the full context for clarity and accuracy. |
| The Church urges local leaders and members not to advocate theories of Book of Mormon geography in official Church settings. | The Church urges local leaders and members not to advocate theories of Book of Mormon geography in official Church settings. **Such advocacy includes illustrations, artwork, media, and exhibits on web pages including lds.org and in Church buildings, publications, visitors centers, etc.** |
| | Explanation: The original version of the essay implied that visual depictions were authorized, while advocacy was not. |
| Speaking of the book's history and geography, President Russell M. Nelson taught: "Interesting as these matters may be, study of the Book of Mormon is | Speaking of the book's history and geography, President Russell M. Nelson taught: "Interesting as these matters may be, study of the Book of |

| | |
|---|---|
| most rewarding when one focuses on its *primary* purpose—to testify of Jesus Christ. By comparison, all other issues are incidental."4 | Mormon is most rewarding when one focuses on its *primary* purpose—to testify of Jesus Christ. By comparison, all other issues are incidental."6 |
| | **Explanation**: No change suggested. |

2. Comments comparing the original version published in January 2019 and the revised version published in February.

| Original (Jan 2019) | Revised (Feb 27, 2019) |
|---|---|
| Book of Mormon Geography Overview<br><br>The Church takes no position on the specific geographic location of Book of Mormon events in the ancient Americas. Church members are asked not to teach theories about Book of Mormon geography in Church settings but to focus instead on the Book of Mormon's teachings and testimony of Jesus Christ and His gospel.<br><br>**Comment. It's not apparent why this overview was deleted, except that it duplicated a later statement in the essay. However, I did note in my comments before that "this policy appears to censor references to or discussion of" the teachings of past prophets and apostles regarding the Hill Cumorah.** | Book of Mormon Geography Overview |
| The Book of Mormon includes a history of an ancient people who migrated from the Near East to the Americas. This history contains | The Book of Mormon includes a history of an ancient people who migrated from the Near East to the Americas. This history contains |

| | |
|---|---|
| information about the places they lived, including descriptions of landforms, natural features, and the distances and cardinal directions between important points. The internal consistency of these descriptions is one of the striking features of the Book of Mormon. | information about the places they lived, including descriptions of landforms, natural features, and the distances and cardinal directions between important points. The internal consistency of these descriptions is one of the striking features of the Book of Mormon. |
| Since the publication of the Book of Mormon in 1830, members and leaders of The Church of Jesus Christ of Latter-day Saints have expressed numerous opinions about the specific locations of the events discussed in the book. Some believe that the history depicted in the Book of Mormon<br><br>occurred in North America, while others believe that it occurred in Central America or South America. Although Church members continue to discuss such theories today,<br><br>the Church takes no position on the geography of the Book of Mormon except that the events it describes took place in the Americas. | Since the publication of the Book of Mormon in 1830, members and leaders of The Church of Jesus Christ of Latter-day Saints have expressed numerous opinions about the specific locations of the events discussed in the book. Some believe that the history depicted in the Book of Mormon **—with the exception of the events in the Near East—**<br><br>occurred in North America, while others believe that it occurred in Central America or South America. Although Church members continue to discuss such theories today,<br><br>**the Church's only position is that the events the Book of Mormon describes took place in the ancient Americas.**<br><br>**Comment:** This changes the former statement of "no position except" to "only position is." Cumorah remains de-correlated. The term "Americas" is a recent development. The Church History Department uses it everywhere now |

| | to replace what the historical documents actually say. Moroni and Joseph Smith both referred to the aborigines in "this country," but that causes problems for M2C, so instead we always see "Americas" instead. The same tactic was used in the *Saints* book to write Cumorah out of Church history. |
|---|---|
| The Prophet Joseph Smith himself accepted what he felt was evidence of Book of Mormon civilizations in both North America and Central America. While traveling with Zion's Camp in 1834, Joseph wrote to his wife Emma that they were "wandering over the plains of the Nephites, recounting occasionally the history of the Book of Mormon, roving over the mounds of that once beloved people of the Lord, picking up their skulls and their bones, as a proof of its divine authenticity."1 In 1842, the Church newspaper Times and Seasons published articles under Joseph Smith's editorship that identified the ruins of ancient native civilizations in Mexico and Central America as further evidence of the Book of Mormon's historicity.2 | The Prophet Joseph Smith himself accepted what he felt was evidence of Book of Mormon civilizations in both North America and Central America. While traveling with Zion's Camp in 1834, Joseph wrote to his wife Emma that they were "wandering over the plains of the Nephites, recounting occasionally the history of the Book of Mormon, roving over the mounds of that once beloved people of the Lord, picking up their skulls and their bones, as a proof of its divine authenticity."1 In 1842, the Church newspaper Times and Seasons published articles under Joseph Smith's editorship that identified the ruins of ancient native civilizations in Mexico and Central America as further evidence of the Book of Mormon's historicity.2<br><br>**Comment.** It's unfortunate that the serious error in this paragraph was not corrected. The first sentence states as a fact what can only be at most an inference. This undermines the credibility of the essay and suggests it was driven by an agenda. |

| | |
|---|---|
| Anthony W. Ivins, a Counselor in the First Presidency, stated: "There has never been anything yet set forth that definitely settles that question [of Book of Mormon geography]. So the Church says we are just waiting until we discover the truth."3<br><br>**Comment.** I had pointed out that this quotation, a favorite of FairMormon and other M2C advocates, was taken out of context and modified with a misleading inserted bracket.<br>I also pointed out that President Ivins, just the year before in General Conference, gave an entire address about the New York Hill Cumorah, affirming that it is, in fact, the Cumorah of Mormon 6:6. Deleting President Ivins from this essay suggests that the authors did not want people researching President Ivins, who made the clear distinction between the two separate teachings of all the prophets:<br>1. Cumorah is in New York.<br>2. We don't know where the other events took place. | |
| The Church urges local leaders and members not to advocate theories of Book of Mormon geography in official Church settings.<br><br>**Comment.** This statement applied to any theories, including the teachings of the prophets, but limited the ban to official Church | |

| | |
|---|---|
| settings. The revision expands the ban to "any setting or manner." | |
| | The Church does not take a position on the specific geographic locations of Book of Mormon events in the ancient Americas. President M. Russell Ballard, Acting President of the Quorum of the Twelve Apostles, reminded members that "the Book of Mormon is not a textbook on topography. Speculation on the geography of the Book of Mormon may mislead instead of enlighten; such a study can be a distraction from its divine purpose."<br><br>**Comment.** This paragraph basically restates the paragraph above about "the Church's only position." Again, we see the term "Americas." President Ballard's quotation replaces President Ivins' but the authors forgot to provide a footnote.<br>It's undoubtedly true that speculation on geography can be a distraction, but isn't it also a distraction to ignore or, worse, reject the teachings of past prophets? At least the previous version cited President Ivins, who took a firm stand that Cumorah is in New York. |
| | Individuals may have their own opinions regarding Book of Mormon geography and other such matters about which the Lord has not spoken. |

**Comment.** This new sentence raises the question, how do we know when the Lord has spoken? Most members think the Lord speaks through his prophets, every one of whom has affirmed the New York Cumorah (at least, every one who has ever addressed the topic). This includes members of the First Presidency speaking in General Conference. Accordingly, this sentence could be interpreted to mean individuals may have their own opinions about geography other than the New York Cumorah. If, on the other hand, the sentence is intended to repudiate the teachings of past prophets, that should be made clear.

However, the First Presidency and Quorum of the Twelve Apostles urge leaders and members not to advocate those personal theories in any setting or manner that would imply either prophetic or Church support for those theories.

**Comment.** This sentence is probably the most important in the essay because it should put an end to the practice of the M2C advocates of claiming prophetic or Church support for their theories. We'll see if they respond on their web sites. But it also raises a question about Church curriculum, media, visitors centers, etc., which advocate M2C. Because the Church now officially has no position on the geography issues, we can expect

| | to see M2C eradicated, or at least balanced with alternative theories. |
|---|---|
| | All parties should strive to avoid contention on these matters.

**Comment.** This is also an important sentence. There's no reason to contend about any of this, so long as people are enabled to make informed decisions as they choose. There's no justification for using claims of prophetic or Church support to justify censorship, logical fallacies, etc. Ideally, everyone involved would simply offer facts and analysis for others to consider. |
| Speaking of the book's history and geography, President Russell M. Nelson taught: "Interesting as these matters may be, study of the Book of Mormon is most rewarding when one focuses on its primary purpose—to testify of Jesus Christ. By comparison, all other issues are incidental."4 | Speaking of the book's history and geography, President Russell M. Nelson taught: "Interesting as these matters may be, study of the Book of Mormon is most rewarding when one focuses on its primary purpose—to testify of Jesus Christ. By comparison, all other issues are incidental."3 |
| Note 1: Letter to Emma Smith, June 4, 1834, in The Joseph Smith Papers, Documents, Volume 4: April 1834–September 1835,ed. Matthew C. Godfrey and others (2016), 57; spelling standardized.

Note 2: "Traits of the Mosaic History, Found among the Azteca Nation," Times and Seasons, June 15, 1842, 818–20; see also "American Antiquities," Times and Seasons, July 15, 1842, 858–60. Although it is not clear how involved Joseph Smith was in | Note 1: Letter to Emma Smith, June 4, 1834, in The Joseph Smith Papers, Documents, Volume 4: April 1834–September 1835,ed. Matthew C. Godfrey and others (2016), 57; spelling standardized.

Note 2: "Traits of the Mosaic History, Found among the Azteca Nation," Times and Seasons, June 15, 1842, 818–20; see also "American Antiquities," Times and Seasons, July 15, 1842, 858–60. Although it is not clear how involved Joseph Smith was in |

| | |
|---|---|
| writing these editorials, he never refuted them.<br><br>Note 3: Anthony W. Ivins, Conference Report (April 1929), 16.<br><br>Note 4: Russell M. Nelson, "A Testimony of the Book of Mormon," Ensign, Nov. 1999, 69. | writing these editorials, he never refuted them.<br><br><br><br>Note 3: Russell M. Nelson, "A Testimony of the Book of Mormon," Ensign, Nov. 1999, 69. |

## 3. Proposals for further revision.

People are unclear about the purpose and authority of these essays and entries. I've understood them to be merely resources to consider, an acknowledgement that these topics remain controversial and unresolved. But others cite them as authoritative.

They don't seem authoritative because they are anonymous. No one takes responsibility for them. They can be, and have been, changed without notice and without an editing history. Worse, they don't cite the teachings of the prophets. Instead, they focus on the teachings and speculations of the scholars who prepared them.

Because they have been changed before, I propose they be changed again to cite the teachings of the prophets more clearly.

For example, the entry currently says, "the Church's only position is that the events the Book of Mormon describes took place in the ancient Americas." That contradicts the 1990 letter from the Office of the First Presidency which reads:

> The Church has long maintained, as attested to by references in the writings of General Authorities, that the Hill Cumorah in western New York state is the same as referenced in the Book of Mormon.

Was that letter incorrect? Unauthorized? We can't tell.

It does make sense to simply ignore such contradictions if the decision has been made to de-correlate past teachings, but the ambiguity that lingers is unsettling and leads to the type of disagreement and debate that the essay seeks to prevent.

The essay should distinguish between (i) claiming prophetic or Church support, and (ii) seeking to support the prophets and the Church.

Version 1 included a mangled 1929 quotation from President Ivins that tried to accommodate M2C. Version 2 deleted President Ivins completely instead of adding President Ivins' 1928 address, here:

http://www.lettervii.com/p/president-ivins-on-new-york-cumorah.html

The essay would have been more informative and would have clarified the matter by including and explaining both quotations by President Ivins instead of deleting them altogether. The problem persists because the Gospel Topics Essay on DNA studies retains the 1929 quotation from President Ivins, but does not include the 1928 address.

Ambiguity is fine. It makes sense to leave it up to each member of the Church to make his/her own informed decisions based on study and faith, as they feel guided by the Spirit. Each person can study the science and the scriptures and reconcile them however they want. That's a sound approach, consistent with Articles of Faith 9 and 11.

But **"having an opinion" is not the same as having an** *informed* **opinion.**

Article of Faith 9 assures us "We believe all that God has revealed, all that He does now reveal, and we believe that He will yet reveal many great and important things pertaining to the Kingdom of God."

No one can believe something God has revealed if they don't know what God has revealed. No one can believe the teachings of the prophets if they don't know what the prophets have taught. The current version of the entry does not quote or cite the teachings of the prophets about Cumorah.

**The essay has already been changed once. It can be changed again.** I hope the next version informs readers about what the prophets have taught about the New York Cumorah.

# Appendix 3. Oliver Cowdery's Essays

In October 1834 the LDS newspaper *Messenger and Advocate*, based in Kirtland, Ohio, published the first of eight essays about Church history. The essays, published as letters to W.W. Phelps who was in Missouri, were the first detailed published accounts of important events in Church history. Oliver wrote the essays with the assistance of Joseph Smith. Oliver introduced the essays with this explanation:

> That our narrative may be correct, and particularly the introduction, it is proper to inform our patrons, that our brother J. [Joseph] Smith jr. has offered to assist us. Indeed, there are many items connected with the fore part of this subject that render his labor indispensible. **With his labor and with authentic documents now in our possession, we hope to render this a pleasing and agreeable narrative, well worth the examination and perusal of the Saints.**—To do justice to this subject will require time and space: we therefore ask the forbearance of our readers, **assuring them that it shall be founded upon facts.**[115]

The essays respond specifically to the claims in *Mormonism Unvailed* (discussed below). The essays were so important that Joseph had them copied into his personal history. With Joseph's approval, they were republished in the *Times and Seasons* (Nauvoo) in 1841 and in the *Gospel Reflector* (Philadelphia), also in 1841. The essays were republished in the *Millennial Star*, in a special pamphlet in Liverpool, England, that sold thousands of copies, in *The Prophet* (an LDS newspaper in New York City) in 1844, and in the 1899 *Improvement Era* by Joseph F. Smith, then editor of the magazine and Second Counselor in the First Presidency.

To appreciate the importance of the eight essays, they should be read in conjunction with *Mormonism Unvailed*, a book published in October 1834 in Painesville, Ohio, a few miles northeast of Kirtland. The book was the culmination of several months of investigation by a disgruntled

---

[115] Oliver Cowdery, Letter I, *Messenger and Advocate* I.1:13 ¶11. Also at https://www.josephsmithpapers.org/paper-summary/history-1834-1836/106

former member of the Church, Doctor Philastes Hurlbut (Doctor being his given name, not a title). The book attacked the character of Joseph Smith, his family, and his followers. It claimed Joseph did not translate the plates but merely read words off a "peep stone" he put in a hat. And it claimed the Book of Mormon was fiction based on a novel by Solomon Spaulding.

In 1835, Joseph Smith referred to Hurlbut as a doctor "of falsehood" and pointed out that "the reverend Mr. Howe" was "the illegitimate author of "Mormonism Unveiled.""[116]

An editorial in the 1838 *Elders' Journal* revisited the topic.

> This is the Hurlburt that was author of a book which bears the name of E. [Edward] D. Howe, but it was this said Hurlburt that was the author of it. But after the affair of Hurlburt's wife and the pious old deacon, the persecutors thought it better to put some other name as author to their book than Hurlburt, so E. D. Howe substituted his name. The change however was not much better. Asahel Howe, one of E. D.'s brothers who was said to be the likeliest of the family, served apprenticeship in the work house in Ohio for robbing the post office. And yet notwithstanding all this, all the pious priests of all denominations were found following in the wake of these mortals.

> Hurlburt and the Howes are among the basest of mankind, and known to be such and yet the priests and their coadjutors hail them as their best friends and publish their lies, speaking of them in the highest terms.[117]

The answers provided by Oliver and Joseph in these essays remain relevant to respond to modern critics. You can read the essays in full in the Joseph Smith Papers. I wrote a short book explaining the context and providing additional background.[118]

---

[116] Joseph Smith, "To the Elders of the Church of the Latter Day Saints," *Messenger and Advocate* II.3 (Dec 1835):228 ¶2

[117] *Elders' Journal* I.4 (August 1838):59

[118] Neville, Jonathan, *Letter VII: Joseph Smith and Oliver Cowdery Explain the New York Cumorah* (Legends Library, Salt Lake City, Utah 2017).

| Claims by *Mormonism Unvailed* and modern critics | Response from Joseph and Oliver (based on facts) |
|---|---|
| 1. Joseph produced the Book of Mormon by reading from a "peep stone" in a hat and didn't even use the plates. Alternate story: he translated the 116 pages with the Urim and Thummim, but used the peep stone to produce the published text. | 1. Joseph translated the plates with the Urim and Thummim, the interpreters that came with the plates. |
| 2. Joseph and his family had bad character. | 2. People seek excuses for rejecting the prophets, none of whom were perfect. They even accused Christ of being a sinner. Imperfect people do not taint the truthfulness of the Gospel. Besides, Joseph and his family had good character. |
| 3. The Book of Mormon is fiction, whether composed by Joseph Smith or copied from Solomon Spalding. | 3. The Book of Mormon is an authentic history because it is a fact that the Hill Cumorah in New York is the scene of the demise of the Nephites and Jaredites. |
| 4. The Book of Mormon is a false history of the aborigines. [Modern: DNA disproves the Book of Mormon because the indigenous people in Latin America came from Eastern Asia.] | 4. Moroni explained the book was written and deposited in western New York and is the record of the aborigines "of this country." DNA shows a link between the Native Americans in New York and Israel (X2 haplotype). The open question is the dating of the migration. |
| 5. The LDS church is based on a "magical world view" and is a delusion. | 5. The facts of Church history involve ministering angels and an authentic ancient history. |
| 6. There was no restoration of the Priesthood. | 6. Oliver was a second witness of the literal restoration of the Priesthood by John the Baptist. |
| 7. Joseph Smith sought money and power. | 7. Joseph learned not to seek money, but instead sought the |

| | gathering and restoration of Israel and the establishment of Zion. |
|---|---|

## Summary and excerpts from the essays (published as letters).

Letters I through VIII include Oliver's unique perspective on the foundational events in the restoration of the Gospel and early Church history. Oliver provides numerous details that help modern-day readers form a better mental picture of the early events.

## Letter I

In Letter I, Oliver describes the restoration of the Aaronic Priesthood. This passage is included in the Pearl of Great Price as a note at the end of Joseph Smith-History.

Excerpts:

… by giving them publicity some thousands who have embraced the same covenant, may learn something more particular upon the rise of this church in this last time….

On Friday, the 5th, in company with our brother JOSEPH SMITH jun., I left Kirtland for this place (New Portage,) to attend the conference previously appointed. To be permitted once more to travel with this brother, occasions reflections of no ordinary kind. Many have been the fatigues and privations which have fallen to my lot to endure for the gospel's sake, since 1828, with this brother. Our road has frequently been spread with the "fowler's snare," and our persons sought with the eagerness of the Savage's ferocity for innocent blood, by men either heated to desperation by the insinuations of those who professed to be "guides and way-marks" to the kingdom of glory, or the individuals themselves! This, I confess, is a dark picture to spread before our patrons, but they will pardon my plainness when I assure them of the truth….

Not only have I been graciously preserved from wicked and unreasonable men, with this our brother, but I have seen the fruit of perseverance in proclaiming the everlasting gospel, immediately after it was declared to the world in these last days, in a manner not to be forgotten while heaven gives me common intellect. And what serves to render the reflection past expression on this point is, that from his hand I received baptism, by the direction of the angel of God—the first received into this church in this day.

Near this time of the setting of the sun, Sabbath evening, April 5th, 1829, my natural eyes for the first time beheld this brother: he then resided in Harmony, Susquehanna county Penn. On Monday, the 6th, I assisted him in arranging some business of a temporal nature, and on Tuesday, the 7th, commenced to write the Book of Mormon.

These were days never to be forgotten; to sit under the sound of a voice dictated by the inspiration of heaven, awakened the utmost gratitude of this bosom! Day after day I continued, uninterrupted, to write from his mouth, as he translated with the Urim and Thummim, or, as the Nephites would have said, "interpreters," the history or record called "The Book of Mormon."

To notice, in even few words, the interesting account given by Mormon and his faithful son Moroni, of a people once beloved and favored of heaven, would supersede my present design; I shall therefore defer this to a future period, and, as I said in the introduction, pass more directly to some few incidents immediately connected with the rise of this church, which may be entertaining to some thousands who have stepped forward, amid the frowns of bigots and the calumny of hypocrites, and embraced the gospel of Christ. No men in their sober senses could translate and write the directions given to the Nephites, from the mouth of the Savior of the precise manner in which men should build up his church and especially when corruption had spread an uncertainty over all forms and systems practised among men, without desiring a privilege of showing the willingness of the heart by being buried in the liquid grave, to answer a "good conscience by the resurrection of Jesus Christ."

After writing the account given of the Saviour's ministry to the remnant of the seed of Jacob upon this continent, it was easily to be seen, as the prophet said would be, that darkness covered the earth and, gross darkness the minds of the people. On reflecting further, it was as easily to be seen, that amid the great strife and noise concerning religion, none had authority from God to administer the ordinances of the gospel. For, the question might be asked, have men authority to administer in the name of Christ who deny revelations, when his testimony is no less than the spirit of prophecy, and his religion based, built, and sustained by immediate revelations in all ages of the world when he has had a people on earth? If these facts were buried and carefully concealed by men whose craft would have been in danger, if once permitted to shine in the faces of men, they were no longer to us, and we only waited for the commandment to be given, "Arise and be baptized."

This was not long desired before it was realized. The Lord, who is rich in mercy, and ever willing to answer the consistent prayer of the humble, after we had called upon him in a fervent manner, aside from the abodes of men, condescended to manifest to us his will. On a sudden, as from the midst of eternity, the voice of the Redeemer spake peace to us, while the vail was parted and the angel of God came down clothed with glory, and delivered the anxiously-looked-for message and the keys off the gospel of repentance. What joy! what wonder! what amazement! While the world were racked and distracted—while millions were groping as the blind for the wall, and while all men were resting upon uncertainty, as a general mass, our eyes beheld—our ears heard, as in the "blaze of day;" yes, more—above the glitter of the May sun-beam, which then shed its brilliancy over the face of nature! Then his voice, though mild, pierced to the centre, and his words "I am thy fellow-servant," dispelled every fear. We listened—we gazed—we admired! 'Twas the voice of the angel from glory—'twas a message from the Most High! and as we heard we rejoiced, while his love enkindled upon our souls, and we were wrapt in the vision of the Almighty! Where was room for doubt? No where; uncertainty had fled, doubt had sunk no more to rise, while fiction and deception had fled forever!

194

But, dear brother, think further, think for a moment what joy filled our out hearts and with what surprise we must have bowed, (for who would not have bowed the knee for such a blessing?) when we received under his hand the holy priesthood, as he said, "upon you my fellow servants, in the name of Messiah I confer this priesthood and this authority, which shall remain upon earth, that the sons of Levi may yet offer an offering unto the Lord in righteousness!"

I shall not attempt to paint to you the feelings of this heart, nor the majestic beauty and glory which surrounded us on this occasion; but you will believe me when I say, that earth, nor men, with the eloquence of time, cannot begin to clothe language in as interesting and sublime a manner as this holy personage. No; nor has this earth power to give the joy, to bestow the peace, or comprehend the wisdom which was contained in each sentence as they were delivered by the power of the Holy Spirit! Man may deceive his fellow man—deception may follow deception, and the children of the wicked one may have power to seduce the foolish and untaught, till naught but fiction feeds the many, and the fruit of falsehood carries in its current the giddy to the grave; but one touch with the finger of his love, yes, one ray of glory from the upper world, or one word from the mouth of the Saviour, from the bosom of eternity, strikes it all into insignificance, and blots it forever from the mind! The assurance that we were in the presence of an angel—the certainty that we heard the voice of Jesus—and the truth unsullied as it flowed from a pure personage, dictated by the will of God, is to me past description, and I shall ever look upon this expression of the Saviour's goodness with wonder and thanksgiving while I am permitted to tarry, and in those mansions where perfection dwells and sin never comes, I hope to adore in that DAY which shall never cease!*

*I will hereafter give you a full history of the rise of this church, up to the time stated in my introduction; which will necessarily embrace the life and character of this brother. I shall therefore leave the history of baptism, &c., till its proper place.

## Letter II

Letter II is largely a discussion of how the world receives the prophets of God.

LETTER II.

DEAR BROTHER, IN the last Messenger and Advocate, I promised to commence a more particular or minute history of the rise and progress of the church of the Latter-day Saints, and publish for the benefit of inquirers and all who are disposed to learn. There are certain facts relative to the works of God worthy the consideration and observance of every individual, and every society:—they are, that he never works in the dark—his works are always performed in a clear, intelligible manner; and another point is, that he never works in vain. This is not the case with men, but might it not be? When the Lord works, he accomplishes his purposes, and the effects of his power are to be seen afterward…

Common undertakings and plans of men may be overthrown or destroyed by opposition. The systems of this world may be exploded or annihilated by oppression or falsehood, but it is the reverse with pure religion. There is a power attendant on truth that all the arts and designs of men cannot fathom; there is an increasing influence which rises up in one place the moment it is covered in another, and the more it is traduced, and the harsher the means employed to affect its extinction, the more numerous are its votaries. It is not the vain cry of "delusion" from the giddy multitude; it is not the sneers of bigots; it is not the frowns of zealots, neither the rage of princes, kings, nor emperors, that can prevent its influence. The fact is, as Tertullian said, no man ever looked carefully into its consistency and propriety without embracing it. It is impossible; that light which enlightens man is at once enraptured; that intelligence which existed before the world was will unite, and that wisdom in the Divine economy will be so conspicuous, that it will be embraced, it will be observed, and it must be obeyed.

Look at pure religion whenever it has had a place on earth, and you will always mark the same characteristics in all its features. Look at truth (without which the former could not exist), and the same peculiarities are apparent. Those who have been guided by them have always shown the same principles; and those who were not have as uniformly sought to destroy their influence.

…

Enoch walked with God, and was taken home without tasting death. Why were not all converted in his day and taken with him to glory? Noah, it is said, was perfect in his generation; and it is plain that he had communion with his Maker, and by HIS direction accomplished a work, the parallel of which is not to be found in the annals of the world! Why were not the world converted, that the flood might have been stayed? Men, from the days of our father Abraham, have talked, boasted, and extolled his faith: and he is even represented in the scriptures—"The father of the faithful." Moses talked with the Lord face to face; received the great moral law, upon the basis of which those of all civilized governments are founded; led Israel forty years, and was taken home to receive the reward of his toils—then Jacob could realize his worth…

But in reviewing the lives and acts of men in past generations, whenever we find a righteous man among them, there always were excuses for not giving heed or credence to his testimony. The people could see his imperfections; or, if no imperfections, supposed ones, and were always ready to frame an excuse upon that for not believing. No matter how pure the principles, nor how precious the teachings—an excuse was wanted-and an excuse was had.

…

One of two reasons may be assigned as the cause why the messengers of truth have been rejected—perhaps both. The multitude saw their imperfections, or supposed ones, and from that framed an excuse for rejecting them; or else in consequence of the corruption of their own hearts, when reproved, were not willing to repent but sought to make a man an offender for a word, or for wearing camels' hair, eating locusts, drinking wine, or showing friendship to publicans and sinners!

When looking over the sacred scriptures, we seem to forget that they were given through men of imperfections, and subject to passions. It is a general belief that the ancient prophets were perfect—that no stain, or blemish ever appeared upon their characters while on earth, to be brought forward by the opposer as an excuse for not believing. The same is said of the apostles; but James said that Elias [Elijah] was a man subject to like passions as themselves, and yet he had that power with God that in answer to his prayer, it rained not on the earth by the space of three years and a half.

There can be no doubt but those to whom he wrote looked upon the ancient prophets as a race of beings superior to any in those days, and in order to be constituted a prophet of God, a man must be perfect in every respect. The idea is, that he must be perfect according to their signification of the word. If a people were blessed with prophets, they must be the individuals who were to prescribe the laws by which they must be governed, even in their private walks. The generation following were ready to suppose, that those men who believed the word of God were as perfect as those to whom it was delivered supposed they must be, and were as forward to prescribe the rules by which they were governed, or rehearse laws and declare them to be the governing principles of the prophets, as though they themselves held the keys of the mysteries of heaven, and had searched the archives of the generations of the world...

I have, then, as you will see, made mention of our Lord, to show that individuals teaching truth, whether perfect or imperfect, have been looked upon as the worst of men. And that even our Savior, the great Shepherd of Israel, was mocked and derided, and placed on a parallel with the prince of devils; and the prophets and apostles, though at this day, looked upon as perfect as perfection, were considered the basest of the human family by those among whom they lived. It is not rumour, though it is wafted by every gale and reiterated by every zephyr, upon which we are to found our judgments of ones merits or demerits: If it is, we erect an altar upon which we sacrifice the most perfect of men, and establish a criterion by which the "vilest of the vile" may escape censure.

But lest I weary you with too many remarks upon the history of the past, after a few upon the propriety of a narrative of the description I have proposed, I shall proceed.

## Letter III

In letter III, Oliver comments on the challenge of preserving history and describes the background for Joseph's prayer in the Sacred Grove.

LETTER III.

… such facts as are within my knowledge, will be given without any reference to inconsistencies in the minds of others, or impossibilities, in the feelings of such as do not give credence to the system of salvation and redemption, so clearly set forth and so plainly written over the face of the sacred scriptures.

… It is known to you that this church has suffered reproach and persecution from a majority of mankind who have heard but a rumor, since its first organization; and further, you are also conversant with the fact, that no sooner had the messengers of the fulness of the gospel began to proclaim its heavenly precepts, and call upon men to embrace the same, than they were vilified and slandered by thousands who never saw their faces, and much less knew aught derogatory of their characters, moral or religious. Upon this unfair and unsaint-like manner of procedure they have been giving, in large sheets, their own opinions of the incorrectness of our system, and attested volumes of our lives and characters.

Since, then our opposers have been thus kind to introduce our cause before the public, it is no more than just that a correct account should be given; and since they have invariably sought to cast a shade over the truth, and hinder its influence from gaining ascendancy, it is also proper that it should be vindicated by laying before the world a correct statement of events as they have transpired from time to time.

Whether I shall succeed so far in my purpose as to convince the public of the incorrectness of those scurrilous reports which have inundated our land, or even but a small portion of them, will be better ascertained when I close than when I commence; and I am content to submit it before the candid for perusal, and before the judge of all for inspection, as I most assuredly believe that before HIM I must stand and answer for the deeds transacted in this life.

Should I, however, be instrumental in causing a few to hear before they judge, and understand both sides of this matter before they condemn, I shall have the satisfaction of seeing them embrace it, as I am certain that one is the inevitable fruit of the other.

## Letter IV

Letter IV includes detailed information about Moroni's first visit to Joseph, including his appearance. One key point: Moroni tells Joseph the record "was written and deposited not far from that place," meaning where Joseph lived. Mormon and Moroni wrote the record; here Moroni is saying they did so in New York.

LETTER IV.

… our brother was urged forward and strengthened in the determination to know for himself of the certainty and reality of pure and holy religion; and it is only necessary for me to say, that while this excitement continued, he continued to call upon the Lord in secret for a full manifestation of divine approbation, and for, to him, the all important information, if a Supreme being did exist, to have an assurance that he was accepted of him. This, most assuredly, was correct—it was right. The Lord has said, long since, and his word remains steadfast, that to him who knocks it shall be opened, and whosoever will, may come and partake of the waters of life freely.

…

On the evening of the 21st of September, 1823, previous to retiring to rest, our brother's mind was unusually wrought up on the subject which had so long agitated his mind; his heart was drawn out in fervent prayer, and his whole soul was so lost to every thing of a temporal nature, that earth to him had lost its charms, and all he desired was to be prepared in heart to commune with some kind messenger who could communicate to him the desired information of his acceptance with God.

At length the family retired, and he, as usual, bent his way, though in silence … he continued still to pray; his heart, though once hard and obdurate, was softened, and that mind which had often flitted, like the "wild bird of passage," had settled upon a determined basis not to be decoyed or driven from its purpose.

In this situation hours passed unnumbered—how many or how few I know not, neither is he able to inform me, but supposes it must have been eleven or twelve and perhaps later, as the noise and bustle of the family in retiring had long since ceased.—While continuing in prayer for a manifestation in some way that his sins were forgiven, endeavoring to exercise faith in the scriptures, on a sudden a light like that of day, only of a purer and far more glorious appearance and brightness, burst into the room; indeed, to use his own description, the first sight was as though the house was filled with consuming and unquenchable fire. This sudden appearance of a light so bright as must naturally be expected, occasioned a shock or sensation, visible to the extremities of the body. It was, however, followed with a calmness and serenity of mind, and an overwhelming rapture of joy that surpassed understanding, and in a moment a personage stood before him.

Notwithstanding the room was previously filled with light above the brightness of the sun, as I have before described, yet there seemed to be an additional glory surrounding or accompanying this personage, which shone with an increased degree of brilliancy, of which he was in the midst; and though his countenance was as lightening, yet it was of a pleasing, innocent and glorious appearance, so much so, that every fear was banished from the heart, and nothing but calmness pervaded the soul.

It is no easy task to describe the appearance of a messenger from the skies, indeed, I doubt there being an individual clothed with perishable clay, who is capable to do this work. To be sure the Lord appeared to his apostles after his resurrection, and we do not learn as they had not the least difficulty in looking upon him; but from John's description upon Patmos, we learn that he is there represented as most glorious in appearance, and from other items in the sacred scriptures we have the fact recorded where angels appeared and conversed with men, and there was no difficulty on the part of the individuals to endure their presence; and others where their glory was so conspicuous that they could not endure. The last description or appearance is the one to which I refer, when I say that it is no easy task to describe their glory.

But it may be well to relate the particulars as far as given: the stature of this personage was a little above the common size of men in this age; his garment was perfectly white, and had the appearance of being without seam.

Though fear was banished from his heart, yet his surprise was no less when he heard him declare himself to be a messenger sent by commandment of the Lord, to deliver a special message, and to witness to him that his sins were forgiven, and that his prayers were heard; and that the scriptures might be fulfilled, which say, "God has chosen the foolish things of the world to confound the things which are mighty; and base things of the world, and things which are despised has God chosen; yea, and things which are not, to bring to nought things which are, that no flesh should glory in his presence. Therefore, says the Lord, I will proceed to do a marvellous work among this people, even a marvellous work and a wonder; the wisdom of their wise shall perish, and the understanding of their prudent shall be hid; for according to his covenant which he made with his ancient saints, his people the house of Israel must come to a knowledge of the gospel, and own that Messiah whom their fathers rejected, and with them the fulness of the Gentiles be gathered in, to rejoice in one fold under one Shepherd.

"This cannot be brought about until first certain preparatory things are accomplished, for so has the Lord purposed in his own mind. He has, therefore, chosen you as an instrument in his hand to bring to light that which shall perform his act, his strange act, and bring to pass a marvelous work and a wonder. Wherever the sound shall go it shall cause the ears of men to tingle, and wherever it shall be proclaimed, the pure in heart shall rejoice, while those who draw near to God with their mouths, and honor him with their lips while their hearts are far from him, will seek its overthrow, and the destruction of those by whose hands it is carried. Therefore, marvel not if your name is made a derision, and had as a by-word among such, if you are the instrument in bringing it, by the gift of God, to the knowledge of the people."

He then proceeded and gave a general account of the promises made to the fathers, and also gave a history of the aborigines of this country, and said they were literal descendants of Abraham. He represented them as once being an enlightened and intelligent people, possessing a correct knowledge of the gospel, and the plan of restoration and redemption. **He said this history was written and deposited not far from that place,** and that it was our brother's privilege, if obedient to the commandments of the Lord, to obtain, and translate the same by the means of the Urim and Thummim, which were deposited for that purpose with the record.

"Yet," said he, "the scripture must be fulfilled before it is translated, which says that the words of a book, which were sealed, were presented to the learned; for thus has God determined to leave men without excuse, and show to the meek that his arm is not shortened that it cannot save."

A part of the book was sealed, and was not to be opened yet. The sealed part, said he, contains the same revelation which was given to John upon the isle of Patmos, and when the people of the Lord are prepared, and found worthy, then it will be unfolded unto them.

On the subject of bringing to light the unsealed part of this record, it may be proper to say, that our brother was expressly informed, that it must be done with an eye single to the glory of God; if this consideration did not wholly characterize all his proceedings in relation to it, the adversary of truth would overcome him, or at least prevent his making that proficiency in this glorious work which he otherwise would.

While describing the place where the record was deposited, he gave a minute relation of it, and the vision of his mind being opened at the same time, he was permitted to view it critically; and previously being acquainted with the place, he was able to follow the direction of the vision, afterward, according to the voice of the angel, and obtain the book.

## Letter V

Letter V contains a discussion of scriptural precedent for divine manifestations and the gathering of Israel.

LETTER V.

You will notice in my last, on rehearsing the words of the angel, where he communicated to our brother, that his sins were forgiven, and that he was called of the Lord to bring to light, by the gift of inspiration, this important intelligence, an item like the following:—"God has chosen the foolish things of the world, and things which are despised, God has chosen;" &c.

This, I conceive to be an important item. Not many mighty and noble, were called in ancient times, because they always knew so much that God could not teach them, and a man that would listen to the voice of the Lord and follow the teachings of heaven, always was despised, and considered to be of the foolish class—Paul proves this fact, when he says, "We are made as the filth of the world—the off-scouring of all things unto this day."

I am aware, that a rehearsal of visions, of angels, at this day, is as inconsistent with a portion of mankind as it formerly was, after all the boast of this wise generation in the knowledge of the truth; but there is a uniformity so complete, that on the reflection, one is led to rejoice that it is so.

In my last I gave an imperfect description of the angel, and was obliged to do so, for the reason that my pen would fail to describe an angel in his glory, or the glory of God. I also gave a few sentences which he uttered on the subject of the gathering of Israel, &c. Since writing the former, I have thought it would, perhaps, be interesting to give something more full on this important subject, as well as a revelation of the gospel. That these holy personages should feel a deep interest in the accomplishment of the glorious purposes of the Lord, in his work in the last days, is consistent, when we view critically what is recorded of their sayings in the holy Scriptures.

[A discussion of religious history is omitted.]

In the last days, to fulfill the promises to the ancient prophets, when the Lord is to pour out his Spirit upon all flesh, he has determined to bring to light his gospel to the Gentiles, that it may go to the house of Israel...

But the time has now arrived, in which, according to his covenants, the Lord will manifest to the faithful that he is the same to-day and forever, and that the cup of suffering of his people, the house of Israel, is nearly filled; and that the way may be prepared before their face, he will bring to the knowledge of the people the gospel as it was preached by his servants on this land, and manifest to the obedient the truth of the same, by the power of the Holy Spirit;

[A discussion of scriptures about the gathering is omitted.]

## Letter VI

Letter VI discusses the gathering of Israel but also explains the difficulty of describing everything one learns in visions.

LETTER VI.

I gave, in my last, a few words, on the subject of a few items, as spoken by the angel at the time the knowledge of the record of the Nephites was communicated to our brother, and in consequence of the subject of the gospel and that of the gathering of Israel's being so connected, I found it difficult to speak of the one without mentioning the other; and this may not be improper, as it is evident that the Lord has decreed to bring forth the fulness of the gospel in the last days, previous to gathering Jacob, but a preparatory work, and the other is to follow in quick succession.

This being of so much importance, and of so deep interest to the saints, I have thought best to give a farther detail of the heavenly message, and if I do not give it in the precise words, shall strictly confine myself to the facts in substance.

[Lengthy discussion of the gathering of Israel omitted.]

I have now given you a rehearsal of what was communicated to our brother, when he was directed to go and obtain the record of the Nephites. I may have missed in arrangement in some instances, but the principle is preserved, and you will be able to bring forward abundance of corroborating scripture upon the subject of the gospel and of the gathering. You are aware of the fact, that to give a minute rehearsal of a lengthy interview with a heavenly messenger, is very difficult, unless one is assisted immediately with the gift of inspiration.

There is another item I wish to notice on the subject of visions. The Spirit you know, searches all things, even the deep things of God. When God manifests to his servants those things that are to come, or those which have been, he does it by unfolding them by the power of that Spirit which comprehends all things, always; and so much may be shown and made perfectly plain to the understanding in a short time, that to the world, who are occupied all their life to learn a little, look at the relation of it, and are disposed to call it false. You will understand then, by this, that while those glorious things were being rehearsed, the vision was also opened, so that our brother was permitted to see and understand much more full and perfect than I am able to communicate in writing. I know much may be conveyed to the understanding in writing, and many marvellous truths set forth with the pen, but after all it is but a shadow, compared to an open vision of seeing, hearing and realizing eternal things. And if the fact was known, it would be found, that of all the heavenly communications to the ancients, we have no more in comparison than the alphabet to a quarto vocabulary. It is said, and I believe the account, that the Lord showed the brother of Jared (Moriancumer) all things which were to transpire from that day to the end of the earth, as well as those which had taken place. I believe that Moses was permitted to see the same, as the Lord caused them to pass in vision before him as he stood upon the mount. I believe that the Lord Jesus told many things to his apostles which are not written, and after his ascension unfolded all things unto them; I believe that Nephi, the son of Lehi, whom the Lord brought out of Jerusalem, saw the same; I believe that the twelve upon this continent, whom the Lord chose to preach his gospel, when he came down to manifest to this branch of the house of Israel, that he had other sheep who should hear his voice, were also permitted to behold the same mighty things transpire in vision before their eyes; and I believe that the angel Moroni, whose words I have been rehearsing, who communicated the knowledge of the same to the Nephites, in this age, saw also, before he hid up the record unto the Lord, great and marvellous things, which were to transpire when the same should come forth; and I also believe, that God will give line upon line, precept upon precept, to his saints, until all these things will be unfolded to them, and they be finally sanctified and brought into the celestial glory, where tears will be wiped from all faces, and sighing and sorrowing flee away!

May the Lord preserve you from evil and reward you richly for all your afflictions, and crown you in his kingdom. Amen.

## Letter VII

Letter VII contains the important Cumorah material. Oliver introduces that section with a discussion of Joseph's deliberations as he experienced the temptation of getting the plates for their monetary value. This is an aspect Joseph never dwelt on in writing, but Oliver could only have learned it from him.

LETTER VII.
You will remember that in my last I brought my subject down to the evening, or night of the 21st of September, 1823, and gave an outline of the

conversation of the angel upon the important fact of the blessings, promises and covenants to Israel, and the great manifestations of favour to the world, in the ushering in of the fulness of the gospel, to prepare the way for the second advent of the Messiah, when he comes in the glory of the Father, with the holy angels.

A remarkable fact is to be noticed with regard to this vision. In ancient time the Lord warned some of his servants in dreams: for instance, Joseph, the husband of Mary, was warned in a dream to take the young child and his mother, and flee into Egypt; also, the WISE men were warned of the Lord in a dream not to return to Herod; and when "out of Egypt the Son was called," the angel of the Lord appeared in a dream to Joseph again: also he was warned in a dream to turn aside into the parts of Galilee. Such were the manifestations to Joseph, the favored descendant of the father of the faithful in dreams, and in them the Lord fulfilled his purposes: But the tone of which I have been speaking is what would have been called an open vision. And though it was in the night, yet it was not a dream. There is no room for conjecture in this matter, and to talk of deception, would be to sport with the common sense of every man who knows when he is awake, when he sees and when he does not see.

He could not have been deceived in the fact that a being of some kind appeared to him: and that it was an heavenly one, the fulfillment of his words so minutely, up to this time, in addition to the truth and word of salvation which has been developed to this generation, in the Book of Mormon, ought to be conclusive evidence to the mind of every man who is privileged to hear of the same. He was awake, and in solemn prayer, as you will bear in mind, when the angel made his appearance; from that glory which surrounded him the room was lit up to a perfect brilliancy, so that darkness wholly disappeared: he heard his words with his ears, and received a joy and happiness indescribable by hearing that his own sins were forgiven, and his former transgressions to be remembered against him no more, if he then continued to walk before the Lord, according to his holy commandments. He also saw him depart, the light and glory withdraw, leaving a calmness and peace of soul past the language of man to paint. Was he deceived?

Far from this; for the vision was renewed twice before morning, unfolding further and still further the mysteries of godliness and those things to come. In the morning he went to his labor as usual, but soon the vision of the heavenly messenger was renewed, instructing him to go immediately and view those things of which he had been informed, with a promise that he should obtain them, if he followed the directions and went with an eye single to the glory of God.

Accordingly he repaired to the place which had thus been described. But it is necessary to give you more fully the express instructions of the angel, with regard to the object of this work in which our brother had now engaged—He was to remember that it was the work of the Lord, to fulfil certain promises previously made to a branch of the house of Israel of the tribe of Joseph, and when it should be brought forth, it must be done expressly with an eye, as I said before, single to the glory of God, and the welfare and restoration of the house of Israel.

You will understand, then, that no motive of a pecuniary, or earthly nature, was to be suffered to take the lead of the heart of the man thus favored. The allurements of vice, the contaminating influence of wealth, without the direct guidance of the Holy Spirit, must have no place in the heart nor be suffered to take from it that warm desire for the glory and kingdom of the Lord, or, instead of obtaining, disappointment and reproof would most assuredly follow. Such was the instruction and this the caution.

Alternately, as we could naturally expect, the thought of the previous vision was ruminating in his mind, with a reflection of the brightness and glory of the heavenly messenger; but again a thought would start across the mind on the prospects of obtaining so desirable a treasure—one in all human probability sufficient to raise him above a level with the common earthly fortunes of his fellow men, and relieve his family from want, in which, by misfortune and sickness they were placed.

It is very natural to suppose that the mind would revolve upon those scenes which had passed, when those who had acquired a little of this world's goods, by industry and economy, with the blessings of health or friends, or by art and intrigue, from the pockets of the day-laborer, or the widow and the fatherless, had passed by with a stiff neck and a cold heart, scorning the virtuous because they were poor, and lording over those who were subjected to suffer the miseries of this life.

Alternately did these, with a swift reflection of the words of the holy messenger,—"Remember, that he who does this work, who is thus favoured of the Lord, must do it with his eye single to the glory of the same, and the welfare and restoration of the scattered remnants of the house of Israel"— rush upon his mind with the quickness of electricity. Here was a struggle indeed; for when he calmly reflected upon his errand, he knew that if God did not give, he could not obtain; and again, with the thought or hope of obtaining, his mind would be carried back to its former reflection of poverty, abuse,—wealth, grandeur and ease, until before arriving at the place described, this wholly occupied his desire; and when he thought upon the fact of what was previously shown him, it was only with an assurance that he should obtain and accomplish his desire in relieving himself and friends from want.

A history of the inhabitants who peopled this continent, previous to its being discovered to Europeans by Columbus, must be interesting to every man; and as it would develope the important fact, that the present race were descendants of Abraham, and were to be remembered in the immutable covenant of the Most High to that man, and be restored to a knowledge of the gospel, that they, with all nations might rejoice, seemed to inspire further thoughts of gain and income from such a valuable history. Surely, thought he, every man will seize with eagerness, this knowledge, and this incalculable income will be mine. Enough to raise the expectations of any one of like inexperience, placed in similar circumstances. But the important point in this matter is, that man does not see as the Lord, neither are his purposes like his. The small things of this life are but dust in comparison with salvation and eternal life.

It is sufficient to say that such were his reflections during his walk of from two to three miles, the distance from his father's house to the place pointed out. And to use his own words it seemed as though two invisible powers were influencing, or striving to influence his mind—one with the reflection that if he obtained the object of his pursuit, it would be through the mercy and condescension of the Lord, and that every act or performance in relation to it, must be in strict accordance with the instruction of that personage who communicated the intelligence to him first; and the other with the thoughts and reflections like those previously mentioned—contrasting his former and present circumstances in life with those to come. That precious instruction recorded on the sacred page—pray always—which was expressly impressed upon him, was at length entirely forgotten, and as I previously remarked, a fixed determination to obtain and aggrandize himself, occupied his mind when he arrived at the place where the record was found.

I must now give you some description of the place where, and the manner in which these records were deposited.

You are acquainted with the mail road from Palmyra, Wayne Co. to Canandaigua, Ontario Co. N. Y. and also, as you pass from the former to the latter place, before arriving at the little village of Manchester, say from three to four, or about four miles from Palmyra, you pass a large hill on the east side of the road. Why I say large, is, because it is as large perhaps, as any in that country. To a person acquainted with this road, a description would be unnecessary, as it is the largest and rises the highest of any on that route. The north end rises quite sudden until it assumes a level with the more southerly extremity, and I think I may say an elevation higher than at the south a short distance, say half or three fourths of a mile. As you pass toward Canandaigua it lessens gradually until the surface assumes its common level, or is broken by other smaller hills or ridges, water courses and ravines. I think I am justified in saying that this is the highest hill for some distance round, and I am certain that its appearance, as it rises so suddenly from a plain on the north, must attract the notice of the traveller as he passes by.

At about one mile west rises another ridge of less height, running parallel with the former, leaving a beautiful vale between. The soil is of the first quality for the country, and under a state of cultivation, which gives a prospect at once imposing, when one reflects on the fact, that here, between these hills, the entire power and national strength of both the Jaredites and Nephites were destroyed.

By turning to the 529th and 530th pages of the Book of Mormon, you will read Mormon's account of the last great struggle of his people, as they were encamped round this hill Cumorah. (It is printed Camorah, which is an error.) In this valley fell the remaining strength and pride of a once powerful people, the Nephites—once so highly favored of the Lord, but at that time in darkness, doomed to suffer extermination by the hand of their barbarous and uncivilized brethren. From the top of this hill, Mormon, with a few others, after the battle, gazed with horror upon the mangled remains of those who, the day before, were filled with anxiety, hope, or doubt. A few had fled to the South, who were hunted down by the victorious party, and all who would not deny the Savior and his religion, were put to death. Mormon himself, according to the record of his son Moroni, was also slain.

But a long time previous to this national disaster it appears from his own account, he foresaw approaching destruction. In fact, if he perused the records of his fathers, which were in his possession, he could have learned that such would be the case. Alma, who lived before the coming of the Messiah, prophesies this. He however, by Divine appointment, abridged from those records, in his own style and language, a short account of the more important and prominent items, from the days of Lehi to his own time, after which he deposited, as he says, on the 529th page, all the records in this same hill, Cumorah, and after gave his small record to his son Moroni, who, as appears from the same, finished it, after witnessing the extinction of his people as a nation.

It was not the wicked who overcame the righteous: far from this: it was the wicked against the wicked, and by the wicked the wicked were punished. The Nephites who were once enlightened, had fallen from a more elevated standing as to favour and privilege before the Lord, in consequence of the righteousness of their fathers, and now falling below, for such was actually the case, were suffered to be overcome, and the land was left to the possession of the red men, who were without intelligence, only in the affairs of their wars; and having no records, only preserving their history by tradition from father to son, lost the account of their true origin, and wandered from river to river, from hill to hill, from mountain to mountain, and from sea to sea, till the land was again peopled, in a measure, by a rude, wild, revengeful, warlike and barbarous race. Such are our Indians.

This hill, by the Jaredites, was called Ramah: by it, or around it, pitched the famous army of Coriantumr their tent. Coriantumr was the last king of the Jaredites. The opposing army were to the west, and in this same valley, and near by. From day to day, did that mighty race spill their blood, in wrath, contending as it were, brother against brother, and father against son. In this same spot, in full view from the top of this same hill, one may gaze with astonishment upon the ground which was twice covered with the dead and dying of our fellowmen. Here may be seen, where once sunk to nought the pride and strength of two mighty nations; and here may be contemplated in solitude, while nothing but the faithful record of Mormon and Moroni is now extant to inform us of the fact, scenes of misery and distress—the aged, whose silver locks in other places, and at other times, would command reverence; the mother, who, in other circumstances would be spared from violence—the infant, whose tender cries would be regarded and listened to with a feeling of compassion and tenderness— and the virgin, whose grace, beauty and modesty, would be esteemed and held inviolate by all good men and enlightened and civilized nations, were alike disregarded and treated with scorn! In vain did the hoary head and man of gray hairs ask for mercy—in vain did the mother plead for compassion—in vain did the helpless and harmless infant weep for very anguish—and in vain did the virgin seek to escape the ruthless hand of revengeful foes and demons in human form—all alike were trampled down by the feet of the strong, and crushed beneath the rage of battle and war! Alas! who can reflect upon the last struggles of great and populous nations, sinking to dust beneath the hand of justice and retribution, without weeping over the corruption of the human heart, and sighing for the hour when the clangor of arms shall no more be heard, nor the calamities of contending armies be any more experienced for a thousand years? Alas! the calamity of war, the extinction of nations, the ruin of kingdoms, the fall of empires, and the dissolution of governments! Oh! the misery, distress and evil attendant, on these. Who can contemplate like scenes without sorrowing, and who so destitute of commiseration as not to be pained that man has fallen so low, so far beneath the station in which he was created?

In this vale lie commingled, in one mass of ruin, the ashes of thousands, and in this vale were destined to be consumed the fair forms and vigorous systems of tens of thousands of the human race—blood mixed with blood, flesh with flesh, bones with bones, and dust with dust! When the vital spark which animated their clay had fled, each lifeless lump lay on one common level—cold and inanimate. Those bosoms which had burned with rage against each other for real or supposed injury, had now ceased to heave with malice; those arms which were a few moments before nerved with strength, had alike become paralyzed, and those hearts which had been fired with revenge, had now ceased to heave with malice; those arms which were a few moments before nerved with strength, had alike become paralyzed, and those hearts which had been fired with revenge, had now ceased to beat, and the head to think—in silence, in solitude, and in disgrace alike, they have long since turned to earth, to their mother dust, to await the august, and to millions, awful hour, when the trump of the Son of God shall echo and re-echo from the skies, and they come forth quickened and immortalized, to not only stand in each other's presence, but before the bar of him who is Eternal!

### Letter VIII

Letter VIII, the last in the series, continues the description of Cumorah.

IN my last I said I should give, partially, a "description of the place where, and the manner in which these records were deposited:" the first promise I have fulfilled, and must proceed to the latter:

The hill of which I have been speaking, at the time mentioned, presented a varied appearance: the north end rose suddenly from the plain, forming a promontory without timber, but covered with grass. As you passed to the south you soon came to scattering timber, the surface having been cleared by art or by wind; and a short distance further left, you are surrounded with the common forest of the country. It is necessary to observe, that even the part cleared was only occupied for pasturage, its steep ascent and narrow summit not admitting the plow of the husbandman with any degree of ease or profit. It was at the second mentioned place where the record was found to be deposited, on the west side of the hill, not far from the top down its side; and when myself visited the place in the year 1830, there were several trees standing: enow [enough] to cause a shade in summer, but not so much as to prevent the surface being covered with grass—which was also the case when the record was first found.

Whatever may be the feeling of men on the reflection of past acts which have been performed on certain portions or spots of this earth, I know not, neither does it add or diminish to nor from the reality of my subject. When Moses heard the voice of God, at the foot of Horeb, out of the burning bush, he was commanded to take his shoes off his feet, for the ground on which he stood was holy. The same may be observed when Joshua beheld the "Captain of the Lord's host" by Jerico. And I confess that my mind was filled with many reflections; and though I did not then loose my shoe, yet with gratitude to God did I offer up the sacrifice of my heart.

How far below the surface these records were placed by Moroni, I am unable to say; but from the fact that they had been some fourteen hundred years buried, and that too on the side of a hill so steep, one is ready to conclude that they were some feet below, as the earth would naturally wear more or less in that length of time. But they being placed toward the top of the hill, the ground would not remove as much as two-thirds, perhaps. Another circumstance would prevent a wearing of the earth: in all probability, as soon as timber had time to grow, the hill was covered, after the Nephites were destroyed, and the roots of the same would hold the surface. However, on this point I shall leave every man to draw his own conclusion and form his own speculation, as I only promised to give a description of the place at the time the records were found in 1823.

It is sufficient for my present purpose, to know that such is the fact, that in 1823, yes, 1823, a man with whom I have had the most intimate and personal acquaintance, for almost seven years, actually discovered by the vision of God, the plates from which the Book of Mormon, as much as it is disbelieved, was translated! Such is the case, though men rack their very brains to invent falsehoods, and then waft them upon every breeze, to the contrary notwithstanding.

I have now given sufficient on the subject of the hill Cumorah—it has a singular and imposing appearance for that country, and must excite the curious enquiry of every lover of the Book of Mormon, though, I hope, never like Jerusalem and the sepulchre of our Lord, the pilgrims. In my estimation, certain places are dearer to me for what they now contain, than for what they have contained. For the satisfaction of such as believed I have been thus particular, and to avoid the question being a thousand times asked, more than any other cause, shall proceed and be as particular as heretofore.

The manner in which the plates were deposited. First, a hole of sufficient depth, (how deep I know not,) was dug. At the bottom of this was laid a stone of suitable size, the upper surface being smooth. At each edge was placed a large quantity of cement, and into this cement, at the four edges of this stone were placed erect, four others, their bottom edges resting in the cement at the outer edges of the first stone. The four last named, when placed erect, formed a box, the corners, or where the edges of the four came in contact, were also cemented so firmly that the moisture from without was prevented from entering. It is to be observed, also, that the inner surface of the four erect, or side stones was smooth. This box was sufficiently large to admit a breast-plate, such as was used by the ancients to defend the chest, &c., from the arrows and weapons of their enemy. From the bottom of the box, or from the breast-plate, arose three small pillars composed of the same description of cement used on the edges; and upon these three pillars was placed the record of the children of Joseph, and of a people who left the tower far, far before the days of Joseph, or a sketch of each, which had it not been for this, and the never failing goodness of God, we might have perished in our sins, having been left to bow down before the altars of the Gentiles, and to have paid homage to the priests of Baal! I must not forget to say that this box, containing the record was covered with another stone, the bottom surface being flat and the upper, crowning. But those three pillars were not so lengthy as to cause the plates and the crowning stone to come in contact. I have now given you, according to my promise, the manner in which this record was deposited; though when it was first visited by our brother, in 1823, a part of the crowning stone was visible above the surface, while the edges were concealed by the soil and grass, from which circumstance you will see, that however deep this box might have been placed by Moroni at first, the time had been sufficient to wear the earth so that it was easily discovered, when once directed, and yet not enough to make a perceivable difference to the passer by. So wonderful are the works of the Almighty, and so far from our finding out are his ways, that one who trembles to take his holy name into his lips, is left to wonder at his exact providences, and the fulfilment of his purposes in the event of times and seasons. A few years sooner might have found even the top stone concealed, and discouraged our brother from attempting to make a further trial to obtain this rich treasure, for fear of discovery; and a few later might have left the small box uncovered, and exposed its valuable contents to the rude calculations and vain speculations of those who neither understand common language nor fear God. But such would have been contrary to the words of the ancients and the promises made to them; and this is why I am left to admire the works and see the wisdom in the designs of the Lord in all things manifested to the eyes of the world: they show that all human inventions are like the vapors, while his word endures forever and his promises to the last generation.

Having thus digressed from my main subject to give a few items for the special benefit of all, it will be necessary to return, and proceed as formerly. And if any suppose I have indulged too freely in reflections, I will only say, that it is my opinion, were one to have a view of the glory of God which is to cover Israel in the last days, and know that these, though they may be thought small things, were the beginning to effect the same, they would be at a loss where to close, should they give a moment's vent to the imaginations of the heart.

You will have wondered, perhaps, that the mind of our brother should be so occupied with the thoughts of the good of this world, at the time of arriving at Cumorah, on the morning of the 22nd of September, 1823, after having been rapt in the visions of heaven during the night, and also seeing and hearing in open day; but the mind of man is easily turned, if it is not held by the power of God through the prayer of faith, and you will remember that I have said that two invisible powers were operating upon his mind during his walk from his residence to Cumorah, and that the one urging the certainly of wealth and ease in this life, had so powerfully wrought upon him, that the great object so carefully and impressively named by the angel, had entirely gone from his recollection that only a fixed determination to obtain now urged him forward. In this, which occasioned a failure to obtain, at that time, the record, do not understand me to attach blame to our brother: he was young, and his mind easily turned from correct principles, unless he could be favored with a certain round of experience. And yet, while young, untraditionated and untaught in the systems of the world, he was in a situation to be lead into the great work of God, and be qualified to perform it in due time.

After arriving at the repository, a little exertion in removing the soil from the edges of the top of the box, and a light pry, brought to his natural vision its contents. No sooner did he behold this sacred treasure than his hopes were renewed, and he supposed his success certain; and without first attempting to take it from its long place of deposit, he thought, perhaps, there might be something more equally as valuable, and to take only the plates, might give others an opportunity of obtaining the remainder, which could be secure, would still add to his store of wealth. These, in short, were his reflections, without once thinking of the solemn instruction of the heavenly messenger, that all must be done with an express view of glorying God.

On attempting to take possession of the record a shock was produced upon his system, by an invisible power, which deprived him, in a measure, of his natural strength. He desisted for an instant, and then made another attempt, but was more sensibly shocked than before. What was the occasion of this he knew not—there was the pure unsullied record, as had been described—he had heard of the power of enchantment, and a thousand like stories, which held the hidden treasures of the earth, and supposed that physical exertion and personal strength was only necessary to enable him to yet obtain the object of his wish. He therefore made the third attempt with an increased exertion, when his strength failed him more than at either of the former times, and without premeditating he exclaimed, "Why can I not obtain this book?" "Because you have not kept the commandments of the Lord," answered a voice, within a seeming short distance. He looked, and to his astonishment, there stood the angel, who had previously given him the directions concerning this matter. In an instant, all the former instructions, the great intelligence concerning Israel and the last days, were brought to his mind: he thought of the time when his heart was fervently engaged in prayer to the Lord, when his spirit was contrite, and when his holy messenger from the skies unfolded the wonderful things connected with this record. He had come, to be sure, and found the word of the angel fulfilled concerning the reality of the record, but he had failed to remember the great end for which they had been kept, and in consequence could not have power to take them into his possession and bear them away.

At that instant he looked to the Lord in prayer, and as he prayed darkness began to disperse from his mind and his soul was lit up as it was the evening before, and he was filled with the Holy Spirit; and again did the Lord manifest his condescension and mercy: the heavens were opened and the glory of the Lord shone round about and rested upon him. While he thus stood gazing and admiring, the angel said, "Look!" and as he thus spake he beheld the prince of darkness, surrounded by his innumerable train of associates. All this passed before him, and the heavenly messenger said, "All this is shown, the good and the evil, the holy and impure, the glory of God and the power of darkness, that you may know hereafter the two powers and never be influenced or overcome by that wicked one. Behold, whatever entices and leads to good, and to do good, is of God, and whatever does not is of that wicked one. It is he that fills the hearts of men with evil, to walk in darkness and blaspheme God; and you may learn from henceforth, that his ways are to destruction, but the way of holiness is peace and rest. You now see why you could not obtain this record; that the commandment was strict, and that if ever these sacred things are obtained, they must be by prayer and faithfulness in obeying the Lord. They are not deposited here for the sake of accumulating gain and wealth for the glory of this world; they were sealed by the prayer of faith, and because of the knowledge which they contain, they are of no worth among the children of men, only for their knowledge. On them is contained the fulness of the gospel of Jesus Christ, as it was given to his people on this land, and when it shall be brought forth by the power of God it shall be carried to the Gentiles, of whom many will receive it, and after will the seed of Israel be brought into the fold of their Redeemer by obeying it also. Those who kept the commandments of the Lord on this land, desired this at his hand, and through the prayer of faith obtained the promise, that if their descendants should transgress and fall away, that a record might be kept, and in the last days come to their children. These things are sacred, and must be kept so, for the promise of the Lord concerning them must be fulfilled. No man can obtain them if his heart is impure, because they contain that which is sacred; and, besides, should they be entrusted in unholy hands the knowledge could not come to the world, because they cannot be interpreted by the learning of this generation; consequently, they would be considered of no worth, only as precious metal. Therefore, remember, that they are to be translated by the gift and power of God. By them will the Lord work a great and a marvelous work: the wisdom of the wise shall become as nought, and the understanding of the prudent shall be hid, and because the power of God shall be displayed, those who profess to know the truth, but walk in deceit, shall tremble with anger; but with signs and with wonders, with gifts and with healings, with the manifestations of the power of God, and with the Holy Ghost, shall the hearts of the faithful be comforted. You have now beheld the power of God manifested and the power of Satan: you see that there is nothing that is

220

desirable in the works of darkness; that they cannot bring happiness; that those who are overcome therewith are miserable, while, on the other hand, the righteous are blessed with a place in the kingdom of God, where joy unspeakable surrounds them. There they rest beyond the power of the enemy of truth, where no evil can disturb them. The glory of God crowns them, and they continually feast upon his goodness and enjoy his smiles. Behold, notwithstanding you have seen this great display of power, by which you may ever be able to detect the evil one, yet I give unto you another sign, and when it comes to pass then know that the Lord is God, and that he will fulfil his purposes, and that the knowledge which this record contains will go to every nation, and kindred, and tongue, and people under the whole heaven.

This is the sign: When these things begin to be known, that is, when it is known that the Lord has shown you these things, the workers of iniquity will seek your overthrow: they will circulate falsehoods to destroy your reputation, and also will seek to take your life; but remember this if you are faithful, and shall hereafter continue to keep the commandments of the Lord, you shall be preserved to bring these things forth; for in due time he will again give you a commandment to come and take them. When they are interpreted, the Lord will give the holy priesthood to some, and they shall begin to proclaim this gospel and baptize by water, and after that they shall have power to give the Holy Ghost by the laying on of their hands. Then will persecution rage more and more; for the iniquities of men shall be revealed, and those who are not built upon the Rock will seek to overthrow this Church; but it will increase the more opposed, and spread further and further, increasing in knowledge till they shall be sanctified and receive an inheritance where the glory of God will rest upon them; and when this takes place, and all things are prepared, the ten tribes of Israel will be revealed in the north country, whither they have been for a long season; and when this is fulfilled will be brought to pass that saying of the prophet—"And the Redeemer shall come to Zion, and unto them that turn from transgression in Jacob, saith the Lord" But, notwithstanding the workers of iniquity shall seek your destruction the arm of the Lord will be extended and you will be borne off conqueror, if you keep all his commandments. Your name shall be known among the nations, for the work which the Lord will perform by your hands shall cause the righteous to rejoice and the wicked to rage: with the one it shall be had in honor, and with the other in reproach; yet, with these it shall be a terror because of the great and marvelous work which shall follow the coming forth of this fulness of the gospel. Now, go thy way, remembering what the Lord has done for thee, and be diligent in keeping his commandments, and he will deliver thee from temptations and all the arts and devices of the wicked one. Forget not to pray, that thy mind may become strong that when he shall manifest unto thee, thou mayest have power to escape the evil, and obtain these precious things."

Though I am unable to paint before the mind, a perfect description of the scenery which passed before our brother, I think I have said enough to give you a field for reflection which may not be unprofitable. You see the great wisdom in God in leading him thus far, that his mind might begin to be more matured, and thereby be able to judge correctly, the spirits. I do not say that he would not have obtained the record had he gone according to the direction of the angel—I say that he would; but God knowing all things from the beginning, began thus to instruct his servant. And in this it is plainly to be seen that the adversary of truth is not sufficient to overthrow the work of God. You will remember that I said, two invisible powers were operating upon the mind of our brother while going to Cumorah. In this, then, I discover wisdom in the dealings of the Lord: it was impossible for any man to translate the book of Mormon by the gift of God, endure the afflictions, and temptations, and devices of Satan, without being overthrown, unless he had been previously benefitted with a certain round of experience: and had our brother obtained the record the first time, not knowing how to detect the works of darkness, he might have been deprived of the blessing of sending forth the word of truth to this generation. Therefore, God knowing that Satan would thus lead his mind astray, began at that early hour, that when the full time should arrive, he might have a servant prepared to fulfil his purpose. So, however afflicting to his feelings this repulse might have been, he had reason to rejoice before the Lord, and be thankful for the favors and mercies shown: that whatever other instruction was necessary to the accomplishing this great work, he had learned, by experience, how to discern between the spirit of

Christ and the spirit of the devil.

From this time to September, 1827, few occurrences worthy of note, transpired. As a fact to be expected, nothing of importance could be recorded concerning a generation in darkness. In the mean time our brother of whom I have been speaking, passed the time as others, in laboring for his support. But in consequence of certain false and slanderous reports which have been circulated, justice would require me to say something upon the private life of one whose character has been so shamefully traduced. By some he is said to have been a lazy, idle, vicious, profligate fellow. These I am prepared to contradict, and that too by the testimony of many persons with whom I have been intimately acquainted, and know to be individuals of the strictest veracity, and unquestionable integrity. All these strictly and virtually agree in saying, that he was an honest, upright, virtuous, and faithfully industrious young man. And those who say to the contrary can be influenced by no other motive than to destroy the reputation of one who never injured any man in either property or person.

While young, I have been informed he was afflicted with sickness; but I have been told by those for whom he has labored, that he was a young man of truth and industrious habits. And I will add further that it is my conviction, if he never had been called to the exalted station in which he now occupies, he might have passed down the stream of time with ease and in respectability, without the foul and hellish tongue of slander ever being employed against him. It is no more than to be expected, I admit, that men of corrupt hearts will try to traduce his character and put a stop upon his name: indeed, this is according to the word of the angel; but this does not prohibit me from speaking freely of his merits, and contradicting those falsehoods—I feel myself bound so to do, and I know that my testimony, on this matter, will be received and believed while those who testify to the contrary are crumbled to dust, and their words swept away in the general mass of lies, when God shall purify the earth!

Connected with this, is the character of the family: and on this I say as I said concerning the character of our brother—I feel myself bound to defend the innocent always when opportunity offers. Had not those who are notorious for lies and dishonesty, also assailed the character of the family, I should pass over them here in silence; but now I shall not forbear. It has been industriously circulated that they were dishonest, deceitful and vile. On this I have the testimony of responsible persons, who have said and will say, that this is basely false; and besides, a personal acquaintance for seven years, has demonstrated that all the difficulty is, they were once poor, (yet industrious,) and have now, by the help of God, arisen to note, and their names are like to, (indeed they will,) be handed down to posterity, and had among the righteous. They are industrious honest, virtuous and liberal to all. This is their character; and though many take advantage of their liberality, God will reward them; but this is the fact, and this testimony shall shine upon the records of the Saints, and be recorded on the archives of heaven to be read in the day of eternity, when the wicked and perverse, who have vilely slandered them without cause or provocation, reap their reward with the unjust, where there is weeping, wailing and gnashing of teeth—if they do not repent.

Soon after this visit to Cumorah, a gentleman from the south part of the State, (Chenango County,) employed our brother as a common labourer, and accordingly he visited that section of the country; and had he not been accused of digging down all, or nearly so, the mountains of Susquehannah, or causing others to do it by some art of necromancy, I should leave this, for the present, unnoticed. You will remember, in the mean time, that those who seek to vilify his character, say that he has always been notorious for his idleness. This gentleman, whose name is Stowell, resided in the town of Bainbridge, on or near the head waters of the Susquehannah river. Some forty miles south, or down the river, in the town of Harmony, Susquehannah county, Pa. is said to be a cave or subterraneous recess, whether entirely formed by art or not I am uninformed, neither does this matter; but such is said to be the case,—when a company of Spaniards, a long time since, when the country was uninhabited by white settlers, excavated from the bowels of the earth ore, and coined a large quantity of money; after which they secured the cavity and evacuated, leaving a part still in the cave, purposing to return at some distant period. A long time elapsed and this account came from one of the individuals who was first engaged in this mining business. The country was pointed out and the spot minutely described. This, I believe, is the substance, so far as my memory serves, though I shall not pledge my veracity for the correctness of the account as I have given. Enough however, was credited of the Spaniard's story, to excite the belief of many that there was a fine sum of the precious metal being coined in this subterraneous vault, among whom was our employer; and accordingly our brother was required to spend a few months with some others in excavating the earth, in pursuit of this treasure.

While employed here, he became acquainted with the family of Isaac Hale, of whom you read in several of the productions of those who have sought to destroy the validity of the book of Mormon. It may be necessary hereafter, to refer you more particularly to the conduct of this family, as their influence has been considerably exerted to destroy the reputation of our brother, probably because he married a daughter of the same, contrary to some of their wishes, and in connexion with this, to certain statements of some others of the inhabitants of that section of country. But in saying this I do not wish to be understood as uttering aught against Mrs. Smith, (formerly Emma Hale.) She has most certainly evinced a decidedly correct mind and uncommon ability of talent and judgment, in a manifest willingness to fulfil, on her part that passage in sacred writ,—"and they twain shall be one flesh."—by accompanying her husband against the wishes and advice of her relatives, to a land of strangers: and however I may deprecate their actions, can say in justice, her character stands as fair for morality, piety and virtue, as any in the world. Though you may say, this is a digression from the subject proposed, I trust I shall be indulged, for the purpose of satisfying many, who have heard so many slanderous reports that they are lead to believe them true because they are not contradicted; and besides, this generation are determined to oppose every item in the form or under the pretence of revelation, unless it comes through a man who has always been more pure than Michael the great prince; and as this is the fact, and my opposers have put me to the necessity, I shall be more prolix, and have no doubt, before I give up the point, shall prove to your satisfaction, and to that of every man, that the translator of the book of Mormon is worthy the appellation of a seer and a prophet of the Lord. In this I do not pretend that he is not a man subject to passion like other men, beset with infirmities and encompassed with weaknesses; but if he is, all men were so before him, and a pretence to the contrary would argue a more than mortal, which would at once destroy the whole system of the religion of the Lord Jesus; for he anciently chose the weak to overcome the strong, the foolish to confound the wise, (I mean considered so by this world,) and by the foolishness of preaching to save those who believe.

On the private character of our brother I need add nothing further at present, previous to his obtaining the records of the Nephites, only that while in that country, some very officious person complained of him as a disorderly person, and brought him before the authorities of the county; but there being no cause of action he was honorably acquitted. From this time forward he continued to receive instruction concerning the coming forth of the fulness of the gospel, from the mouth of the heavenly messenger, until he was directed to visit again the place where the records was deposited.

For the present I close, with a thankful heart that I am permitted to see thousands rejoicing in the assurance of the promises of the Lord, confirmed unto them through the obedience of the everlasting covenant.

# Appendix 4: Comparison charts

Differences of opinion and interpretation can be difficult to compare unless they are presented side-by-side. In this Appendix, I offer some comparison charts.

There's also a useful Cumorah decision tree here:

http://bookofmormonconsensus.blogspot.com/2017/02/cumorah-decision-tree-for-book-of.html

As you read the table below, ask yourself these questions.
Which column makes more sense to you?
Which column would make more sense to people you know?

Traditional vs. Revisionist Church history

| Revisionist history as taught by Joseph's critics and modern scholars | Traditional history as taught by JS and OC, the scriptures, and the prophets |
|---|---|
| At great sacrifice, Mormon preserved ancient Nephite records and abridged them. Moroni deposited the abridgment in a hill in western New York. | At great sacrifice, Mormon preserved ancient Nephite records and abridged them. Moroni deposited the abridgment in a hill in western New York. |
| Joseph didn't use the plates to translate. | Joseph Smith translated the abridged plates. |
| Joseph didn't use the Urim and Thummim that came with the plates; instead, he read words that appeared on a seer stone he put in a hat when he covered his face with the hat. He didn't really translate anything. | Joseph translated the plates into English through the medium of the Urim and Thummim that came with the plates |

| | |
|---|---|
| The Book of Mormon tells the history of either (i) a small group of Israelites among Mayan societies in Mesoamerica or (ii) unknown former inhabitants somewhere in the Western Hemisphere. | The Book of Mormon tells the history of the aborigines of this country; their descendants are the Indians that now live in this country. |
| The Hill Cumorah in New York had nothing to do with the Book of Mormon; i.e., the scene of the final battles of the Jaredites and the Nephites is somewhere in southern Mexico. | The Hill Cumorah in New York is a Book of Mormon site; i.e., it was the scene of the final battles of the Jaredites and the Nephites. |
| Oliver Cowdery, David Whitmer, Lucy Mack Smith, Heber C. Kimball, Brigham Young, Parley P. Pratt and others created a false narrative about the New York Cumorah. | Oliver Cowdery, David Whitmer, Lucy Mack Smith, Heber C. Kimball, Brigham Young, Parley P. Pratt and others told the truth about the New York Cumorah. |
| D&C 128:20 reflects Joseph Smith's adoption of the false narrative about the New York Cumorah. | D&C 128:20 explains that glad tidings came from the Hill Cumorah of Mormon 6:6 in western NY. |

―――

## Cumorah advocates, NY vs not NY.

People who say Cumorah is in New York and people who say Cumorah is not in New York.

| People who say Cumorah is in New York | People who say Cumorah is not in New York |
|---|---|
| Joseph Smith | LDS scholars who promote a Mesoamerican setting for the Book of Mormon |
| Oliver Cowdery | LDS scholars who promote a Baja Californian setting for the Book of Mormon |
| David Whitmer | LDS scholars who promote a Panamanian setting for the Book of Mormon |
| Lucy Mack Smith | LDS scholars who promote a Peruvian setting for the Book of Mormon |
| Brigham Young | LDS scholars who promote a Chilean setting for the Book of Mormon |
| John Taylor | |
| Heber C. Kimball | |
| Wilford Woodruff | |
| Orson Pratt | |
| Parley P. Pratt | |
| Joseph F. Smith | |
| Heber J. Grant | |
| George Albert Smith | |
| Joseph Fielding Smith | |
| Marion G. Romney | |
| Mark E. Peterson | |
| **Simple, clear, definitive** | **Mass of confusion** |

———

## Agree and Agree-to-Disagree list

| Proposition | M2C | Moroni's America |
|---|---|---|
| 1. The most important aspect of the Book of Mormon is its message. | Agree | Agree |
| 2. The Book of Mormon is an inspired translation of an actual ancient record of actual people who lived in the real world. | Agree | Agree |
| 3. The ultimate objective of our research/writing is to motivate people to read the Book of Mormon and strengthen their faith in Christ as a result. | Agree | Agree |
| 4. Another objective of our research and writing is to help people better understand the text of the book by understanding its setting, culture and context. | Agree | Agree |
| 5. The Church has no official position on where Book of Mormon events took place. | Agree | Agree |
| 6. In Letter VII, Oliver Cowdery identified the valley west of the Hill Cumorah in New York as the location of the final battles of the Nephites and Jaredites. | Agree | Agree |
| 7. Joseph Smith instructed his scribes to copy Oliver's letters, including Letter VII, into his journal as part of his life story. | Agree | Agree |
| 8. Joseph Smith gave permission to Benjamin Winchester to republish Oliver's letters, including Letter VII, in his newspaper called the *Gospel Reflector* | Agree | Agree |
| 9. Don Carlos republished Oliver's letters, including Letter VII, in the 1842 Church | Agree | Agree |

| | | |
|---|---|---|
| newspaper called the *Times and Seasons* (T&S). | | |
| 10. On Sept. 9, 1841, Dr. Bernhisel gave Wilford Woodruff a copy of the Stephens' popular archaeology books about Central America to give to Joseph Smith | Agree | Agree |
| 11. On Nov. 5, 1841, Wilford Woodruff wrote a letter to Dr. Bernhisel that is not extant. | Agree | Agree |
| 12. A thank-you letter dated Nov. 16, 1841, was sent to Bernhisel on Joseph Smith's behalf. No one knows who wrote the letter because the handwriting remains unidentified and no journals mention it. | Agree | Agree |
| 13. A series of editorials were published in the T&S during 1842 that linked the Book of Mormon to archaeological findings in North and Central America. They cited the Stephens books and archaeology books by Josiah Priest. All were published either anonymously or over the signature of Ed. for Editor. | Agree | Agree |
| 14. From February 15 through October 15, 1842, the boilerplate of the T&S said the paper was edited, printed, and published by Joseph Smith. | Agree | Agree |
| 15. Joseph Smith originally obtained the plates from a stone box Moroni constructed out of stone and cement in the Hill Cumorah in New York. | Agree | Agree |
| 16. Brigham Young said Oliver told him that he (Oliver) and Joseph had made at least two visits to a room in the Hill Cumorah in New York that contained | Agree | Agree |

| | | |
|---|---|---|
| piles of records and ancient Nephite artifacts. | | |
| 17. Mormon said he buried all the Nephite records in the Hill Cumorah (Morm. 6:6), the scene of the final battles of the Nephites, except he kept out the plates he gave to his son Moroni to finish the record. | Agree | Agree |
| 18. D&C 128:20 reads, "And again, what do we hear? Glad tidings from Cumorah! Moroni, an angel from heaven, declaring the fulfilment of the prophets—the book to be revealed," followed by references to other events that took place in New York. | Agree | Agree |
| 19. The geography passages in the Book of Mormon are subject to a variety of interpretations. | Agree | Agree |
| 20. To date, apart from Moroni's stone box and the plates and other objects Joseph Smith possessed and showed to the Witnesses, no artifact or archaeological site that can be directly linked to the Book of Mormon has been found anywhere. | Agree | Agree |
| 21. Cultural characteristics can be discerned from the text. | Agree | Agree |
| 22. The New Jerusalem Ether wrote about is located in Jackson County, Missouri. | Agree | Agree |
| 23. Mayan civilization collapsed around 800 A.D. and Mayans migrated to North America, where they lived for several hundred years before returning to Central America. | Agree | Agree |
| 24. The Newark Ohio earthworks are the largest earthworks in the world and | Agree | Agree |

| | | |
|---|---|---|
| demonstrate knowledge of astronomy and geometry. | | |
| 25. There were a million ancient mounds in North America before the Europeans arrived. | Agree | Agree |
| 26. There are two million skeletons buried in mounds in Illinois alone. | Agree | Agree |
| 27. As an Apostle and Church Historian, Joseph Fielding Smith said the two-Cumorah theory caused members to become confused and disturbed in their faith in the Book of Mormon. He reiterated this when he was President of the Quorum of the Twelve in the 1950s in his book *Doctrines of Salvation.* | Agree | Agree |
| 28. The land of Zarahemla is north of the land of Nephi and lower in elevation than the land of Nephi. | Agree | Agree |

**And here's where we agree to disagree. Everyone can choose which position he/she agrees with on each topic. Other ideas are also fine.**

| Topic | M2C | Moroni's America |
|---|---|---|
| 1. Location of the Hill Cumorah | The hill in New York had nothing to do with ancient Nephites or Jaredites (apart from Moroni traveling to the area). The real Hill Cumorah which contains Mormon's repository of records and was the scene of the final battles is elsewhere. | The hill in New York is the actual Hill Cumorah and Hill Ramah where both the Nephites and the Jaredites were destroyed. It also contained Mormon's repository of the Nephite records. |

| | | |
|---|---|---|
| 2. Two-Cumorah theory described | There are two Cumorahs. The one in New York where Joseph Smith found the plates was just the place where Moroni buried his record. Unknown early Mormons gave this hill the name Cumorah and Joseph Smith later adopted this tradition. The real Cumorah where Mormon deposited the Nephite records is the scene of the final battles and it is in Mesoamerica. | There is only one Cumorah and it is in New York. |
| 3. Joseph Fielding Smith's comments on the two-Cumorah theory | Joseph Fielding Smith's criticisms of the two-Cumorah theory are invalid because 50 years ago, someone heard a BYU professor say Pres. Smith told him he could teach whatever he wanted about Cumorah. | Joseph Fielding Smith's criticisms of the two-Cumorah theory are valid, have caused and continue to cause members to become confused and disturbed in their faith of the Book of Mormon. |
| 4. Oliver Cowdery's Letter VII | Oliver Cowdery was speculating and was factually wrong about the New York location of the Hill Cumorah. | Oliver Cowdery stated a fact about the New York Cumorah based on his own experience in Mormon's repository as related to Brigham Young and others. |
| 5. Anonymous T&S article, | The articles linking the Book of Mormon to | The articles linking the Book of Mormon to |

| Sept/Oct 1842 | Central America were written, or at least approved by, Joseph Smith | Central America were not written, approved of, or even seen by Joseph Smith prior to publication |
| --- | --- | --- |
| 6. *Times and Seasons* Editor | Joseph was a hands-on editor of the T&S | Joseph was a nominal editor only. The paper was actually edited by William Smith and/or W.W. Phelps. |
| 7. Book of Mormon overall geography | The text describes an overall hourglass shape. | The text does not describe an overall hourglass shape. Instead, Cumorah is a pin in the map in New York and Zarahemla is a pin in the map in Iowa. |
| 8. Setting in Central America vs. North America | The description in the text best fits someplace in Central America, including Guatemala and Mexico. | The description in the text best fits North America, from Florida to New York and west to Missouri and Iowa. |
| 9. Cultural elements in the text | The text describes an ancient Mesoamerican culture. Towers in the text refer to massive stone pyramids. Horses may be tapirs. The Nephites sacrificed agouti or other large rodents. | The text describes an ancient North American culture. Towers in the text refer to wooden towers. Horses are horses. The Nephites strictly observed the Law of Moses, including species. |
| 10. Joseph Smith's knowledge | Joseph did not leave a first-hand record of a revelation about Book of | Joseph Smith knew where the Book of Mormon events took |

|  | Mormon geography, so he had no revelation or inspiration regarding Book of Mormon geography | place because Moroni had shown him, as mentioned in the Wentworth letter and by his mother Lucy. |
|---|---|---|
| 11. "Plains of the Nephites" (Joseph's letter to Emma refers to Ohio, Indiana and Illinois as the "plains of the Nephites") | Joseph speculated about a location not specifically mentioned in the text ("the plains of the Nephites"). | Joseph recognized the plains referred to in the text of the Book of Mormon; i.e., "meet them upon the plains between the two cities" (Alma 52:20); "pitch their tents in the plains of Nephihah" (Alma 62:18) and "battle against them, upon the plains" (Alma 62:19). |
| 12. Zelph | Zelph was a warrior killed in Illinois who was known to some of Lehi's descendants who migrated northward from Mesoamerica into the Hinterland (areas not covered by the text) | Zelph was a warrior in the final battles of the Nephites, killed in Illinois between Zarahemla and Cumorah. |
| 13. Location of Zarahemla | Zarahemla is located somewhere in Mexico or Guatemala; D&C 125:3 does not refer to the Nephite Zarahemla | Zarahemla is located across from Nauvoo as indicated by D&C 125:3 (near Montrose Iowa) |
| 14. River Sidon | Because the land of Nephi is south of the land of Zarahemla and people travel down to the | Because the land of Nephi is south of the land of Zarahemla and people travel down to |

| | | |
|---|---|---|
| | land of Zarahemla from Nephi, and because the river Sidon flows past the city of Zarahemla, the River Sidon flows north. Sidon is the Umacita or Grijalva river in Mesoamerica | the land of Zarahemla from Nephi, the river between the two lands flows North. This is the Tennessee River, unnamed in the text. The text says that the river Sidon flows past the city of Zarahemla and along the land of Zarahemla, but not that it goes to the land of Nephi. These descriptions fits the Iowa location; Sidon is the upper Mississippi River. |
| 15. Correspondences in Central America between BoM and ancient cultures | Many correspondences suggest the BoM took place in Central America, including Mayan banners, pyramids, stone temples, warfare, symbols of the tree of life, state-level society, etc. | These correspondences are typical of most cultures and, to the extent they are unique to BoM, they reflect culture brought to Central America from North America when the Mayans returned after 900 AD. |
| 16. Jaredites | The Jaredites lived in Central America and were destroyed at the Hill Cumorah (Ramah) in Mexico | The Jaredites likely expanded throughout the western hemisphere and only those who lived in "this north country" were Ether's ancestors who were |

| | | discussed in the Book of Ether and were destroyed at Cumorah |
|---|---|---|
| 17. Presence of ancient writing | The text requires the presence of ancient writing systems, which are found only in Mesoamerica | The text excludes the presence of ancient writing systems because Lamanites destroyed any records they could find, which is why Mormon had to hide the plates. |
| 18. Western Hemisphere setting | Although Joseph merely speculated about BoM geography, he knew it took place somewhere in the Western Hemisphere | Joseph knew by revelation that the Book of Mormon took place in the Western Hemisphere because he identified the plains of the Nephites, identified the western tribes of Indians as Lamanites, etc. |
| 19. 1842 Wentworth letter statement that the "Lamanites are Indians in this country." | This refers to all indigenous people in the Western Hemisphere. | Joseph was writing from Nauvoo, Illinois, to Mr. Wentworth who lived in Chicago, Illinois. Joseph's statement refers to the Native American Indians in Illinois and what was then the United States. |
| 20. 1830-31 Mission to the Lamanites (D&C 28, 30 and 32) | Early Mormons believed the American Indians were Lamanites, but the term actually refers to all indigenous people in the | Referred specifically to those tribes they visited (and other culturally connected tribes) in New York, Ohio and |

|  | Americas | Missouri |
|---|---|---|
| 21. Archaeological evidence in North America between BoM and ancient cultures | The archaeology in North America during BoM times shows a tribal level society, but BoM describes a state-level society | The archaeology shows a tribal level society but also a long-lost state-level society with monumental architecture among Adena and Hopewell societies, just as BoM describes |
| 22. Modern prophets/apostles have identified Lamanites in Latin America | These statements corroborate the Mesoamerican setting. | These statements are not limited to Mesoamerica and reflect post-Book of Mormon migrations (Mayans moving north after 800 AD, then returning to Mesoamerica). |
| 23. DNA evidence | All known DNA in Mesoamerican is Asian in origin, but DNA evidence is inconclusive; cannot prove or disprove the Book of Mormon. | Only northeastern (Great Lakes) Indian tribes have DNA other than Asian; dating of X2 haplotype (Middle-Eastern) remains an open issue because scientists currently say the X2 haplotype appeared in the Great Lakes region thousands of years before Lehi. |
| 24. Promised land covenant | Promised land and covenant land includes entire Western hemisphere | Promised land and covenant land refers to the United States |

| | | |
|---|---|---|
| 25. Statements recorded by Wilford Woodruff and Martha Coray and attributed to Joseph Smith say that Zion is all of North and South America | These statements mean Lehi's descendants filled the hemisphere, but BoM took place in a limited geography (Mesoamerica) | These statements originally meant Northern and Southern states, but Zion is anywhere the pure in heart live. Winchester's wing concept of the continents of North and South America was adopted by Hyrum Smith and successors, then applied retroactively (Wilford Woodruff, Martha Coray) |
| 26. Uto-Aztecan languages have Hebrew and Egyptian influence | These language influences show transoceanic interaction with Indians in western U.S. and Mexico. | These language influences show transoceanic interaction with Indians in western U.S. and Mexico, but not on Mayans. In addition, Algonquin (Great Lakes Indians) languages also have Hebrew and Egyptian influence. |
| 27. General Conference talks that affirm the New York Cumorah | Presidents Ivins and Romney of the First Presidency were merely expressing their own opinions and were wrong. Same with Elder Mark E. Petersen. | Presidents Ivins and Romney of the First Presidency testified to the truth of what President Oliver Cowdery and others taught. Same with Elder Mark E. Petersen. |

## Translation: seer stone vs Urim and Thummim
Who taught what

| Peep stone in a hat (stone from a well) | Urim and Thummim (Nephite interpreters) |
|---|---|
| Book: *Mormonism Unvailed* | Book: Joseph Smith - History |
| William E. McLellin | Joseph Smith |
| Anthony Sweat (BYU) | Oliver Cowdery |
| David Whitmer | Brigham Young |
| *Saints*, volume 1* | Wilford Woodruff |
| Gospel Topics Essay on Book of Mormon Translation | Heber C. Kimball |
| Book of Mormon Central | John Taylor |
| Emma Smith (according to Joseph Smith III) | Erastus Snow |
| Martin Harris | Lucy Mack Smith |

*https://saintsreview.blogspot.com/2019/08/peep-stone-vs-urim-and-thummim-in-saints.html

―――

# Appendix 5: Wentworth letter and Orson Pratt's pamphlet

This table compares Joseph Smith's article titled "Church History," popularly known as the Wentworth letter,[119] with Orson Pratt's 1840 pamphlet titled *A[n] Interesting Account of Several Remarkable Visions*.[120] A revised version of the Wentworth letter was republished as "Latter-Day Saints" in 1844.[121]

| 1842 Wentworth Letter | 1840 Orson Pratt pamphlet |
|---|---|
| In this important and interesting book the history of ancient America **is unfolded**, from its **first** settlement by a colony that came from the tower of Babel, at the confusion of languages to the beginning of the fifth century of the Christian era. | In this important and **most** interesting book, **we can read** the history of ancient America, from its **early** settlement by a colony who came from the tower of Babel, at the confusion of languages, to the beginning of the fifth century of the Christian era. |
| **We are informed by these records** that America in ancient times has been inhabited by two distinct races of people. | By these Records we are informed, that America, in ancient times, has been inhabited by two distinct races of people. |
| The first **were called Jaredites** and came directly from the tower **of Babel.** The second race came directly from the city of Jerusalem, about six hundred years before Christ. They were **principally** Israelites, of the descendants of Joseph. | The first, **or more ancient race**, came directly from the **great** tower, being called Jaredites. The second race came directly from the city of Jerusalem, about six hundred years before Christ, **being** Israelites, **principally** the descendants of Joseph. |

---

[119]    https://www.josephsmithpapers.org/paper-summary/church-history-1-march-1842/2

[120]    https://www.josephsmithpapers.org/paper-summary/appendix-orson-pratt-an-interesting-account-of-several-remarkable-visions-1840/17

[121] https://www.josephsmithpapers.org/paper-summary/latter-day-saints-1844/3

Joseph explained that Lehi's people were "principally Israelites," leaving open the possibility of other nationalities. Pratt claimed they were all Israelites, principally descendants of Joseph.

| | |
|---|---|
| The Jaredites were destroyed about the time that the Israelites came from Jerusalem, who succeeded them in the inheritance of the country. | **The first nation, or** Jaredites, were destroyed about the time that the Israelites came from Jerusalem, who succeeded them in the inheritance of the country. |
| The principal nation of the second race fell in battle towards the close of the fourth century. | The principal nation of the second race, fell in battle towards the close of the fourth century. |
| **The remnant are the Indians that now inhabit this country.** | The remaining remnant, having dwindled into an uncivilized state, still continue to inhabit the land, although divided into a "multitude of nations," and are called by Europeans the "American Indians." |

This is a critical change because Joseph deleted Pratt's theory about the identity of the remnant of Lehi's descendants.

Pratt claimed the remnant are "a multitude of nations" extending far beyond the United States to the western coast of South America. At one point, Pratt wrote "The Lamanites, at that time, dwelt in South America, and the Nephites in North America."

Pratt expounded his theories for several pages. Below we include only the portions relevant to geography and anthropology.

Joseph deleted all of Pratt's theory. He replaced it with the simple declaration that Lehi's descendants are "the Indians that now inhabit this country."

Joseph's deletion of Pratt's theory appears to be a rejection of that theory. The revelations Joseph received, including D&C 28, 30 and 32, are consistent with what he wrote in the Wentworth letter.

Orson Pratt lived until October 3, 1881. He survived Joseph by 37 years, preaching frequently as a member of the Quorum of the Twelve.

He frequently taught the concepts he set out in his 1840 pamphlet without mentioning the significant edit Joseph made in the Wentworth letter.

In 1879, Pratt published a new edition of the Book of Mormon that contained footnotes referencing geography. He acknowledged the speculative nature of some of his conclusions by prefacing them with "it is believed," but regarding Cumorah, he stated without equivocation that it was located in western New York.

One wonders if Orson realized how Joseph had edited his pamphlet or if he ever discussed the changes with Joseph. That seems unlikely. The Wentworth letter was published at a time of significant turmoil in Orson Pratt's life. His wife Sarah was accused of adultery and made allegations against Joseph Smith. When Pratt sided with his wife, he was excommunicated on August 20, 1842. He was rebaptized in January 1843 and ordained to his former position in the Quorum of the Twelve.

Nor is it likely that Orson read the revised version, published as "Latter Day Saints," because that article appeared in *He Pasa Ekklesia* (the whole church), a compilation edited by Israel Daniel Rupp and published in Lancaster, Pennsylvania.

| | |
|---|---|
| | We learn from this very ancient history, that at the confusion of languages, when the Lord scattered the people upon all the face of the earth, the Jaredites, being a righteous people, obtained favour in the sight of the Lord, and were not confounded. |
| | And because of their righteousness, the Lord miraculously led them from the tower to the great ocean, where they were commanded to build vessels, in which they were marvellously brought across the great deep to the shores of North America. |
| | And the Lord God promised to give |

| | |
|---|---|
| | them America, which was a very choice land in his sight, for an inheritance. |
| | And He swore unto them in his wrath, that whoso should possess this land of promise, from that time henceforth and forever, should serve him, the true and only God, or they should be swept off when the fulness of his wrath should come upon them, and they were fully ripened in iniquity. |
| | Moreover, he promised to make them a great and powerful nation, so that there should be no greater nation upon all the face of the earth. |

| | |
|---|---|
| | Accordingly, in process of time, they became a very numerous and powerful people, occupying principally North America; building large cities in all quarters of the land; being a civilized and enlightened nation. |
| | But they gave no heed to these warnings; therefore the word of the Lord was fulfilled; and they were entirely destroyed; leaving their houses, their cities, and their land desolate; and their sacred records also, which were kept on gold plates, were left by one of their last prophets whose name was Ether, in such a situation, that they were discovered by the remnant of Joseph, who soon afterwards were brought from Jerusalem to inherit the land. |
| | This remnant of Joseph were also led in a miraculous manner from |

| | Jerusalem, in the first year of the reign of Zedekiah, king of Judah. |
| --- | --- |
| | They were first led to the eastern borders of the Red Sea; then they journeyed for some time along the borders thereof, nearly in a southeast direction; after which, they altered their course nearly eastward, until they came to the great waters, where, by the commandment of God, they built a vessel, in which they were safely brought across the great Pacific ocean, and landed upon the western coast of South America. |
| | In the eleventh year of the reign of Zedekiah, at the time the Jews were carried away captive into Babylon, another remnant were brought out of Jerusalem; some of whom were descendants of Judah. |
| | They landed in North America; soon after which they emigrated into the northern parts of South America, at which place they were discovered by the remnant of Joseph, something like four hundred years after. |
| | From these ancient records, we learn, that this remnant of Joseph, soon after they landed, separated themselves into two distinct nations. |
| | This division was caused by a certain portion of them being greatly persecuted, because of their righteousness, by the remainder. |
| | The persecuted nation emigrated towards the northern parts of South America, leaving the wicked nation in possession of the middle and |

| | |
|---|---|
| | southern parts of the same. |
| | The former were called Nephites, being led by a prophet whose name was Nephi. The latter were called Lamanites, being led by a very wicked man whose name was Laman.... |
| | And the Nephites began to prosper in the land, according to their righteousness, and they multiplied and spread forth to the east, and west, and north; building large villages, and cities, and synagogues, and temples, together with forts, and towers, and fortifications, to defend themselves against their enemies.... |
| | And in the days of their righteousness, they were a civilized, enlightened, and happy people. |
| | But, on the other hand, the Lamanites, because of the hardness of their hearts, brought down many judgments upon their own heads; nevertheless, they were not destroyed as a nation; but the Lord God sent forth a curse upon them, and they became a dark, loathsome, and filthy people. |
| | Before their rebellion, they were white and exceedingly fair, like the Nephites; but the Lord God cursed them in their complexions, and they were changed to a dark colour; and they became a wild, savage, and ferocious people; |
| | being great enemies to the Nephites, whom they sought, by every means, to destroy, and many times came against them, with their numerous |

| | hosts to battle, but were repulsed by the Nephites, and driven back to their own possessions, not, however, generally speaking, without great loss on both sides; |
| --- | --- |
| | for tens of thousands were very frequently slain, after which they were piled together in great heaps upon the face of the ground, and covered with a shallow covering of earth, which will satisfactorily account for those ancient mounds, filled with human bones, so numerous at the present day, both in North and South America. |
| | The second colony, which left Jerusalem eleven years after the remnant of Joseph left that city, landed in North America, and emigrated from thence, to the northern parts of South America; and about four hundred years after, they were discovered by the Nephites, as we stated in the foregoing… |
| | And in process of time, the Nephites began to build ships near the Isthmus of Darien, and launch them forth into the western ocean, in which great numbers sailed a great distance to the northward, and began to colonize North America. Other colonies emigrated by land, and in a few centuries the whole continent became peopled. |
| | North America, at that time, was almost entirely destitute of timber, it having been cut off by the more ancient race, who came from the great tower, at the confusion of |

| | |
|---|---|
| | languages; but the Nephites became very skilful in building houses of cement; also, much timber was carried by the way of shipping from South to North America…. |
| | After Jesus had finished ministering unto them, he ascended into heaven; and the twelve disciples, whom he had chosen, went forth upon all the face of the land, preaching the gospel; baptizing those who repented for the remission of sins, after which they laid their hands upon them, that they might receive the Holy Spirit. |
| | Mighty miracles were wrought by them, and also by many of the church. The Nephites and Lamanites were all converted unto the Lord, both in South and North America: and they dwelt in righteousness above three hundred years; but towards the close of the fourth century of the Christian era, they had so far apostatized from God, that he suffered great judgments to fall upon them. |
| | The Lamanites, at that time, dwelt in South America, and the Nephites in North America. |
| | A great and terrible war commenced between them, which lasted for many years, and resulted in the complete overthrow and destruction of the Nephites. This war commenced at the Isthmus of Darien, and was very destructive to both nations for many years. |
| | At length, the Nephites were driven before their enemies, a great |

|  | distance to the north, and north-east; and having gathered their whole nation together, both men, women, and children, they encamped on, and round about the hill Cumorah, where the records were found, which is in the State of New York, about two hundred miles west of the city of Albany. |
|--|---|
|  | Here they were met by the numerous hosts of the Lamanites, and were slain, and hewn down, and slaughtered, both male and female—the aged, middle aged, and children. Hundreds of thousands were slain on both sides; and the nation of the Nephites were destroyed, excepting a few who had deserted over to the Lamanites, and a few who escaped into the south country, and a few who fell wounded, and were left by the Lamanites on the field of battle for dead, among whom were Mormon and his son Moroni, who were righteous men. |

# Appendix 6: Overview of scholarly arguments

Over the years many readers have asked about my response to the arguments of the advocates of the Mesoamerican/two Cumorahs theory (M2C) who oppose the New York Cumorah. This requires setting forth their arguments fairly, in their own words.

That takes a lot of time, but to recognize multiple working hypotheses, as I do, you have to put in the time. Or else just defer to whichever hypothesis confirms your bias and ignore the rest.

While I have my own bias, I fully accept M2C as an alternative working hypothesis. That doesn't mean I ignore the problems with it.

In this appendix, we'll look at some of the major points made in the dozens of books and articles that support M2C. Some of these have been widely quoted and cited. I'll offer my responses.

In making a case for the New York Cumorah, I didn't spend a lot time relating the back-and-forth about the "Book of Mormon wars" over Cumorah and geography. As I explained in the Preface and Chapter 1, for me the Cumorah question begins and ends with one's approach to the credibility and reliability of the prophets who have taught the New York Cumorah.

If you **accept** the teachings of the prophets, there is plenty of corroborating evidence, both internally (within the text) and externally (in the fields of archaeology, anthropology, geology, geography, etc.).

If you **reject** the teachings of the prophets, whether overtly or implicitly by framing their teachings as their private opinions that were wrong, there is plenty of corroborating evidence, both internally (within the text) and externally (in the fields of archaeology, anthropology, geology, geography, etc.).

That's a simple, binary choice.

Beyond that is the complexity of all the arguments, pro and con.

Once we pass through complexity, we can reach the simplicity on the other side of complexity—the product of informed decisions.

-----

M2C *by definition* rejects the teachings of the prophets about the New York Cumorah.

I repeat: I do not see this as a right or wrong issue. Rejecting the prophets doesn't make M2C inherently "wrong." Maybe, as they claim, the prophets *were* wrong.

Instead of absolutes, I prefer the framework of multiple working hypotheses. That gives everyone flexibility to incorporate new information as it become available.

That flexibility also requires a give-and-take among the hypotheses. Many of the most prominent Church scholars disagree. They have concluded that M2C is "the" explanation of the Book of Mormon that must be promoted. M2C has become the de facto standard. If it is correct, M2C will become stronger as it responds to criticism—just like the New York Cumorah will.

Hence this Appendix.

People employ logical fallacies and thinking errors to confirm their biases. For that reason, the debates are not all that fruitful. Basic psychology requires people to validate their life's work. Rare are the individuals who change their minds about things they've taught for decades, have published and lectured about, and have raised and spent millions of dollars advocating.

For me, changing my mind about Cumorah and Book of Mormon geography was comparatively easy. Although I had believed M2C for decades, it was merely an interest of mine. It was not my career. I had not led tours or published books or taught students.

For years, I read the FARMS newsletters, the articles, the books, and then the web pages. I attended conferences and watched videos. I visited sites in Central and South America. I was "all in" for M2C.

But then I started noticing problems with M2C. I attended lectures and conferences about the "Heartland" model of geography. I read books and articles, many of them by Wayne May. I went on a tour of Ohio with Rod Meldrum. I highly recommend both.

Soon, the problems with M2C became obvious. I studied more,

asked around, started blogging, and the rest is history.

As I said, it was easy for me to change my mind. But I recognize the difficulty faced by M2C scholars and their followers and supporters. That's why I spent the first part of this book reviewing the psychological filters that impede our mental flexibility.

I completely respect and personally like the M2C scholars I have met. They are all fine people, faithful Latter-day Saints, etc. I think they have good intentions and want to share the gospel through the Book of Mormon. They believe they are providing useful evidence, and from their perspective, they undoubtedly are. But I think they are in a bubble of their own creation and they don't recognize it. They probably think the same about me. Which is fine. Unity through diversity.

My disagreements involve facts and explanations, proposals and hypotheses. None of it is personal. But we face a serious problem because the dominant, well-funded organizations such as Book of Mormon Central have taken an editorial stance in favor of M2C that misleads members of the Church (and the entire world).

As I wrote in the beginning of this book, I'm fine with people believing whatever they want, for whatever reasons they want. I encourage people to make informed decisions, but many people don't have the time or interest to do so. They defer to experts. That's why I think it's incumbent on those experts to recognize and accommodate multiple working hypotheses.

Those who seek more detail can consult my blogs listed in the Appendix. They are not organized by topic so it can be difficult to find what you want. (Hint: use the search box.)

## The trip to Cumorah

There must have been an important reason for the move to Fayette because it required miracles to bring about. As I explained in Part Five: Cumorah and the Two Sets of Plates, one important reason was to enable Joseph to fulfill the commandment in D&C 10 to translate the plates of Nephi, which he had not obtained from Moroni's stone box.

The move was prompted by the striking commandment Joseph received through the Urim and Thummim to contact David Whitmer. Joseph had never met David, but Oliver had. Oliver wrote the letter.

David received miraculous help on his farm to enable him to make the two-day trip to Harmony in the middle of planting season.

Oliver told David that Joseph had tracked David's entire trip. Oliver had written down the names of the taverns where David stayed, the people he met, and other details. As they retraced David's trip back to Fayette, David was astonished because every detail was correct.

David remembered encountering the divine messenger who was taking the plates to Cumorah because (i) it was the first time he heard of Cumorah and (ii) the same messenger showed the plates to David's mother Mary Whitmer. Mary reported that the man identified himself as "Brother Nephi."

To the extent scholars have paid attention to the 1829 trip to Fayette, they have generally expressed skepticism, dismissed it as the product of David's faulty memory, or changed the details.

In his influential book *Opening the Heavens: Accounts of Divine Manifestations, 1820-1844* (second edition), John W. Welch omitted the direct statements David gave to Stevenson in 1886 and to Joseph F. Smith/Orson Pratt in 1879. Instead Welch quoted from an unauthenticated, typewritten account dated April 25, 1918, that contradicted the earlier accounts (see page 108). Then Welch stated, "The plates were carried to Fayette by Moroni in a bundle on his back."

That claim directly contradicts the main point of David's account, the detail that caused David to remember; i.e., that the messenger said he was taking the plates to Cumorah. The New York Cumorah contradicts M2C, which Professor Welch has promoted for decades.

The disinformation in *Opening the Heavens* is especially troublesome because the original sources are difficult to find. Welch provides an internet link only to the 1918 typescript. He cites the long out-of-print book *David Whitmer Interviews*. , but even then does not cite the pages where David quotes the messenger saying "I am going to Cumorah," which is on pages 42 and 182. Unsuspecting readers will understandably believe what they read in *Opening the Heavens* and will never learn what David actually reported.

Another M2C scholar, after citing the Pratt/Smith report, wrote,

> This report would be much more conclusive had it not been recorded nearly fifty years later. The passage of time and the accepted designation of "Cumorah" as the name of the New York hill by the time of the recollection argue against this second-hand report from Whitmer as being a definitive statement.[122]

Notice the sophistry in this comment. "Much more conclusive" does not mean "inconclusive," but that is the implication. It was not a second-hand report; it was Whitmer's direct testimony of what he saw, which he told to at least two different interviewers.

This effort to undermine David's credibility relies on the premise that David never related the account until 49 years after the fact.

Of course, we don't know that David did *not* relate the account of the messenger going to Cumorah with the plates much earlier—we just do not have a specific written account of that happening. However, when Edward Stevenson interviewed David in 1886 and asked about the incident, he was prompted to do so before he left Salt Lake City by Zina Young. Her only known contact with David Whitmer was in 1832 when he was one of the missionaries who converted her family. She would have had to learn about it back then, not long after David picked up Joseph and Oliver.[123]

It is also possible she read about the account when the *Deseret News* published the Pratt/Smith interview on 16 November 1878. In that case, though, one wonders why Stevenson would not have read or heard about the account from that publication. Stevenson makes no reference to the *Deseret News* version in his diary.

Stevenson did write about his February 1886 interview in his diary,

---

[122] Brant A. Gardner, *Traditions of the Fathers*, (Greg Kofford Books, 2015), pp. 375-6.

[123] I discussed this on my blogs here http://www.lettervii.com/2019/09/david-whitmer-and-cumorah-messenger.html and here https://saintsreview.blogspot.com/2020/11/fake-moroni-story-zina-diantha-young.html.

in a letter to Daniel H. Wells that was published in the *Millennial Star*, and in a letter to the Editor of the Utah Journal. In January 1887 Stevenson visited David again and wrote about it in his Journal, in an article published in the *Juvenile Instructor*, an article in the *Millennial Star*, and yet another article in the 1889 *Juvenile Instructor* that changed some of the details.

The 7-8 September 1878 interview of David by Orson Pratt and Joseph F. Smith generated four known versions. Smith wrote about it in his journal. Pratt and Smith wrote a formal report to President John Taylor and the Council of the Twelve which was published in the *Deseret News* on Nov. 16, 1878. Orson Pratt wrote a private letter about the interview. In 1918, typewritten notes attributed to Smith for the first time identify the messenger as Moroni.

The Moroni identification is implausible because (i) David Whitmer personally met Moroni within a month and never made the connection, (ii) Moroni was a resurrected being described as taller than average (iii) the messenger was heavy set, about 5'8-9" with white hair and a white beard. The idea that resurrected beings change their appearance like legendary shape-shifters contradicts basic doctrine about the resurrection.

Comparing these accounts is beyond the scope of this book, but they are all included in Lyndon W. Cook, *David Whitmer Interviews*, which I highly recommend if you can find a copy. David's story about encountering the stranger carrying the plates to Cumorah is consistent each time he related it.

David was also adamant that Joseph had given the plates to a messenger before leaving Harmony. In 1881, he was interviewed by the *Kansas City Journal*. The article quoted David to say the following:

> Soon after I received another letter from Cowdery, telling me to come down into Pennsylvania and bring him and Joseph to my father's house, giving as a reason therefor that they had received a commandment from God to that effect. I went down to Harmony, and found everything just as they had written me. The next day after I got there **they packed up the plates** and we proceeded on our journey to my father's house where

we arrived in due time, and the day after we commenced upon the translation of the remainder of the plates.[124] (emphasis added)

After this article was published, David wrote to the editor of the paper to complain about "several errors in the interview."

In regard to my going to Harmony, my statement was that "I found everything as Cowdery had written me, and that they packed up the next day and went to my father's, (**did not say 'packed up the plates'**) and that he, Smith, (not 'we') then commenced the translation of the remainder of the plates."[125]

David knew Joseph and Oliver did not pack up the plates because the man he encountered on the road to Fayette had them in his knapsack.

## Archaeology and Mormon's Codex

This section addresses some of the principal arguments made by the M2C scholars regarding the connection between the text and archaeology.

In *Mormon's Codex*, p. 706, John Sorenson notes how modern Biblical archaeology is producing convergences and correspondences with the text of the Bible. Based on this, William Dever insists that Israel "must not be written out of history." Then Sorenson compares Biblical archaeology to the Book of Mormon:

Archaeologist John Clark has pointed out a similar trend in the relationship between Mesoamerican archaeology and scholarship on the Book of Mormon: 'The trend over the last 50 years is one of convergence between the Book of Mormon and Mesoamerican archaeology. Book of Mormon claims [have] remain[ed] unaltered since 1830, so all the accommodation has been on the archaeology side.'30 This book carries

---

[124] David Whitmer, as interviewed by the Kansas City Journal (1881), *Opening the Heavens*, p. 148.

[125] David Whitmer (1881), *Opening the Heavens*, p. 149.

that trend much further. Consequently, in the spirit of Dever, I maintain that 'the Nephites must not be written out of Mesoamerican history.'

[Note 30 is John E. Clark, "Archaeology, Relics, and Book of Mormon Belief," Journal of Book of Mormon Studies 14/2 (2005): 49; and Clark, "Archaeological Trends and Book of Mormon Origin," BYU Studies 44/4 (2005): 83-104.]

Brother Clark is often quoted by other M2C scholars. He is frequently quoted by FairMormon. Brant Gardner includes 10 of Clark's papers in his Bibliography in *Traditions of the Fathers.* I'll address Clark's work on Cumorah later, but for now I want to look at the claim Sorenson made in *Mormon's Codex.*

First, he quotes **Clark:** "The trend over the last 50 years is one of convergence between the Book of Mormon and Mesoamerican archaeology. **Book of Mormon claims** remain unaltered since 1830, so all the accommodation has been on the archaeology side."

Brother Clark seems to mean that the text has not changed since 1830 (presumably setting aside changes in punctuation, grammar, and terminology, as well as formatting). If that's what he means, then I agree.

But when you read Clark's work (as well as the work of the other M2C scholars), you see that is not what he means at all, in two ways.

**Text-based claims.** "Book of Mormon claims" can refer to the text itself, but such claims are not self-executing. Such claims are necessarily interpretations, particularly where the text is vague (such as what the text means by "northward" or "narrow neck of land").

**Context-based claims**. "Book of Mormon claims" can also refer to claims made *about* the text. This includes the description of the plates, where Joseph found them, the box they were in, what the angel told Joseph, what he told others, how the translation took place, etc.

In both senses, Book of Mormon claims, as viewed through the M2C lenses, have changed substantially since 1830. In fact, to the extent there is "accommodation" between the Book of Mormon and Mesoamerican archaeology, it has all come from the expansion of M2C.

**Here's an example of a changed text-based claim.**

Nowhere does the text use the term "headwaters," but every M2C scholar reads that term into the text. Why? Because the principal rivers in Mesoamerica flow northward, so the theory requires a river flowing north past Zarahemla. Of course, the text says no such thing. This is a new text-based claim that accommodates a particular geography. To say, as Clark and Sorenson do, that Mesoamerican archaeology is accommodating the text is exactly backward.

Other text-based claims, such as finding mountains throughout the text where they don't appear, assuming Joseph mistranslated animals and plants, imposing Mayan concepts of directions, etc., are all nothing but efforts by M2C scholars to accommodate the archaeology in their preferred setting. This flexible methodology would make it possible to fit the Book of Mormon just about anywhere in the world, into just about any culture.

**Here's an example of a changed contextual claim.** In 1830 (through at least 1842), it was universally understood that the Hill Cumorah of Mormon 6:6 was in western New York. This was published explicitly as a fact in multiple Church newspapers and embraced by Joseph Smith, who had it copied directly into his personal journal.

Now, Brothers Clark and Sorenson, as well as the other M2C scholars, insist the Hill Cumorah is *not* in New York. Clark writes, in direct opposition to Oliver Cowdery, that "the Cumorah of the golden plates is not the Cumorah of the final battles."

The reason given? Because of archaeology.

Archaeological findings in their preferred setting have led M2C scholars to change course regarding this basic, previously unambiguous and universally accepted Book of Mormon claim.

To compound the problem, M2C scholars attack those who seek to retain—unaltered—the Book of Mormon claims that prevailed when it was first published.

All that said, it turns out there is an increasing accommodation, convergence, correspondence, etc., between archaeology and the Book of Mormon—but it is in North America, not Mesoamerica.

If you're an M2C scholar, or a follower of M2C, you are probably unaware of this archaeology.

———

Back to Brother Sorenson's claim. After quoting Clark, he writes, "This book carries that trend much further."

If you read *Mormon's Codex*, you see that Brother Sorenson accurately describes his book. He definitely carries the trend of accommodation forward. For example, he famously writes, "There remain Latter-day Saints who insist that the final destruction of the Nephites took place in New York, but any such idea is manifestly absurd."

That sounds a lot like, "if you believe Oliver Cowdery, you're crazy."

Brother Sorenson continues: "Hundreds of thousands of Nephites traipsing across the Mississippi Valley to New York, pursued (why?) by hundreds of thousands of Lamanites, is a scenario worthy only of a witless sci-fi movie, not of history."

This is a classic straw man fallacy. First, he insists the Nephites lived in Mesoamerica. Then he points out it is foolish to believe they "traipsed" from Mesoamerica to New York. But no one (there may be someone somewhere) seriously advocates such a scenario.

Setting aside Brother Sorenson's straw man argument, we have an either/or question. Either you accept the New York Cumorah, or you accept a Mesoamerican Cumorah. If you accept a Mesoamerican Cumorah, then you have to adjust Book of Mormon claims, both text-based and context-based, to accommodate your theory. However, if you accept the New York Cumorah, you don't have to adjust either the text or the context.

Pretty simple, really.

Finally, Brother Sorenson writes, "Consequently, in the spirit of Dever, I maintain that 'the Nephites must not be written out of Mesoamerican history.'"

This is the fallacy of thinking past the sale.

The Nephites could not be written *out* of Mesoamerican history unless they were first written *into* that history.

No Mesoamerican experts have found Nephites in Mesoamerica. Mesoamerican history is well documented in the monuments and paintings. Experts can read the language. They know the names and dates of the kings, the extent of the kingdoms, the kinds of trading they engaged in, etc. And yet, they have never found the Nephites there.

You can't write something out if it's not there to begin with.

It is Brother Sorenson himself who is writing the Nephites *into* Mesoamerican history—and then asking everyone else not to write them out.

At over 800 pages, with voluminous references, *Mormon's Codex* is an impressive book. But it boils down to an effort to write Nephites into Mesoamerican history by finding "correspondences" that are usually typical of human societies everywhere. The logic goes like this:

Nephites were farmers.
Mayans were farmers.
Therefore, Nephites were Mayans.

Ironically, the only reason M2C scholars are focusing on Mesoamerica is because Joseph, Oliver and the other prophets said the events took place in America. The text is silent on the setting. Without the teachings of the prophets, the Book of Mormon events could have happened anywhere in the world.

But the same prophets who taught the events took place in America also taught that Cumorah is in New York!

## Reasons why Cumorah cannot be the location of the final Nephite battle

Brother John Clark published an article in the *Journal of Book of Mormon Studies* that Brother Gardner cited as containing "the reasons that the New York hill could not have been the location of the final Nephite battle."

Brother Clark cited a report from an archaeological survey conducted before highway construction in the Genesee Valley of New York in the 1970s. Curious, I obtained a copy of the report. Not surprisingly, I found some things readers of this blog might be interested in.

Brother Clark's long citation (footnote 9) ends with this sentence: "This implies that a population decline took place during the Middle Woodland Period." (The Middle Woodland Period, as defined in the report, is 500 BC-AD 1000.) However, Brother Clark omits the final sentence from the original paragraph, which is this: "At present there is no apparent explanation for such a decline."

Had Brother Clark removed his M2C lenses, he might have seen the connection between the final war between the Nephites and Lamanites in the area and the "unexplained" decline in population in western New York.

The report also notes that "Mortuary ceremonialism declined during the Late Woodland Period, as shown by the lack of grave goods or burial mounds following the Middle Woodland cultures." These burial practices were "patterned after those found in Ohio (Hopewell Tradition)." In Book of Mormon terms, Ohio was Bountiful and the Hopewell were the Nephites. If we read the text, we would expect the Nephite traditions to decline after they were vanquished by the Lamanites.

[Note: The term *Hopewell* comes from the last name of the man who owned the property upon which a particular mound was excavated. Had his last name been Nephi instead of Hopewell, archaeologists would be referring to these people as the Nephi culture.]

———

Brother Clark described the highway survey this way:

For the nearby Genesee Valley in New York, Neal L. Trubowitz gives detailed information from an intensive survey carried out in conjunction with the construction of a recent highway. For the wide strip of land involved, there is 100 percent coverage, so the information for relative changes in occupation is unusually good, as such things go in archaeology.

Trubowitz himself has a different perspective. He first explains that the report is his PhD dissertation. Then he notes that when he returned for a visit,

I found that the entire Genesee Expressway had gone to construction since I left, and that a major proportion of the archaeological sites identified in our research, notably the concentration of sites at the junction of the Genesee River with Canaseraga Creek, **had been destroyed by that construction without the benefit of any research beyond the work noted in this study.**

The history of highway salvage archaeology peculiar to New York, in combination with the political power structure within the state government at that time, **contributed to the loss of many sites in the Genesee Valley** that doubtless were eligible for nomination to the National Register of Historic Places and deserved further research. **These sites cannot be replaced and their loss represents a serious depletion of the archaeological record.** Yet, the Genesee Expressway investigations still represent a quantum leap in quality over the highway archaeological research that was possible before 1973 in New York. At least with this expressway, archaeologists were able to undertake systematic reconnaissance and **some minimal test excavations,** as compared to the almost nonexistent levels of research that were done on older major highways.

To Brother Clark, Trubowitz's dissertation represents detailed information of an intense survey of 100% coverage of the area. To Trubowitz himself, though, there were only "minimal test excavations" followed by destruction of "the concentration of sites," which cannot be replaced. Trubowitz says "their loss represents a serious depletion of the archaeological record," to which Brother Clark responds, "Possibilities and probabilities of destroyed evidence have become an excuse for avoiding serious archaeological research altogether."

———

Trubowitz also notes that while Ritchie, the other author Brother Clark cited, "did investigate mounds and other non-Seneca sites, very little organized research on cultures earlier than Late Woodland Period had been undertaken" prior to the highway study.

He also notes that

Practically every landowner who has any close connection with his or her property (farming, etc.) has a collection ranging from a few stray projectile points to thousands of artifacts. **Many collectors are known to have found sites which have not been recorded at any institution.** Some of the earlier private collections have been broken up at auctions and are no longer available to researchers... **It would take the lifetime of a number of investigators to track down all the extant collections,** and any survey of these collections would suffer from the collecting biases of those people who accumulated them.

Yet, based on the Trubowitz study, Brother Clark reaches this conclusion: "sufficient information is available for the surrounding regions to make a critical assessment. Mormon's hill and Moroni's hill are not one and the same... Archaeologically speaking, it is a clean hill. No artifacts, no walls, no trenches, no arrowheads. The area immediately surrounding the hill is similarly clean."

The author of the study Brother Clark cites says there are innumerable landowners who have collections that number in the thousands of artifacts, but Brother Clark doesn't mention that. Instead, he tells his readers that there are no artifacts.

I have spent time with an archaeologist in New York. We visited a site and he expertly picked up artifacts laying around. He gave me a couple. He told me that the University of Buffalo has over a million artifacts that they don't have the time or space to completely organize, let alone display. They have identified dozens of Hopewell sites in western New York.

Little if any archaeological work has been done around the Hill Cumorah. When he visited in 1832, Heber C. Kimball observed parts of the embankments still there. The are has been farmed continuously for 180 years, but you can still see one embankment feature on detailed elevation maps of the valley west of Cumorah.

Willard Bean's book about Cumorah references numerous arrow points and other artifacts found in the area, including skeletons. Because they were so abundant, his son used to skip arrowheads instead of rocks in local ponds. They dug up human skeletons with skulls large enough to put over their heads. Similar reports were made throughout the eastern and midwestern United States in the 1800s as people dug into the mounds and plowed the plains for farming.

Brother Clark found just enough information in the Trubowitz study to confirm his bias against the New York Cumorah. The study is difficult to obtain, but now that I have a copy, I'm happy to share it with anyone who wants to see it.

## Who Promotes M2C

**Lately, people want to know who, exactly, is promoting M2C.** They have children and/or grandchildren attending BYU or in CES and they want to prepare them for what they will learn and from whom. I'm reluctant to identify individuals because people change their views from time to time. Just because someone promotes M2C (or, worse, BYU's fantasy map of the Book of Mormon) doesn't mean he/she won't later change course.

Besides, as I keep emphasizing, people can have strong testimonies and can promote faith regardless of what they think about Book of Mormon geography. M2C is not a scarlet letter.

But, in my opinion and experience, M2C does have the long-term impact of causing confusion and disturbing faith, especially because it's a gateway drug to rejecting what the prophets teach about other topics.

As I explain below, I think anyone who starts with the premise that the prophets and apostles were wrong about Cumorah is not only embarking on a futile effort, but is leading others to doubt the prophets and apostles in their respective areas of expertise.

Students at BYU and CES are especially vulnerable because they trust their teachers (as they should).

**But when their teachers tell them to disbelieve the prophets and apostles about the Hill Cumorah, they introduce the idea that they, the intellectuals, are the final say on what students should believe.** As long as the prophets and apostles agree with the intellectuals, according to the M2C BYU/CES teachers, then students should believe the prophets and apostles. But when the intellectuals disagree with the prophets and apostles, then the students should believe the M2C intellectuals.

Long-time readers of my blog know that in the early days, I took an academic approach of critiquing specific publications from what I called the "M2C citation cartel" of FARMS, FairMormon, BookofMormonCentral, *BYU Studies*, the *Interpreter*, etc. Some of the scholars whose work I cited and assessed objected. While unwilling to discuss these things with me personally, they said it was inappropriate for me to cite them by name. In the interests of civility, I agreed to leave names out of the discussions going forward.

Besides, I personally like the LDS scholars and intellectuals who promote M2C and I don't think personalities have anything to do with the merits of an academic argument. I certainly have never intended any offense. I've always said I would prefer private conversations and resolution of disagreements, but because they are unwilling to engage in that effort, I've written blogs instead.

That said, anyone who wants to know who promotes M2C can visit the directory pages of the Interpreter Foundation and BookofMormonCentral, two organizations that dogmatically promote M2C to the point of excluding and uniformly criticizing alternatives, contrary to the Church's position of neutrality. People publicly affiliated with these groups embrace the editorial positions of these organizations; i.e., they reject the teachings of the prophets and apostles about the New York Cumorah, as well as the Church's position of neutrality.

## The Final Battle for Cumorah

Brother John Clark wrote an article titled "The Final Battle for Cumorah," *Review of Books on the Book of Mormon* 6/2 (1994): 79-113. You can access it directly from the Neal A. Maxwell Institute here: https://publications.mi.byu.edu/pdf-control.php/publications/review/6/2/S00005-51b10ada1f8b75Clark.pdf

BookofMormonCentral references it here: https://archive.bookofmormoncentral.org/content/final-battle-cumorah.

This is a seminal article because Brother Clark lays out the reasons why so many intellectuals in the Church reject what the prophets and apostles have taught about Cumorah. His arguments here have endured as an important part of the foundation for M2C.

The article is presented as a "Review of Christ in North America" (1993), by Delbert W. Curtis. Here is the Abstract: "Clark examines the scholarship and logic involved in assuming a one-Cumorah theory for Book of Mormon geography."

Notice the editorial position here. The "one-Cumorah theory" is merely an "assumption" that can be assessed by examining its "scholarship and logic." That statement is a poetically concise description of M2C.

Brother Clark usually does a nice job cutting to the key issues, and this article is no exception. In fact, one of his observations on page 84 helped lead me to embark on this review of Cumorah issues.

> "But these other scholars are never cited, nor is it clear that Curtis has read them with anything but disdain...."

I agree with Brother Clark that it is important to cite scholars specifically and to read them with respect and due consideration.

Here's another important observation from p. 84.

> Anyone with over a month's experience in the Church knows that interpretation of scriptures is tricky business and that differences of opinion are rarely resolved, especially when it concerns what someone "meant." The existence of Curtis's book is clear evidence that the scriptures for Zion and the land of promise can be read in a narrow sense. The question, however, is whether they should be.

The semantic debates are, ultimately, **nothing more than bias confirmation.** If you want to believe a scripture means one thing, you can interpret it that way. If I want to believe it means something else, I can interpret it my way. Most of the debates about Book of Mormon geography involve this type of bias confirmation that can never be resolved. That's how we have ended up with dozens of different theories about Book of Mormon geography.

**The futility of private interpretation that Brother Clark describes here is precisely why we have prophets and apostles, a point that doesn't seem to dawn on him, as we'll see.**

The specific example that prompted Brother Clark's comment was the quotation from History, 1838-1856 of a sermon given by Joseph Smith on 8 April 1844.[126]

> The whole of America is the land of Zion itself from the north to the south, and it is described by the prophets, who declare that it is the Zion where the mountain of the Lord should be, and that it should be in the center of the land.

This is often quoted as evidence that Zion is the entire western hemisphere, meaning the continents of North and South America, and Brother Clark adopts that interpretation as we'll see in a moment.

Back in 1994, people were citing *Teachings of the Prophet Joseph Smith*, which put this passage in italics. People rarely read the rest of the sermon, but Joseph went on to say this:

> I have received instructions from the Lord that from henceforth wherever the Elders of Israel shall build up churches and branches unto the Lord throughout the States, there shall be a stake of Zion; in the great cities as Boston, New York &c. there shall be stakes.

---

[126]    http://www.josephsmithpapers.org/paper-summary/history-1838-1856-volume-e-1-1-july-1843-30-april-1844/354

This observation, along with other contemporary references to the United States as "America" and the historical context of the division between the states in the North and South, suggest that Joseph used the term "the whole of America" to refer to the United States. Twelve years earlier, Joseph had received a revelation that said, "For behold, the Southern States shall be divided against the Northern States..." D&C 87:3. He was, in effect, telling his listeners that all of America, meaning the entire United States and not just the northern states where they lived, was Zion.

Of course, my interpretation is not binding on anyone else, and that's the point that Brother Clark tries to make.

> "The citation from Joseph Smith, *as I understand it,* appears to include "the whole of America." That this is "singular" only appears to weaken Curtis's reading that "Zion is from Mexico on the south to Canada on the north." Curtis appears to read the statement to mean that the land of Zion is in the center of the land; I think "center" refers to "the mountain of the Lord" as being in the center of the land.
>
> In any event, why would anyone want to read this statement so narrowly? The obvious suspicion is that it is the only reading that will support Curtis's geography.
>
> The same is true of the "Zion" scriptures. These appear to mention a Zion in "the tops of the mountains," a reference that many have considered as an accurate description of the Salt Lake City intermountain region. It would be a poor description indeed for the Great Lakes area." pp. 84-5.

Here, Brother Clark simply disagrees with Brother Curtis' interpretation, which he characterizes as "narrow," supposedly in contrast to Brother Clark's more "expansive" interpretation. He prefers his own view to Brother Curtis' because "The obvious suspicion is that it is the only reading that will support Curtis's geography." This is precisely the type of accusation to which I thought Brother Clark objected, yet he doesn't seem to realize what he is doing.

Parsing the grammar of someone's hand-written account of Joseph's spoken, extemporaneous sermon is silly enough, but characterizing someone else's interpretation as "narrow" and therefore invalid is worse. Prior revelations had identified Missouri as the land of Zion. How can it be unreasonable to ask what land Missouri is in the center of?

My point is not to resolve the question of Zion's extent, but to show how even a writer as precise and careful as Brother Clark can be blind to his own analytical errors.

———

In the next part of his article, Brother Clark sets forth the Columbus argument that so many M2C writers have relied upon. I engage this just to show how easy it is to support one's argument by attacking an easy target and ignoring arguments that contradict what you're advocating.

Fortunately for Brother Clark, Brother Curtis is an easy target. Brother Clark quotes him as writing, "Columbus didn't actually come to North America..." Of course, that's factually wrong. The Bahamas and Cuba are north of southern Mexico and are part of North America.

In fact, the first place Columbus landed (probably--the location remains open for debate) was the island of San Salvador in the Bahamas. This is less than 400 miles from Florida. (Some LDS think Lehi landed in Florida.) On that first voyage, Columbus also visited Cayo Cruz in Cuba, which is only 134 miles from Florida.

By contrast, San Salvador is 1,400 miles from the *east coast* of southern Mexico. M2C scholars claim Lehi landed on the *west coast* of southern Mexico or Guatemala, which of course is even farther away from San Salvador, Cayo Cruz, and the other places Columbus visited in 1492.

Columbus landed within 134 miles of Florida, but over 1,400 miles from Mexico.

M2C scholars invoke all of Columbus' voyages, because on his fourth voyage in 1502 he visited Trujillon on the east coast of Honduras, which is *closer* to their Mesoamerican setting. But it is still far away. In addition to being the wrong coast, Trujillo is 300 miles away from Guatemala City—farther than he was from Florida on his first voyage.

Plus, before Columbus' fourth voyage in 1502, Cabot landed in Newfoundland (1497) and Cabral landed in Brazil (1500), so it's difficult to justify Columbus 4th voyage as the one Nephi described in 1 Nephi 13:12. Before the time of the events in verse 13, when "other Gentiles" were coming, the man in verse 12 had already sailed upon the many waters "unto the seed of my brethren, who were in the promised land." This means the Bahamas and Cuba, not Mesoamerica. Columbus' fourth voyage to Honduras was too late to qualify.

If, as I believe, Lehi and Nephi crossed the Atlantic and landed in Florida, they would have sailed roughly the same route Columbus did through the Caribbean. The Mulekites sailed along a similar route.

There's another important point. Assuming Lehi sailed all the way to Florida through the area Columbus visited, it's not surprising that Nephi, having had a vision of the promised land, recognized the place when they sailed through the area on their way to the landing site in Florida. The M2C theory requires that Lehi landed on the *west coast of Mexico*, an area Columbus never saw or even came close to, which raises the question of how Nephi would have recognized it from his vision.

I realize all of this is getting in the weeds, but when M2C scholars insist Columbus visited Mesoamerica and not North America (meaning the U.S.), we have to assess their claims. No matter how you look at it, Columbus and Nephi are aligned with Caribbean voyages but not with a theory that has Lehi landing on the west coast of Mesoamerica.

This is a digression from Cumorah, obviously, but Brother Clark's Columbus discussion fails to take into account these critical elements.

As do the Columbus arguments of all the M2C proponents.

———

On, finally, to Cumorah.

On pages 93-4, Brother Clark gives a nice biographical introduction that contains good persuasion techniques:

For the first 22 years of my life I thought the location of Cumorah was well-known. as Joseph Smith received the plates from Moroni at that spot.

My father occasionally told us stories about the New York Cumorah that he had heard while serving a mission there during World War II. I was told of tremendous earthworks and defensive trenches encountered by the earliest settlers in Palmyra, and of large deposits of metal weapons.

I also heard of a vision wherein his mission president saw a red-headed Moroni lamenting over the destruction of his people. These were moving images in my youth. As with Curtis, I was extremely offended when I first heard the two-Cumorah theory. and I reacted strongly against it.

Until I heard the two-Cumorah theory after returning from my mission, I had no idea that the location of Cumorah was even a question or that the location of Book of Mormon lands was a topic of research.

My initial reaction was to take offense and to argue the point with my roommate who was taking a class in Book of Mormon archaeology from M. Wells Jakeman. In the course of our arguments, **it soon dawned on me that I had unthinkingly accepted a traditional view of the matter** and had never seriously looked at the statements from the Book of Mormon.

The internal evidence from the Book of Mormon eventually convinced me that I had been naive in accepting the traditional view and that there must be two hills called Cumorah: that of the Book of Mormon and one in New York.

I especially enjoyed this biohistory because it's the inverse of the one I use all the time; i.e., that I had been an M2C believer/proponent for decades before, to use Brother Clark's words, "it dawned on me that I had unthinkingly accepted a traditional view of the matter."

In other words, by the time I went to BYU, **Brother Clark and his fellow M2C promoters had successfully reversed the "traditional view of the matter" by replacing the words of the prophets with the words of the scholars.**

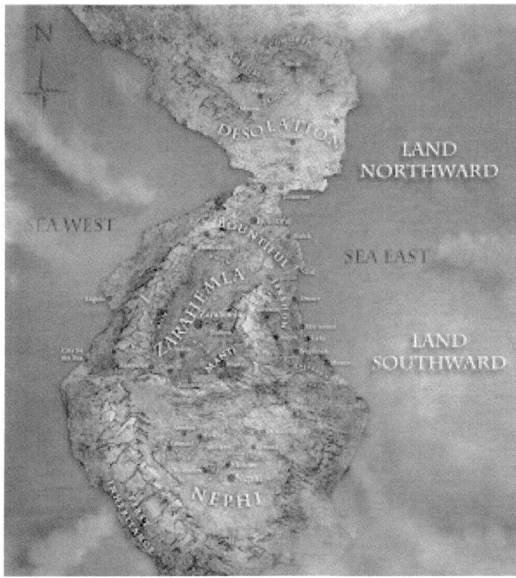

As of 2020, students at BYU and in CES are never taught what the prophets and apostles have consistently taught about the Hill Cumorah.

Instead, they are presented with this fantasy map of Book of Mormon geography that is computer generated and based on the M2C interpretation of the text!

The map is supposedly based on the "best interpretation" of the text, by which the intellectuals mean their own interpretation, driven by M2C ideology. The map makes sure that students never make a connection between Cumorah and New York.

If they ask about this, their teachers tell them that the prophets have never taught anything about Book of Mormon geography.

When confronted with Letter VII and other references, the teachers say these were merely their private opinions.

"But were they wrong?" students ask.

The teachers will seek to avoid answering, but if students persist, every M2C believer will eventually say, essentially, that Joseph and Oliver were ignorant speculators who misled the Church about the true location of Cumorah.

(Or words to that effect.)

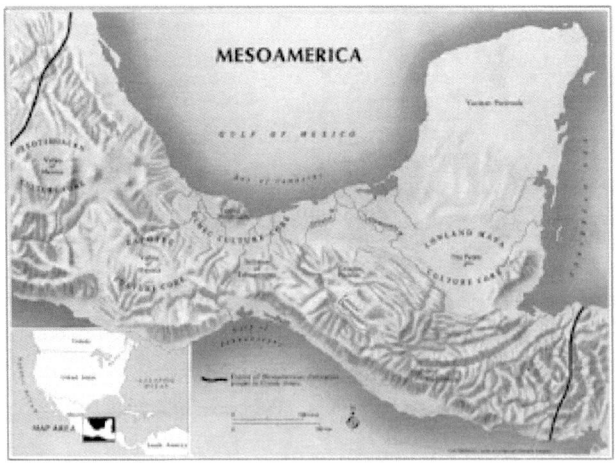

Figure 24 - BYU Studies M2C map

For the only alternative point of view permitted at BYU and CES, BYU/CES students can go to the home page of *BYU Studies* and find another "plausible" map that is the only one presented by *BYU Studies*.

Like BYU's fantasy map, the *BYU Studies* map also teaches students that (i) Cumorah cannot be in New York; (ii) Joseph and Oliver were ignorant speculators who misled the Church; (iii) all the prophets and apostles who have spoken about Cumorah were also wrong and should not have accepted what Joseph and Oliver taught; and (iv) students should believe their BYU/CES teachers instead of the prophets and apostles.

If you go to the BookofMormonCentral web page directory, you'll see that the people responsible for these maps are BYU professors who drive the M2C editorial policy.

———

In the next section of his article, Brother Clark explains and justifies this reversal of the traditional view from the New York Cumorah to M2C.

First, he cites David Palmer's "excellent" book, *In Search of Cumorah: New Evidences for the Book of Mormon from Ancient Mexico.*

We need to digress a moment to discuss Brother Palmer's book.

———

Brother Palmer wrote the entry about Cumorah that is still found in the *Encyclopedia of Mormonism (EoM)*.[127] There, he cites his own book, John L. Sorenson, and John Clark. This practice of citing oneself, and citing people who cite you in turn, constitutes a citation cartel. I call it the M2C citation cartel.

Brother Palmer himself reviewed one of Brother Curtis' pieces in another article from the *Review of Books on the Book of Mormon*.[128] In that article, Brother Palmer wrote,

> The Church of Jesus Christ of Latter-day Saints has never taken an official position on issues of Book of Mormon geography. Some unofficial books, written before modern archaeological methods were applied, assumed that Mormon's Cumorah and the New York hill were the same. This tradition, begun by Oliver Cowdery, has continued to the present.
>
> The New York hill came to be known as the one Book of Mormon location known with certainty. However, it was generally believed that Mesoamerica was the cradle of those cultures."

I provided that quotation to help explain Brother Clark's views and why he characterizes the Palmer book as "excellent." Brother Palmer frames the New York Cumorah as a "tradition begun by Oliver Cowdery," presumably referring to Letter VII *without citing it*. "Some unofficial books" assumed the tradition was correct, but they were "written before modern archaeological methods were applied."

**This dismissive attitude toward Letter VII is the opposite of how Joseph Smith viewed these letters.**

Joseph referred to the eight historical letters that include Letter VII

---

127

http://contentdm.lib.byu.edu/cdm/compoundobject/collection/EoM/id/4391/show/5649

128

https://scholarsarchive.byu.edu/cgi/viewcontent.cgi?article=1040&context=msr

as "President Cowdery's letters." Why? Because when he wrote Letter VII, Oliver Cowdery was the Assistant President of the Church--a calling that placed him senior in authority to the First and Second Counselors in the First Presidency. Joseph designated President Cowdery as spokesman.

Letter VII was published in the official Church newspaper, the *Messenger and Advocate*, copied into Joseph Smith's history, and republished in other official Church newspapers, including the *Times and Seasons*, the *Millennial Star* and the *Improvement Era*. Neither Brother Palmer nor Brother Clark mention any of that.

You can read everything published by the citation cartel--and everything in *Encyclopedia of Mormonism*--and never learn a thing about Letter VII and its context.

Declining to quote, or even cite, President Cowdery's letters when discussing the Hill Cumorah is not polite or serious scholarship.

Which brings us back to Brother Clark's article.

---------

After citing Brother Palmer's book, Clark continues his article with the following paragraph. I'll proceed by inserting my comments after each paragraph of Clark's article.

**Clark:** It is noteworthy that this [i.e., Palmer's] book is not cited by Curtis, nor are its arguments for the internal evidence for the hill Cumorah considered. **This is not polite or serious scholarship.**

[**Comment.** Is it impolite and unserious because Brothers Palmer and Clark are both part of the citation cartel? Is Curtis supposed to cite and consider Palmer because Palmer cited Clark in the *Encyclopedia of Mormonism?* There is no requirement to cite and address every book on a topic. It is just as impolite and unserious for Palmer and Clark to not cite and consider Letter VII.]

**Clark:** The location of the hill Cumorah is the primary strut in Curtis's argument for Book of Mormon lands, yet he presents no analysis of the statements from the Book of Mormon which reveal features of this hill.

[**Comment**. When we read the Palmer/Clark list of "features of this hill" supposedly "revealed" by the statements in the Book of Mormon, we see they are merely self-serving, circuitous interpretations designed to point to Central America.]

For the rest of my comments on this article, see http://www.1cumorah.com/2020/10/the-final-battle-for-cumorah.html

## "The Worlds of Joseph Smith" Conference

In 2005, BYU and the Library of Congress sponsored a two-day academic conference to commemorate the 200th anniversary of Joseph Smith's birth. The press release on lds.org is here. An example of more publicity, including the list of speakers, is here.

This symposium was one of the most high-profile discussions of Joseph Smith to date. In addition to the presentations, "An exhibit of books and other materials related to Joseph Smith, drawn from the collections of the Library of Congress and Brigham Young University, will be on display in the foyer." Among the displays were a first-edition Book of Mormon, original letters and other important historical documents, portraits, etc.

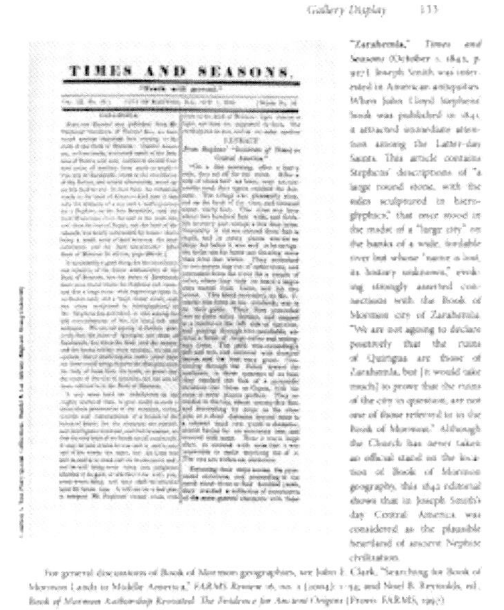
*Gallery Display* 133

TIMES AND SEASONS.

"Zarahemla," *Times and Seasons* (October 1, 1842, p. 927). Joseph Smith was interested in American antiquities. When John Lloyd Stephens' book was published in 1841 it attracted immediate attention among the Latter-day Saints. This article contains Stephens' descriptions of "a large round stone, with the sides sculptured in hieroglyphics," that once stood in the midst of a "large city" on the banks of a wide, fordable river but whose "name is lost, its history unknown," evoking strongly asserted connections with the Book of Mormon city of Zarahemla. "We are not agoing to declare positively that the ruins of Quirigua are those of Zarahemla, but [it would take much] to prove that the ruins of the city in question, are not one of those referred to in the Book of Mormon." Although the Church has never taken an official stand on the location of Book of Mormon geography, this 1842 editorial shows that in Joseph Smith's day Central America was considered as the plausible heartland of ancient Nephite civilization.

For general discussions of Book of Mormon geographies, see John E. Clark, "Searching for Book of Mormon Lands in Middle America," *FARMS Review* 16, no. 2 (2004): 1–54; and Noel B. Reynolds, ed., *Book of Mormon Authorship Revisited: The Evidence for Ancient Origins* (Provo: FARMS, 1997).

Figure 25 - Worlds of JS - Times and Seasons

**M2C was prominent.** The exhibit included a page from the *Times and Seasons*: the infamous "Zarahemla" article from Oct. 1, 1842.

Plus, they exhibited a page from John Lloyd Stephens'

*Incidents of Travel in Central America, Chiapas, and Yucatan.*

Needless to say, they did not display the issue of the *Times and Seasons* that contained Letter VII, or the page from Joseph's journal that contained Letter VII, or the *Messenger and Advocate* page that contained Letter VII, or the *Gospel Reflector* issue that contained Letter VII. The exhibitors had nothing at all about Cumorah. The term Cumorah doesn't even appear in the index of the proceedings.

The symposium portrayed to the world the Mesoamerican setting for the Book of Mormon that repudiates what the prophets have taught about the New York Cumorah.

The proceedings were published by *BYU Studies* 44:4 (2005). One of the presentations became the well-known article, "Archaeological Trends and Book of Mormon Origins" by John E. Clark. This article is also on the BOMC site here.

Figure 26 - Worlds of JS - BYU Studies

It was originally a **May 2004 BYU forum address**, then **a presentation at the May 2005 Worlds of Joseph Smith Symposium** at the Library of Congress, and finally **a presentation at the August 2005 FAIR Conference**. It is one of the best-known explanations of M2C and has been frequently cited by other M2C proponents.

The article is too long to reproduce in its entirety, so I'll comment on excerpts. Basically, Brother Clark makes an unchallenged case for the Mesoamerican theory of Book of Mormon geography that was presented to the world as the current consensus about the subject.

**Clark.** Any fair understanding of Joseph Smith must derive from a plausible explanation of the Book of Mormon, and both science and reason can and should be involved in the evaluation. Because the book makes claims about American prehistory, archaeology has long been implicated in assessments of the book's credentials as ancient history, and, by direct implication, of the veracity, sanity, or honesty of Joseph Smith. I revisit issues of archaeology and the Book of Mormon here in addressing the character of Joseph Smith. Archaeology shows that almost everyone involved in the running quarrel over Joseph and the book have misrepresented and misunderstood both.

[**Comment.** This is a thoughtful and useful statement of the issues, except for the presumptuous last sentence.]

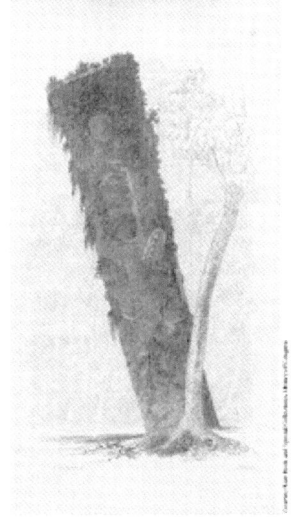

Figure 27 - Worlds of JS - Stephens

**Clark.** For Mormons, Joseph Smith is a prophet, seer, and revelator, and the Book of Mormon is the word of God. Detractors ridicule both as blasphemous frauds. There is no secure middle ground between positions, but there is one spectacular point of agreement. Champions on both sides see the Book of Mormon as the key to Joseph Smith's claim to be a prophet."

[**Comment.** This is an excellent framing of the fundamental issue about Joseph Smith. It parallels the debate among Mormons about the setting for the Book of Mormon, in which there is also no secure middle ground between positions; i.e., Cumorah was either in New York or in Mesoamerica. (There are a few proponents of the idea that Cumorah was in New York while most of the events took place in Mesoamerica, but it is difficult to reconcile those theories with the text.)

**Clark.** Critics see Joseph Smith as author of a romantic fiction, the Book of Mormon, and in doing so they distort both the man and the book beyond belief. They see the book as a logical product of its 1820s intellectual environment, combined with Joseph Smith's native intelligence and deceitful propensities.

[**Comment.** This is a good summary of the anti-Mormon position, but it is also a description of the premise for M2C. In the early 1830s, Parley P. Pratt faced this argument and invoked Central America as a partial answer; i.e., in 1829 Joseph did not know about the extravagant ruined cities in Central America, so the book could not be a product of his own knowledge. Benjamin Winchester and others made similar arguments, and modern LDS scholars have embraced these arguments as well. However, in my view these arguments have caused more problems than they've solved--and they weren't necessary in the first place.]

**Clark.** Most Mormons fall into a more subtle error that also inflates Joseph's talents; they confuse translation with authorship.

[**Comment.** Few if any Mormons confuse this. In fact, I've never met one who did, nor have I read any books, articles, or blogs that make this error. I think Brother Clark is building a straw man here.]

**Clark.** They presume that Joseph Smith knew the contents of the book as if he were its real author, and they accord him perfect knowledge of the text.

[**Comment.** One citation would be very helpful here, but I don't expect one because this is a straw man argument.]

**Clark.** This presumption removes from discussion the most compelling evidence of the book's authenticity—Joseph's unfamiliarity with its contents.

[**Comment.** [This is the "most compelling evidence?" Critics have long said Sydney Rigdon wrote the text by copying Solomon Spalding and inserting Christian sermons and ideas. Some claim that Joseph (and/or Oliver) copied it from Ethan Smith or someone else. To these critics, Joseph's unfamiliarity would be evidence that supports their theory; i.e., that he *didn't* translate it! More importantly, the text itself claims the most compelling evidence is the spiritual witness people receive when the read the book and pray about it. Beyond that, there is no evidence that Joseph was unfamiliar with its contents. He re-read it several times and twice made detailed changes for new editions. It's a strange argument that Joseph was unfamiliar with its contents when he changed punctuation, spelling, and even terminology.]

**Clark.** To put the matter clearly: Joseph Smith did not fully understand the Book of Mormon.

[**Comment.** In a sense, this is true—in an axiomatic way. How could anyone "fully understand" any text? Every reader brings his/her own background, knowledge, experience, etc. to a text; there is no such thing as an objective "full understanding" of a text. If Brother Clark is implying that scholars today "fully understand" the text, he is establishing an impossible standard.]

**Clark.** I propose that he transmitted to readers an ancient book that he neither imagined nor wrote.

[**Comment.** That's not a novel idea; that's what Joseph claimed and what every believer accepts. Clark probably means "composed" here, because Oliver Cowdery wrote it. Joseph dictated it.]

**Clark.** One thing all readers share with Joseph is a partial understanding of the book's complexities.

[**Comment.** One thing no reader shares with Joseph is the four-year tutorial from Moroni that Joseph summarized this way in the Wentworth letter: "I was also informed concerning the aboriginal inhabitants of this country and shown who they were, and from whence they came; a brief sketch of their origin, progress, civilization, laws, governments, of their righteousness and iniquity..." In addition,

Joseph's mother said he described the people as if he lived among them.]

**Clark.** Indeed, many things about the book were simply unknowable in 1830.

[**Comment.** Unknowable because Moroni was incapable of teaching them? Or unknowable because those who weren't tutored by Moroni had no way of knowing these things? I assume Brother Clark means the latter. Indeed, many things about the book are simply unknowable even today, but this includes things Moroni knew and apparently taught Joseph Smith.]

**Clark.** Over the last sixty years, Hugh Nibley, John Sorenson, and other scholars have shown the Book of Mormon to be "truer" than Joseph Smith or any of his contemporaries could know.[7]

[**Comment.** This elevation of scholarship over experience invites dispute. Joseph knew the book was true because Moroni told him about it, he translated it with divinely prepared instruments, he hauled around the ancient plates, and he accompanied others when they, too, saw the plates and the angel.

Brother Clark cites books by Nibley and Sorenson, neither of whom claimed actual experience comparable to Joseph's. Sorenson insists on a Mesoamerican setting, which is problematic in part because it contradicts the men who actually saw the plates and the angel. Brother Clark presumably means that Joseph didn't appreciate the indicia in the book of ancient origins, such as chiasmus. But chiasmus is a subject of as much debate as the origin of the Book itself, and those who "see" Mesoamerica in the text are bringing their own biases with them.]

**Clark.** Consequently, what Joseph Smith knew and understood about the book ought to be research questions rather than presumptions. Thanks in large part to his critics, it is becoming clear that Joseph Smith did not fully understand the geography, scope, historical scale, literary form, or cultural content of the book.

[**Comment.** The only way we can know what Joseph Smith understood is to look at what he said and did, but even if we had every word he ever *spoke*, we still wouldn't know what he *understood*. In Joseph explicitly said he *couldn't* relate everything he knew. (And even when he did explain what Moroni taught him, as in the Wentworth letter, we have modern scholars dismissing what he said.)

As we'll see, Brother Clark means that Joseph didn't agree with the Mesoamerican theory, so therefore Joseph didn't understand the text as well as the modern-day Mesoamerican scholars do. In a sense, I agree with him; Joseph didn't fully understand M2C, which to him and his peers was unthinkable.]

For the rest of my comments, see

http://www.1cumorah.com/2020/10/worlds-of-joseph-smith-conference.html

## Archaeology and Cumorah Questions

One of the primary sources that M2C proponents rely on to reject the New York Cumorah from an archaeological standpoint is an article by John E. Clark titled "Archaeology and Cumorah Questions,"

Figure 28 - Cumorah Questions cover

published by the *Journal of Book of Mormon Studies*, 13/1-2 (2004): 144-51, 174.

Brant Gardner cites it on p. 377 of his 2015 *Traditions of the Fathers*, introducing the second part of the quotation below with this: "Countering the force of traditional association is the archaeological data for the hill and the surrounding area. John E. Clark discusses the **reasons** that the New York hill **could not have been** the location of the final Nephite battle." (emphasis added)

In this article, Brother Clark reaches a definitive conclusion: "I am unaware of any archaeological investigation of the hill itself, but **sufficient information is available** for the surrounding regions **to make a critical assessment.** Mormon's hill and Moroni's hill are not one and the same... Archaeologically speaking, **it is a clean hill.** No artifacts, no walls, no trenches, no arrowheads. **The area immediately surrounding the hill is similarly clean.** Pre-Columbian people did not settle or build here. **This is not the place of Mormon's last stand.** We must look elsewhere for that hill."

Brother Gardner's deference to Clark's article appears typical among M2C advocates. "Archaeology and Cumorah Questions" is cited on the FairMormon page here. It is found on the BMAF page here.

When you read the article along with me you will see how much my interpretation varies from Brother Clark's. This is part of the process of recognizing multiple working hypotheses.

### Archaeology and Cumorah Questions by John E. Clark

**Clark.** If known truth were accepted, Joseph Smith's recovery of the golden plates from the Hill Cumorah would rank as one of the greatest archaeological finds of all time; coupled with the subsequent translation of this golden record into the Book of Mormon, there is nothing comparable in the annals of history.

[**Comment.** Very well said.]

**Clark.** The story of the coming forth of the Book of Mormon reveals a constant tension between the miraculous and the mundane— angels and inscribed golden plates on the one hand, and on the other the work of lifting and carrying heavy objects, periodically hiding the plates, and translating a portion of them character by character. Surely there must have been easier ways. If divine intervention were necessary, why not have an angel just hand young Joseph an English copy of the sacred text and be done with it? Why the drudgeries of exhumation, translation, and transcription, line for line? Was it necessary that Joseph deal with ancient artifacts and spend months with palpable relics dictating paragraphs to scribes? Apparently so.

[**Comment.** This is an excellent point. I've addressed this specific question elsewhere, but for now I suggest that Joseph Smith was an empiricist. He feared being deceived in spiritual things, as he expressed to Emma, which is why he needed the plates to know the history he was reading off the seer stone was real. (King Benjamin told his sons the same thing in Mosiah 1.) One lesson from this is the importance of evidence to enable and encourage faith. It's why the historicity of the Book of Mormon is such an important issue.]

**Clark.** We await answers for most questions evoked by this miracle of divinely supervised archaeological toil. What we do know is that Joseph Smith Jr. found the golden plates and other relics in a stone box in a hill near his home, a prominence now known as Cumorah. And as many believe, Cumorah was also the place of the final battles described in the Book of Mormon that destroyed the Nephites and, centuries earlier, the Jaredites. If any place merits archaeological attention, it is Cumorah. The very word elicits a series of empirical questions that can only be addressed through archaeology.

[**Comment.** I completely agree with all of this.]

**Clark.** Things are rarely as simple as labels make them appear. For the past 50 years, some scholars have suggested that common Latter-day Saint usage of *Cumorah* confuses two different places and that the modest hill where Joseph Smith recovered the plates is not the eminence of the genocidal battles.

[**Comment.** Fair enough; *some* scholars have suggested that. But it's a *direct contradiction* to what Oliver Cowdery said was a fact in Letter VII.]

**Clark.** Further, the Cumorah battlefield is seen by many scholars as the key for identifying the location of the ancient lands described in the book. Hence, much rests on its correct placement.

[**Comment.** That makes sense.]

**Clark.** All these observations lead to a paradox explored here: before archaeology can reveal Cumorah's secrets, it must first be employed to identify its location.

[**Comment.** It's only a paradox if we disregard what Oliver and Joseph and David Whitmer said. Each of them had personal encounters with Moroni, unlike any archaeologist. They gave us a specific pin in the map: the Book of Mormon Cumorah is in New York.]

**Clark.** The hill the plates came from is not at issue; the question is whether this final resting place is the same hill where the ending battles occurred.

[**Comment.** That's the specific question Oliver answered in Letters VII and VIII. This is not a new question; it arose early on, which is why Oliver answered it and why Joseph had it republished so often while he was alive.]

For the rest of my comments on this article, see

http://www.1cumorah.com/2020/10/archaeology-and-cumorah-questions.html

## In Search of Cumorah - David Palmer

I previously discussed Brother Palmer's book *In Search of Cumorah*. This is such a fundamental text for the M2C scholars that it is quoted with approval by both Sorenson in *Mormon's Codex* and Gardner in *Traditions of the Fathers*.

The citation cartel is oblivious to the following fun aspects of Palmer's book.

1. On p. 20 of the 1981 edition, Palmer writes "There is no record of Moroni having told Joseph Smith that the place where the abridgment was buried was Cumorah, or that the hill was once a great battleground. If this had been the place of those great battles, it would be rather surprising that it was not mentioned. We have only the scantiest of inferences that Joseph ever called the hill "Cumorah." (D&C 128:20). However, he does not appear to have corrected Oliver Cowdery, who may have been the one to first name the New York hill "Cumorah." (Cowdery, 1835)."

Every sentence here deserves attention.

First sentence: we have a record of Joseph referring to the hill as Cumorah even before he got the plates (in his mother's history). Who else but Moroni could have told him this? Then we have David Whitmer's recollection of hearing the name Cumorah in 1829 from a heavenly messenger (in the presence of Joseph and Oliver) before he even read the manuscript (and before Joseph and Oliver had even finished the translation). To the M2C citation cartel, though, these don't count as "records" because they contradict their thesis that the location of Cumorah was never revealed.

Second sentence: Brother Palmer has a good point that it would be surprising if the New York location was not mentioned; but since we have accounts that Moroni did mention it, what is actually surprising is that Palmer ignores the records of Joseph and 2 of the 3 witnesses knowing about Cumorah even before the text was published.

Third sentence: The canonized scriptures don't normally qualify as "scanty inferences." D&C 128:20 was written in the context of universal knowledge among Mormons of the day that the New York hill was Cumorah. Oliver's Letter VII made this as clear as possible. It was published in the *Messenger and Advocate* in 1835, in the *Gospel Reflector* in 1841, and in the *Times and Seasons* in 1841. No Mormon alive during Joseph's lifetime could have not known what he meant by Cumorah when he wrote this letter to the Church. There was such demand for Oliver's letters that they were republished in England as a separate pamphlet in 1844.

Fourth sentence: Joseph "does not appear to have corrected Oliver Cowdery." Why would he *correct* Oliver when he helped him write the letters that identified Cumorah in New York, and then had his scribes copy those letters into his own journal as part of his history? Far from correcting him, he embraced these letters!

---

In fairness, Palmer revised his book a little in later editions. In the 1999 edition (7th Printing, Feb. 2005), the first two sentences are the same, but the third and fourth are different: "The first record we have that identifies the hill in New York with the last Nephite and Jaredite battleground was written by Oliver Cowdery (referencing Letter VII in the *Messenger and Advocate*). In a revelation given seven years later there was a hint of a possible connection. "And again, what do we hear? Glad tidings from Cumorah! Moroni, an angel from heaven declaring the fulfillment of the prophets--the book to be revealed." (DC 128:20).

Obviously, this isn't much of an improvement. Palmer ignores the reprinting of Letter VII in the Times and Seasons and Gospel Reflector, and in Orson Pratt's pamphlet. He tells readers there was a 7-year gap between Letter VII and D&C 128:20, instead of the "gap" of a year and a half in the *Times and Seasons* itself, or six months if you count the Wentworth letter. Issues of the *Times and Seasons* and *Gospel Reflector* containing Letter VII were bound and on sale in Nauvoo right through the publication of D&C 128. D&C 128 is hardly a "hint of a possible connection." With the full historical context, there is no doubt that in D&C 128. Joseph was referring to the New York hill.

What I find amazing about this is that in 24 years, from the first edition in 1981 to the latest printing in 2005, no one pointed out this basic error to Brother Palmer. Either that, or he declined to correct it. Worse, as I'll show next, the M2C scholars *adopt* Palmer's approach!

---

Another fun part of this book is on pages 84-86 when he discussed Ritchie's book on New York archaeology. I'm guessing this is where John Clark got the idea to cite Ritchie. Like Clark after him, Palmer concludes Cumorah cannot be in New York because there were no large cities dating to Book of Mormon times near Cumorah. Of course, the text doesn't say the Nephites had large cities near Cumorah, so Ritchie's findings actually corroborate the Book of Mormon text. Apparently the Mesoamerican translation describes large Nephite cities near Cumorah though.

Another link between Palmer and Clark is on page 21. Palmer writes, "A 'two-Cumorah' theory is thus more appropriate, since records were hidden in both Mormon's Cumorah and Moroni's Cumorah. Therefore, it matters little whether it was Joseph Smith or one of his associates who called the hill in New York 'Cumorah.'"

John Clark, in the article I had fun with here, wrote "Mormon's hill and Moroni's hill are not one and the same."

Of course, both of these authors are misleading their readers with this false distinction between Mormon's hill and Moroni's hill. In Letter VII, Oliver Cowdery unequivocally declared that it was a *fact* that the final battles took place in the valley west of the Hill Cumorah in New York (Mormon's Cumorah)--the same hill from which Joseph retrieved the plates (Moroni's Cumorah).

M2C scholars are free to say Oliver Cowdery was mistaken (or deceived, or even dishonest, or whatever excuse they're giving lately); they are even free to misinform their readers about what he wrote. But when they do, I'll point it out here.

---

A third fun aspect of this book is its treatment of the book by McGavin and Bean titled *Book of Mormon Archaeology*. On p. 81, Brother Palmer writes, "McGavin and Bean presented significant amounts of data on antiquities of New York state in support of their position. From that I conclude that there must have indeed been some wars in western New York among the Indians. I will also grant that there might have been scores or even hundreds of drumlin hills with stoneworks that might have served as fortifications.

"What I am not prepared to accept is an age for those remains going back to Nephite times, much less Jaredite times. McGavin and Bean (1949) did not have the advantage of modern dating techniques when they published. Radiocarbon dating was just around the corner, but in its absence even the best of the archaeologists made gross errors in assigning dates to early American cultures. Today, we are in a much better position to evaluate the archaeological data from the state of New York. In doing so, we will first look at the archaeology of the eastern half of the United States, and then will examine the specifics of archaeology in New York to see whether there is consistency with the Book of Mormon model."

Palmer at least recognizes he's "not prepared to accept" data that conflicts with his preferred theory, yet he doesn't discuss a single one of the specific sites mentioned by McGavin and Bean. He cites not a single radiocarbon date from any of those sites. Instead, he generalizes from Ritchie's own generalizations.

McGavin and Bean quoted excerpts from several books by early explorers who personally witnessed the extensive ancient forts the Europeans found when they arrived in western New York. These were so well known, and so ancient (as shown by trees growing over them for hundreds of years), that critics contemporary with Joseph Smith claimed he merely used well-known Indian legends and common knowledge of antiquities in the area to write the Book of Mormon. (In fact, one of the motivations for looking at Mesoamerica was to respond to the early critics, some of whom said Joseph just related well-known legends and others who said the Indians were too savage to have ever lived the way the text described.)

If Palmer and other Mesoamerican advocates want to cite radiocarbon data to refute the New York Cumorah, they should at least be specific and relate the dating of the ancient fortifications identified by the French (the first Europeans to arrive there) and other explorers.

## Encyclopedia of Mormonism on geography

The M2C citation cartel often cites Brother John E. Clark. Brother Clark wrote the entry in the *Encyclopedia of Mormonism* titled "Book of Mormon Geography." I think he did an excellent job summarizing the official Church positions on this topic and setting out the cautions we should all keep in mind when we study the geography and historicity issues. However, he spends a lot of time on criteria that don't appear in the text, which is problematic.

I don't know how many people read the *Encyclopedia of Mormonism* any longer, but it's online and comes across as authoritative. I'd like to see it corrected and edited, so I offer my peer review here.

Here is the article, with emphasis added and my comments in brackets.

Book of Mormon Geography
See this page in the original 1992 publication.
Author: Clark, John E.

**Article:** Although the Book of Mormon is primarily a religious record of the Nephites, Lamanites, and Jaredites, enough geographic details are embedded in the narrative to allow reconstruction of at least a rudimentary geography of Book of Mormon lands. In the technical usage of the term "geography" (e.g., physical, economic, cultural, or political), no Book of Mormon geography has yet been written. **Most Latter-day Saints who write geographies** have in mind one or both of two activities: first, **internal reconstruction** of the relative size and configuration of Book of Mormon lands based upon textual statements and allusions; second, speculative attempts to match an internal geography to a location within North or South America.

[**Comments.** Many people do attempt an internal reconstruction, but they soon discover that no two people can independently come up with the same "internal geography." That's because the text does not give two basic requirements: distance and direction.

The effort to develop a consensus about any particular "internal geography" is a pointless academic exercise. At best, you might get a few people to agree on some assumptions.

Academics typically claim "expertise" and seek to impose their assumptions on others. When enough of them agree, they produce a consensus that, through the academic cycle, becomes the de facto standard within a generation or two.

In my view, the only possible way to develop a geography is to start with a known location--a pin in the map. I see no way to get around this.]

Three questions relating to Book of Mormon geography are discussed here: (1) How can one reconstruct a Book of Mormon geography? (2) What does a Book of Mormon geography look like? (3) What hypothetical locations have been suggested for Book of Mormon lands?

[For the rest of the article and my observations, see my article at http://www.1cumorah.com/2020/10/encyclopedia-of-mormonism-on-geography.html

## Mayan experts

Most archaeologists know little to nothing about the Book of Mormon, but there are a few Mayan experts who do. One is Dr. Michael Coe, who died at age 90 on September 25, 2019. He had known LDS archaeologists for decades and had strong opinions about the Book of Mormon.

An interview with Dr. Coe was posted on Facebook. It is evident that Dr. Coe still thought Joseph Smith wrote the anonymous articles in the 1842 *Times and Seasons* that linked the Book of Mormon to Mesoamerica. He had other misconceptions based on M2C.

Here is the link on Facebook:

https://www.facebook.com/mormonstories/videos/10156488092564301/

In my comments, I'm using only the initials of the people involved. As always, I emphasized that everyone involved with this topic is an awesome, nice, well-meaning person. People just have different biases they seek to confirm.

Some M2C intellectuals asked questions during the presentation. E.g., M.A. asked, "So Joseph read Stephen's widely read books (published 1841/2) while he was writing the BoM (1830)?"

And Z.S., who works for Book of Mormon Central America, wrote "Good question by Michael Ash."

If you watch the video, Dr. Coe **had never made such a claim**.

The M2C promoters stated it and Dr. Coe easily responded by explaining that after Joseph read these travel books, he identified the Mayan ruins as having been built by Book of Mormon people.

The historical evidence indicates that Joseph never had the time to read those books and never commented on them. The entire premise of M2C is a mistaken attribution of anonymous articles in the 1842 *Times and Seasons* to Joseph Smith. Dr. Coe takes that premise on its face and uses it to undermine faith.

Dr. Coe also points out that all ancient civilizations had roads.

Z.S. asked, "Did roads connect to marketplaces in the Maya world, as mentioned in the Book of Mormon?"

The question reflects M2C confirmation bias because the Book of Mormon mentions exactly one market (Helaman 7:10). Naturally, roads everywhere exist to connect places, and where there are people, there are products and services.

Dr. Coe points out that warfare, defensive structures, etc. are ubiquitous; every human civilization has them. "The Mayans were like everyone else. They had wars..."

The Book of Mormon says the people had wars, but so did every other human civilization. M2C believers seek and find such illusory correspondences. It is pure bias confirmation. But on the basis of these illusory correspondences, they want people to disbelieve the prophets and apostles about the New York Cumorah.

Coe pointed out that "One thing Joseph Smith didn't get was the Mayan inscriptions.... They're not in an old world language."

This is the compound fallacy of M2C regarding language. While the Book of Mormon describes the Nephites as literate, the larger group they joined (people of Zarahemla) were explicitly illiterate. And the even larger group of Lamanites were not only illiterate, but they sought to destroy the Nephite records, from beginning to end (Enos and Mormon both talk about this). Mormon had to conceal the Nephite records in the Hill Cumorah in New York specifically because the Lamanites would destroy them if they found them. And the only written languages mentioned in the text are Hebrew and Egyptian. The last place the Book of Mormon could have taken place is in the midst of a literate society with widespread writing and records that are neither Hebrew nor Egyptian.

This is why I think the last place the Nephites could have lived was in Mesoamerica, where Mayan writing exists everywhere, even after the Spanish destroyed so many records. This was a highly literate society, with careful historical records and stone monuments, all in Mayan language that is never mentioned or even alluded to in the Book of Mormon.

———

In the face of all the evidence about Mayan civilization, M2C intellectuals have resorted to the argument that the huge, sophisticated Nephite society was also a tiny, unnoticed minority of Hebrews embedded within Mayan culture. The Nephites happened to have kings and a system of judges who interacted with the illiterate Lamanite royalty, all without being impeded in the least by the Mayans. Instead, the M2C intellectuals claim the Nephites influenced the Mayans.

When asked about whether the Nephites could have lived apart from the Mayans somehow, Coe said, "These explanations are so involved..." He points out that the Mayans were fully literate and they lived throughout the area for thousands of years. None of their extensive literature has anything to do with the Book of Mormon. There are thousands of examples, with no indication of ancient Hebrew or Egyptian.

According to Coe, John Sorenson's writings are a fantasy, an insult to the people who made the inscriptions.

While I agree that M2C is an alternative working hypothesis, those who are not promoting M2C usually recognize that Coe's points about Mesoamerica and the Book of Mormon are sound, factual, and rational.

He notes many similarities between the civilizations of Southeast Asia and Mesoamerica that are difficult to explain. If you really want to look for overseas connections, look to Asia, not the Middle-East. (1:52:00). Dr. Coe says he couldn't even publish his findings about the links to Southeast Asia because he'd be ridiculed.

These connections have been published by others, though, and I think they deserve more attention.

Dr. Coe pointes out that different directions have different colors among Navajo. Also among Mayans and Asians. But not in the Bible. In East Asia, the full moon don't see the man in the moon, they see a rabbit, with a woman holding it. Also in Mesoamerica.

Central Asians migrated to Mesoamerica, according to DNA, language, culture, etc. They didn't go with empty minds.

The paradox of large Nephite civilizations against the absence of their influence.

> Z.S. · 1:16:39 So the National Geographic said, "Most people had been comfortable with population estimates of around 5 million," said Estrada-Belli, who directs a multi-disciplinary archaeological project at Holmul, Guatemala. "With this new data it's no longer unreasonable to think that there were 10 to 15 million people there—including many living in low-lying, swampy areas that many of us had thought uninhabitable."

This is the Tikal Area. The Book of Mormon goes up to 400AD.

This explains the M2C claim that there Book of Mormon describes large populations. However, in my view, **the larger the Mayan population, the less it fits the Book of Mormon.** Plus, the larger the claimed Nephite population, the more striking it is that none of the Book of Mormon appears in the extensive Mayan writings.

M.A. · 1:19:50 So Dr. Coe _admits_ that he hasn't followed the current LDS scholarship addressing BoM issues. No offense to Dr. Coe-- who is obviously a brilliant scholar on Mesoamerica, but if he isn't familiar with LDS scholarly arguments, he can't really address them.

M.A. · 1:20:54 Cara Amsden. Try earlier FARMS, Book of Mormon Central, the Interpreter. John Sorenson, & Mark Wright. Lots to read.

Look at how M.A. cites the M2C citation cartel. "Current LDS scholarship" consists of repudiating the LDS prophets and apostles, while trying to impose M2C on members of the Church by suppressing those teachings, all because the only "evidence" to support M2C consists of illusory correspondences and wishful thinking.

Z.A. · 1:25:24 Coe does not understand the LDS argument that the Nephites were a small, small group among the vast Maya. NOT the Maya themselves.

This is not an "LDS" argument; it's an M2C argument. If you watch the video, you see how Dr. Coe specifically addressed this M2C argument.

M.A. · 1:27:43 Are you seriously wanting me to write the equivalent of a multi-volume library that already addresses these issues? I'll pass.

This is the age-old argument that more volume = more substance. There is nothing in the M2C argument apart from these twin assumptions:

(i) The modern prophets and apostles are wrong about the New York Cumorah.

(ii) Evidence for the Book of Mormon consists of illusory correspondences; i.e., the common attributes of most human societies are present in both the Book of Mormon and Mayan culture, which means the Nephites were Mayans (or lived among the Mayans, depending on which version of M2C you follow).

Dr. Coe boils this M2C argument down to its essence: **The**

**Nephites were a bunch of "secret people" no one has heard of or found.**

> M.A. · 1:34:32 My point is that neither of these two men know the current LDS scholarship so they can't adequately address it. Perhaps Dr. Coe should read the writings of Brant Gardner & then formulate a response.

Dr. Coe points out that propositions should not only be provable, but also falsifiable. **How do you disprove something that is so small you can't see them or detect them. "It's a complete fantasy from beginning to end."**

Brother Gardner's work is voluminous and makes the case for M2C as well as anyone else, but it still boils down to the same twin M2C points:

(i) The prophets and apostles are wrong about the New York Cumorah.

(ii) Illusory correspondences between Mayan culture and the Book of Mormon (actually, Brother Gardner's view of how Joseph *should have translated the text*) are evidence to justify point #1.

> Z.S. · 1:37:31 Coe isn't aware that there are things we see, but just not to the extent that Dehlin has been phrasing things this whole interview. Would Coe be willing to sit down with another organization for an interview?

> T.B. · 1:37:35 We are dealing with the popular understanding of Mormons and their prophet leaders, not obscure apologetic responses about how it could still be shown.

Dr. Coe points out that "What is true is so much more interesting than what is fanciful. In science, we deal with things that can be verified or falsified."

This is an interesting point. The M2C intellectuals like to claim their work is scientific and peer-reviewed, but when you read it closely, it is really only peer-approved; the citation cartel never submits its work to people who disagree with M2C, whether members of the Church or not. That's why I ended up doing my own peer reviews for a while. http://interpreterpeerreviews.blogspot.com/2015/08/intro-why-peer-reviews.html

I invite anyone interested to do your own peer reviews of the M2C citation cartel. You'll quickly discover that if you don't accept the twin premises of M2C, their work doesn't hold up.

**J.D.: Mormon apologists are shrinking the target to something so small that we can't verify or falsify it.**

The problem with J.D.'s comment is he lumps all "Mormon apologists" into the same M2C camp.

Dr. Coe reiterated the M2C position about the *Times and Seasons* when he said **Smith himself said Zarahemla was in Guatemala, so why look elsewhere?**

The anonymous Times and Seasons articles have caused a tremendous amount of confusion and damage.
Next they talk about Cumorah.

2:29:54 It is page 12 of the CES letter but I got my people mixed up. It was John E. Clark. Nothing whatsoever has been found at this site. John E. Clark, director of BYU's archaeological organization, wrote in the *Journal of Book of Mormon Studies* 17:

> In accord with these general observations about New York and
> Pennsylvania, we come to our principal object – the Hill Cumorah.
> Archaeologically speaking, it is a clean hill. No artifacts, no walls, no
> trenches, no arrowheads. The area immediately surrounding the hill
> is similarly clean. Pre-Columbian people did not settle or build here.
> This is not the place of Mormon's last stand. We must look elsewhere for
> that hill.

This is the John Clark article we discussed in previous sections in this Appendix. It has been widely quoted and accepted, but no one has examined it critically because it fits the M2C narrative.

Then there was this comment about the hemispheric model.

R.S. · 2:29:30 Joseph was presented a travel book that described the great cities of Meso America and identifies them as proof of the great civilizations in the BoM. But also most every prophet and apostle since has described the BoM and the Lamanites covering all indigenous "from Barrow to Terra del Fuego".

It is most likely and evidence points that all prophets including Joseph had a hemispheric interpretation of the BoM. The text of the BoM points that direction as well. As does it discount the melding of the Nephites and Lamanites being subsumed into larger populations. I've read it over twenty times.

To me, and being tutelage by the Church educational system, I was taught that the Jaredites and Lehi came to an empty continent preserved for them.

This is an interesting point that reflects multiple common misperceptions.

First, many LDS have been taught that the entire Jaredite civilization was destroyed at Cumorah, but Moroni specifically limits his account to the people living "in this north country," meaning the area around Cumorah. Ether was writing about his own family line, but the Jaredites had spread throughout the continent.

Recent evidence indicates that the earliest Americans arrived by sea, not overland across Beringia, and then migrated north to Alaska and Canada as well as south. This is consistent with the Book of Mormon account of the Jaredites, aside from the dating issue, which we discussed briefly in this book. The DNA of the indigenous people in the Americas is consistent with this evidence.

There are indications in the text that Lehi's group encountered people when they arrived, but the text explicitly excludes "nations" such as the Mayans. They encountered hunter/gatherer groups, which is consistent with the archaeological record in the Southeastern U.S. Science contradicts M2C but supports the Moroni's America scenario.

Dr. Coe also points out that the Mayans never had large armies, but Aztecs had a force of 400,000, others 200,000. Maybe 700,000 men in Aztec army. 5,600,000 people slain in a battle. -26:00

I don't think the Nephites have very large armies. Mormon describes an army as "a great number of men, even to exceed the number of thirty thousand." The largest army Mormon ever enumerates was 50,000 (Lamanites) and 42,000 (his Nephite army). (I know, some say Mormon had 230,000 men at Cumorah, but I think that's a misreading of the text.)

In this sense, one could say that, if Dr. Coe is correct, the Nephites fit the Mayan model because they both had small armies. But ironically, the M2C intellectuals are trying to say a much more numerous Mayan civilization is a better fit for the Book of Mormon than the actual numbers Mormon gave us.

J.D.: "What millions of Mormons are trying to figure out is whether their Church has told them the truth."

On this point, J.D. understandably but incorrectly conflates M2C intellectuals with the Church. Church leaders have consistently taught two things about the Book of Mormon historicity/geography:

1. The Hill Cumorah is in New York.
2. We don't know where the other events took place.

M2C intellectuals have generated confusion by conflating those two clear points, replacing them with these:

1. The prophets and apostles were wrong about the New York

Cumorah.

2. We know the Book of Mormon took place in Mesoamerica.

The rejection of the prophets by the M2C intellectuals has led millions of believers in the Book of Mormon confused and disturbed in their faith—exactly as Joseph Fielding Smith warned when he tried to prevent M2C from taking over.

**Members of the Church who trust the prophets have no problem. But those who trust the M2C intellectuals definitely have a problem.**

Dr. Coe: "If it's [faith in the Gospel] resting on the Book of Mormon, it's not resting on a firm foundation."

Paraphrasing: If you believe the Mormon religion gives you a set of values that are good, don't leave it. But if it depends on the truthfulness of the Book of Mormon, it's a bad foundation. Stay Mormon if it makes you happy and gives you a better life and for your children and grandchildren. But don't use it to tell scientists that they're wrong.

**This is the inevitable outcome of M2C. It leaves people such as Dr. Coe with a false interpretation of the Book of Mormon that doesn't line up with archaeology, anthropology, geology, etc.**

———

## Cumorah artifacts

The *Journal of Book of Mormon Studies* published an article titled "Looking for Artifacts at New York's Hill Cumorah" in 2005. Here's the abstract:

> Landon Smith gives an account of artifact hunting in the fields surrounding Hill Cumorah, near Palmyra, New York. He presents evidence that the archaeology of New York does not support the idea that Book of Mormon peoples lived in that region or that New York's Hill

Cumorah was the scene of the final battles between the Nephites and the Lamanites.

The article is mainly a letter written to a BYU professor, an M2C proponent, by a guy who went artifact hunting around the New York Cumorah. He assumed that hundreds of thousands of people died at Cumorah. He was apparently unfamiliar with Letter VII, so he spent a lot of time looking east and north of the hill.

The hunter wrote,

> Wherever early American sites are, collectors will find them, plowed fields being the best place to look. Having been to the Hill Cumorah Pageant at other times, I knew that there were plowed fields nearby. Since I had the experience of searching and finding sites, my interest in finding sites of possible Nephite/Lamanite arrowheads was high. There were also stories of how Brother Willard Bean found arrowheads by the basketful around the hill and sold them to tourists. If battles took place at the hill, and a lot of people took part—everything sounds about right—the area should be covered with all kinds of artifacts.

Willard Bean lived in Palmyra a hundred years ago. The fields were intensively plowed before and after. Eventually you plow up whatever is below the ground to a certain depth.

There are fields in Palmyra that are devoid of rocks, yet there are rock walls everywhere. How did this happen? Farmers plow up rocks and move them. Eventually, you get fields with no rocks in them.

Bean and others collected arrowheads. Barrels full, reportedly. The Bean children skipped them in ponds. Farmers knew they could get rid of them that way. It's the same way farmers in Israel export stones from their fields throughout the world for free. They take the stones to the valley of Elah and tourists do the rest.

This is another case of assumptions producing conclusions. We could go down the list. Bias confirmation, cognitive dissonance, straw man fallacy, etc.

If you assume that hundreds of thousands of people were killed at Cumorah—or millions if you believe the *BYU Studies* chart—then you would expect there were once hundreds of thousands—or millions—of weapons left behind.

Your expectations will not be satisfied, not because there is "no evidence" of what actually happened, but because there is no evidence that matches your unrealistic expectations.

This is an example of how M2C lenses blind you to what would be obvious if you just took them off for a moment. I reviewed the article at

http://www.1cumorah.com/2020/10/cumorah-artifacts.html.

## Why Central America?

A fundamental question to ask is, why look at Central America (Mesoamerica) in the first place?

Everyone who has read the Book of Mormon knows it never mentions volcanoes, jungles, pyramids, or even buildings made of stone. No mention of jade, jaguars, tapirs. **There is literally nothing in the text that relates to Central America in any way** (beyond generic mention of mountains, rivers, and rain, which describe pretty much everywhere on the planet). This is why including depictions of Mesoamerica in the missionary editions is so problematic; they raise expectations that the text does not meet.

So why look at Central America?

I've asked M2C proponents. Here are typical answers.

**1. Because Joseph Smith said Zarahemla was in Guatemala.** This claim refers to the anonymous articles in the 1842 *Times and Seasons.* For all the reasons I've discussed elsewhere, it is well established that Joseph didn't write or edit those articles. Not even John Taylor or Wilford Woodruff thought he did. The long-held belief that he wrote those articles is a historical mistake, evident now thanks to the Joseph Smith Papers. Beyond that, though, LDS scholars and educators reject what Joseph and Oliver said about the Hill Cumorah being in New York, so why would they care what Joseph said about *anything* related to geography? They don't, really. They just use the *Times and*

*Seasons* articles to claim Joseph thought (mind-reading) that these were intellectual questions to be answered by scholars. Convenient for their job security.

**2. Because early Church members wrote about Central America.** It's true that W.W. Phelps, the Pratt brothers, William Smith, John E. Page, Benjamin Winchester, and others wrote about Central America. But it's also true that Joseph Smith and Oliver Cowdery did not. In fact, in the Wentworth letter, Joseph edited out Orson Pratt's hemispheric model to specify that the Lamanites are the Indians that live in this country (the U.S.). Early Church authors had two objectives. First, discoveries of exotic ruins discovered in Central America excited the public and these authors thought linking the ruins to the Book of Mormon would attract readers (and converts). Second, they sought to counter anti-Mormon arguments that Joseph had copied (or used) the work of other authors to create the Book of Mormon. These other authors were incorporating aspects of the Moundbuilder legends, and critics saw many similarities between these legends and the Book of Mormon. Today, we realize the text has important differences from those legends. Plus, we realize we would expect legends to reflect Book of Mormon history if the events took place in North America.

**3. Because there are correspondences between Mayans and Book of Mormon people.** LDS scholars and educators have compiled lists of what they call "correspondences" between their interpretations of the Book of Mormon text and features of ancient Mayan civilization. These correspondences require two elements: first, the assumption that Joseph mistranslated the text (e.g., by dictating *horses* instead of *tapirs*) and second, the assumption that these features are unique to the two cultures. However, these correspondences are features common in many human cultures. We could find similar correspondences between many ancient civilizations and the text.

**4. Because the text describes an isthmus, which is only found in Central America.** The M2C proponents assume three terms in the text are referring to the same geographical feature, and that it's an isthmus: small neck of land, narrow neck, and narrow neck of land. The also assume that the phrase "nearly surrounded by water" can only mean "nearly surrounded by seas." While those assumptions are not irrational, they are not required. There is an alternative assumption that disqualifies Central America; i.e., the assumption that different terms refer to different features.

**5. Because the text doesn't describe North America.** I showed in *Moroni's America* that the text describes North America quite well, once you assume different terms refer to different features.

**6. Because Cumorah cannot be in New York.** This has become perhaps the most fundamental reason for claiming Cumorah is in Mexico. The conclusion is based primarily on the work of two LDS authors: David A. Palmer and John Clark. Their work has never been carefully evaluated before because it confirmed the biases of M2C proponents. Contrary to their conclusions, the hill in New York matches the description in the text. At a minimum, the New York Cumorah should be considered one of multiple working hypotheses.

---

If anyone knows of another reason to look in Central America, I'd like to know about it.

## The *Times and Seasons* articles

I'm still hearing, occasionally, that the *Times and Seasons* articles don't matter to Book of Mormon archaeology because the archaeology in Mesoamerica supports the Book of Mormon.

First, there can be no doubt that Mesoamerican proponents looked to Mesoamerica because of those articles. For example, an article titled "Archaeology, Relics, and Book of Mormon Belief" from the Journal of Book of Mormon Studies is available on most of the M2C websites. You can download it here:
https://scholarsarchive.byu.edu/jbms/vol14/iss2/6/

Excerpt:

**Article**. An argument against the hemispheric model was provided by Joseph Smith. The year 1842 in Nauvoo had been hectic as the Prophet moved the work along on the Book of Abraham and the temple, all the while dodging false arrest. He even assumed editorial responsibility for the *Times and Seasons*, the Nauvoo newspaper.

[Comment. At first, I thought he was going to cite the Wentworth letter, which expressly repudiated the hemispheric model—including Mesoamerica. Instead, he references the anonymous Mesoamerican articles.]

**Article:** Months earlier he received a copy of the recent best-seller by John Lloyd Stephens, *Incidents of Travel in Central America, Chiapas, and Yucatan*, the first popular English book to describe and illustrate Maya ruins.

[**Comment.** Wilford Woodruff brought the two volumes to Nauvoo as a gift to Joseph from John Bernhisel. During the journey, Woodruff read the books and wrote about them in his journal.]

**Article:** This book amazed the English-speaking world with evidence of an advanced civilization that no one imagined existed—no one, that is, except Latter-day Saints. The Prophet was thrilled, and excerpts from the book were reprinted in the *Times and Seasons* with unsigned commentary, **presumably** his.

[**Comment.** Two problems here.

1. The only evidence Joseph was "thrilled" was a short paragraph in a thank-you note he didn't write or even sign. I've provided considerable evidence that Woodruff drafted the short paragraph, that someone else drafted the second paragraph (dealing with land sales), and that John Taylor hand-wrote the letter. There is no evidence Joseph dictated or even knew about its contents.

2. "Presumably" is an assumption, but there is no evidence that the unsigned commentary was Joseph's and plenty of evidence that it was not. I've written three detailed books about the topic with lots of

references anyone can see for themselves. *The Lost City of Zarahemla, Brought to Light,* and *The Editors: Joseph, Don Carlos, and William Smith.* Critics focus on dubious "stylometry" but they don't share their methodology, assumptions, or even their reference database.]

**Article: What Joseph recorded** is significant for the issues at hand: Since our "Extract" [from Stephens's book] was published . . . we have found another important fact relating to the truth of the Book of Mormon. Central America . . . is situated north of the Isthmus of Darien and once embraced several hundred miles of territory from north to south. The city of Zarahemla . . . stood upon this land. . . . It will not be a bad plan to compare Mr. Stephens' ruined cities with those in the Book of Mormon.[12]
**As is evident in his comments, Joseph Smith believed** Maya archaeology vindicated the Book of Mormon.

[**Comment.** Here the article shifts from "presumably" to stating as a fact that Joseph wrote the article. Then it reads his mind to determine what Joseph believed.

The article misleads readers by using ellipses to omit the claim that Zarahemla is at Quirigua, a site that does not fit the text. Not even M2C proponents accept that site.

Plus, what "important fact" was "found" between September 15 and October 1, 1842? This *Times and Seasons* article is so ridiculous it's difficult to understand why anyone would want to attribute it to Joseph in the first place, but after stylometry data proved Joseph didn't write it, and historical research points to Benjamin Winchester and William Smith as the authors, no one should be perpetuating this claim.]

**Article:** His [Joseph's purported] placement of Zarahemla in eastern Guatemala implied that the Land Southward described in the Book of Mormon was north of Darien, as Panama was then called; thus his commentary presupposed a smallish geography that excluded South America. The Prophet regarded the location of Book of Mormon lands as an open question, and one subject to archaeological confirmation. In the past 50 years, friends and foes have adopted Joseph's "plan" of comparing "ruined cities with those in the Book of Mormon." Both sides believe archaeology is on their side.

[**Comment.** By attributing anonymous articles to Joseph Smith and then reading his mind, scholars can confirm their biases—especially their bias that these questions can only be answered by credentialed scholars. These *Times and Seasons* articles say nothing about Cumorah anyway. Scholars use these articles as a stepping stone to their M2C theory that justifies them in rejecting what the prophets have taught.

## FairMormon Answers

FairMormon is an excellent source for answers to commonly raised questions. However, the editors have a strong pro-M2C bias that taints much of their content.

I've commented on several of the pro-M2C arguments made by FairMormon. I am not saying that FairMormon could make better arguments. I think they are making the best arguments possible to defend M2C. Their problem is trying to defend and promote the idea that the prophets are wrong.

People should be aware, when they go to fairmormon.org, that they are reading a point of view that has evolved (or devolved) to the point of misinformation. They use a variety of persuasion techniques, including selective censorship and logical fallacies, that cause readers to "think past the sale."

With that background, consider the FairMormon entry on the Hill Cumorah.
https://www.fairmormon.org/answers/Book_of_Mormon/Geography/New_World/Hill_Cumorah
It is a response to this question:

> If Mormon chapter 6 is a literal description of the destruction of the Nephites by the Lamanites — approximately 100 thousand were killed by swords and axes — why hasn't any evidence of the battle been found at the site that was traditionally identified as the hill Cumorah in western New York state?

FairMormon and anti-Mormons both claim the New York setting is impossible because there is no evidence that hundreds of thousands--or millions--of men were killed there in a great battle. One of many examples is John Clark's piece, published by the Maxwell Institute here.

And yet, there is no question that the early members of the Church believed the New York Hill Cumorah was the same as the Book of Mormon Hill Cumorah; i.e., the site of the final battles.

FairMormon and Anti-Mormons share these three premises:

1. Jaredites and Nephites died in the hundreds of thousands or millions at Cumorah;
2. There is no archaeological evidence of such massive battles in New York;
3. The early LDS believed the New York Cumorah was the Book of Mormon Cumorah.

Notice the difference:
- Anti-Mormons accept these three premises on their face and conclude the Book of Mormon is false.
- FairMormon accepts these three premises on their face and conclude the early LDS were wrong.

Instead, M2C proponents claim the Book of Mormon Cumorah is in Mesoamerica; i.e., they promote a "two Cumorah" theory.

This is where the Orwellian rhetoric comes in. Obviously, for M2C believers, the early LDS beliefs are troubling. Oliver Cowdery wrote an essay on Church history containing a detailed description of New York Cumorah and the final battles taking place there. His essay was published as a letter multiple times during Joseph Smith's lifetime, and Oliver claimed Joseph helped him write the letter.

D&C 128 expressly identifies the hill near Palmyra as Cumorah.

Joseph Fielding Smith expressly rejected the two Cumorah theory. How do the Mesoamericans justify their two Cumorah theory?

They write articles that cast doubt on the early LDS view.

For example, Joseph Fielding Smith wrote an article available here, that is six pages long.

Instead of giving a link to Pres. Smith's analysis, FairMormon merely cites a critical "review" that itself casts doubt on Pres. Smith's conclusion. Readers have to search for themselves to find what Smith actually wrote.

You can read my detailed observations on
http://www.1cumorah.com/

## Joseph's final word on Book of Mormon geography

Joseph Smith didn't say much about Book of Mormon geography, but he said enough to make it clear and simple.

He wrote the letter to Emma, describing Ohio, Indiana and Illinois as the "plains of the Nephites" and the bones in the mounds as evidence of the divine authenticity of the Book of Mormon.

He helped Oliver Cowdery write the essays on Church history, including Letter VII.

Letter VII was explicit and unambiguous: the New York hill where Joseph obtained the plates was the hill Cumorah in the Book of Mormon. The mile-wide valley to the west of the hill was the location of the final battles of the Nephites and Jaredites took place. No one who reads Letter VII can be mistaken about this. There is no room for confusion about this point.

Joseph had Letter VII copied into his own history where everyone can read it, thanks to the Joseph Smith Papers.[129]

In late 1840 or early 1841, Joseph gave Benjamin Winchester express permission to republish Oliver's letters in the *Gospel Reflector*.[130] This was

---

[129] https://www.josephsmithpapers.org/paper-summary/history-1834-1836/83

[130] Benjamin Winchester is a long-forgotten character who was a close friend of Joseph Smith and played important roles in Church history. I extradited him from the past in my books, especially Lost City of Zarahemla. He published the Gospel Reflector as a Mormon newspaper in Philadelphia in 1841 before moving to Nauvoo to work at the *Times and Seasons*. There is a complete facsimile here: https://archive.org/details/gospelreflectori00winc/page/164/mode/2up?q=Cumorah.

significant because by then, Oliver had left the Church.

Joseph gave the essays, including Letter VII, to his brother Don Carlos to republish in the 1841 *Times and Seasons* in Nauvoo.[131]

In 1842, Joseph wrote a letter to the Saints (now D&C 128), published in the *Times and Seasons*, that built on Letter VII by referring to Cumorah.

In 1844, these letters were so popular in England (where they had been republished in the *Millennial Star*) that a special pamphlet containing these letters was published.

Joseph's brother William, as publisher of the Mormon newspaper in New York titled *The Prophet*, republished again, this time for the New York market. Sadly, and maybe ironically, Letter VII was published on June 29, 1844—two days after the martyrdom.[132]

I consider Letter VII as Joseph's final word on Cumorah because it was clear, definitive, unambiguous, and published by the Assistant President of the Church.

Why would Joseph have to say anything more on the topic?

---

[131] Some historians apparently overlooked this because Don Carlos titled the essays "Rise of the Church" instead of identifying them as Oliver's letters. He also edited the beginning of Letter VII and omitted the term "Letter VII." A facsimile of the issue is on page 378 at this link. http://www.latterdaytruth.org/pdf/100147.pdf

[132] A facsimile of the issue of *The Prophet* is on page 26 at this link. https://archive.org/details/TheProphet18441845/page/n25/mode/2up

# Appendix 7 - Bibliography

## Web pages

Thousands of web pages discuss the Book of Mormon. The ones on this list are grouped according to their editorial position on the Hill Cumorah.

**Reference pages.** These pages provide information and data without overtly advocating one position about Cumorah.

https://archive.org/ The Internet archive that contains a library of millions of free books and other material.

https://www.churchofjesuschrist.org/?lang=eng Main page of the Church of Jesus Christ of Latter-day Saints.

https://catalog.churchofjesuschrist.org/ The Church History catalog. It includes the Wilford Woodruff Journals.

https://www.josephsmithpapers.org/ The best source for finding anything related to Joseph Smith. The editors have an M2C bias you will see in their annotations, but they don't censor original documents.

http://www.latterdaytruth.org/ provides references to Mormon-related historical publications without editorial comments.

https://www.mobom.org/ The Museum of the Book of Mormon is a new way to understand and share the Book of Mormon with the entire world. It presents information about the origins, teachings, and evidence of the Book of Mormon from multiple perspectives, with links to most of the other web pages on this list. I help curate it so I make sure it presents Cumorah accurately, but I also make sure it recognizes other ideas, including M2C and critical perspectives.

https://scripturenotes.com/ scripture study tool.

https://thechurchofjesuschrist.org/ one of several Restoration churches that accept the Book of Mormon. Offers an app integrating the KJV Bible with the 1830 Book of Mormon.

**New York Cumorah advocacy.** These web pages focus on prophetic and scriptural teachings and advocate the New York Cumorah.

http://ldsarchaeology.com/ discusses the archaeology of North America and how it relates to the Book of Mormon.

https://bookofmormonevidence.org/ offers videos, podcasts, and article about the North American setting.

https://bookofmormonanswers.com has answers to nearly 400 common questions about the Book of Mormon.

https://josephsmithfoundation.org/ focuses on traditional interpretations of Church history, including the New York Cumorah.

https://www.josephknew.com/ discusses the Book of Mormon in America's heartland.

http://moronisamerica.com/ collects my blogs and adds additional information, including maps.

**M2C advocacy.** These web pages focus on intellectual approaches, and advocate M2C exclusively.

https://bookofmormon.online/home presents facsimiles of every edition of the Book of Mormon, as well as maps, timelines, and other helpful information. It originally was an awesome, factual resource, but unfortunately, it was acquired by Book of Mormon Central and now promotes M2C.

http://bmaf.org/ Book of Mormon Archaeological Forum is the corporate owner of Book of Mormon Central. The site archives articles and other information to promote M2C.

https://bookofmormoncentral.org/ Book of Mormon Central spends millions of dollars on its web page and internet outreach, but it promotes M2C exclusively. It provides useful resources, but its editorial advocacy of M2C is a disservice to unsuspecting users.

https://www.fairmormon.org/ provides faithful answers to criticisms of the Church of Jesus Christ of Latter-day Saints, but only within the parameters of M2C.

https://interpreterfoundation.org/ The Interpreter Foundation focuses on LDS scriptures, history, and related subjects, with a strong editorial stance in favor of M2C and an intellectual approach.

https://latterdaysaintmag.com/ Meridian Magazine has a strong editorial position to promote M2C in conjunction with Book of Mormon Central.

https://byustudies.byu.edu/ BYU Studies has promoted M2C for decades, rejects alternative perspectives, and still promotes M2C maps on its website.

https://bom.byu.edu/ BYU's Virtual Book of Mormon that teaches M2C.

https://scriptureplus.org/ App that promotes M2C with attractive graphics, videos, and other features

**Critical sites.** These web pages focus on intellectual approaches, advocate against the Book of Mormon, and oppose alternative viewpoints.

https://cesletter.org/ focuses on the author's "search for answers to my Mormon Doubts," many of which arise from the author's own assumptions and inferences.

https://www.mormonstories.org/ conducts podcast interviews focusing on "post-Mormons and progressive Mormons."

http://www.mormonthink.com/ claims to be "neither an anti-Mormon website nor an LDS apologist website" but features and focuses on critical perspectives.

**Scientific resources.** These web pages are unrelated to the Book of Mormon. They provide useful scientific context.

https://www.nps.gov/hocu/index.htm National Park Service page on Hopewell Culture.

https://ilarchsurv.org/ Illinois archaeology.

https://www.in.gov/dnr/historic/2827.htm Indiana archaeology.
http://www.maya-archaeology.org/ Mayan archaeology.
https://nysarchaeology.org/ New York archaeology.
https://www.ohiohistory.org/ Ohio archaeology.
http://www.tn4me.org/era.cfm/era_id/2 Tennessee archaeology.

**My blogs.** These are my blogs on these topics. You can subscribe to get email whenever I post something new.

http://www.lettervii.com/ focuses on Cumorah in the context of Church history.

http://bookofmormonconsensus.blogspot.com/ focuses on the psychology involved with seeking consensus and harmony.

http://www.bookofmormoncentralamerica.com/ focuses on M2C and its implications.

https://howtozion.blogspot.com/ focuses on the larger picture of how to establish Zion.

http://www.1cumorah.com/ focuses on debates about Cumorah.

## Books

Allen, Joseph L., *Exploring the Lands of the Book of Mormon* (SA Publishers, Orem, UT 1989).

Alrutz, Robert W., *Newark Holy Stones: The History of an Archaeological Tragedy*, (The Johnson-Humrickhouse Museum, Coshocton, OH 2010).

Anderson, Richard Lloyd, *Investigating the Book of Mormon Witnesses* (Deseret Book Company, Salt Lake City, UT 1981).

Barney, Ronald O., *Joseph Smith: History, Methods & Memory*, University of Utah Press, Salt Lake City, UT 2020).

Bean, Willard W., *Willard's Cumorah Land*, Edited by Wayne M. May and Vicki Bean Topliff (Ancient American Archaeology, Colfax, WI 2012).

Bean, Willard, & McGavin, Cecil, *Book of Mormon Geography: In Search of Ramah-Cumorah* (Bookcraft, Salt Lake City, UT 1948).

Book of Mormon (Religion 121-122) *Student Manual* (The Church of Jesus Christ of Latter-day Saints, Salt Lake City, UT 1979).

Book of Mormon Onomasticon, The Laura F. Willes Center for Book of Mormon Studies. Online at https://onoma.lib.byu.edu/index.php/Main_Page

Bradley, Don, *The Lost 116 Pages: Reconstructing the Book of Mormon's Missing Stories* (Greg Kofford Books, Salt Lake City, UT 2019).

*Newark "Holy Stones": Context for Controversy*, Public Symposium, (Johnson-Humrickhouse Museum, Coshocton, Ohio, 1999).

Brown, David B., *A Messiah Among the Maya: A Case for Christianity in Pre-Columbian America* (DJ Brown Publishing, Buckner, MO 2019).

Brown, Matthew B., *The Plates of Gold: The Book of Mormon Comes Forth*, Covenant Communications, American Fork, UT 2003).

Brockenshire, Norman, *The Lost Mounds of Western New York: The relationship between the Indian Burial Mounds in Western NY & the Book of Mormon* (N.D.B. Publishing, Batavia, NY 2006).

Bushman, Claudia, *America Discovers Columbus: How an Italian Explorer Became an American Hero* (University Press of New England, Hanover, NH, 1992).

Bushman, Richard Lyman, *Joseph Smith: Rough Stone Rolling,* (Knopf, New York, NY, 2005).

Connolly, Robert P. and Lepper, Bradley T. (Eds), *The Fort Ancient Earthworks* (Ohio Historical Society, Columbus, OH 2004).

Coughanour, Kelli, *The Book of Mormon for Young Readers* (Liberty Press, Springville, UT 2015).

Cook, Lyndon W. Ed., *David Whitmer Interviews: A Restoration Witness* (Grandin Book Company, Orem, UT 1991).

De Bono, Edward, *Six Thinking Hats* (Back Bay Books, New York, NY, 1999).

Dewhurst, Richard J., *The Ancient Giants Who Ruled America: The Missing Skeletons and the Great Smithsonian Cover-Up* (Bear & Company, Rochester, VT 2014).

Diamond, Jared, *Guns, Germs and Steel: The Fates of Human Societies*, W.W. Norton & Company, New York, NY, 1999).

Diamond, Jared, *Collapse: How Societies Choose to Fail or Succeed*, (Penguin Books, London, UK, 2005).

Dixon, Riley L., *Just One Cumorah* (Bookcraft, Inc., Salt Lake City, UT 1958)

Dragoo, Don W., *Mounds for the Dead* (Annals of Carnegie Museum, Pittsburgh, PA 1963).

*Whitmer Farm Historic Site Guide* (The Church of Jesus Christ of Latter-day Saints, Salt Lake City, UT 2015).

*Guide to Exhibits at the Joseph Smith Historic Farm Site* (The Church of Jesus Christ of Latter-day Saints, Salt Lake City, UT 2004).

*Guide to Exhibits at the Book of Mormon Historic Publication Site* (The Church of Jesus Christ of Latter-day Saints, Salt Lake City, UT 2007)

Ferguson, Thomas Stuart and Warren, Bruce W., *The Messiah in Ancient America* (Book of Mormon Research Foundation, Provo, Utah, 1987).

Givens, Terryl L., *By the Hand of Mormon: The American Scripture that Launched a New World Religion* (Oxford Univ. Press, NY, NY 2002).

Gardner, Brant A., *Traditions of the Fathers: The Book of Mormon as History* (Greg Kofford Books, Salt Lake City, UT 2015).

Hills, L.D., *Geography of Mexico and Central America from 2234 B.C. to 421 A.D.* (Independence, MO 1917).

Hammond, Fletcher B., *Geography of the Book of Mormon* (Utah Printing Company, Salt Lake City, UT 1959).

Hocking, David, *Annotated Edition of the Book of Mormon* (Digital Legend Press, Salt Lake City, UT 2018).

Hunter, Milton R., *Christ in Ancient America: Archaeology and the Book of Mormon,* Vol. II (Deseret Book Company, Salt Lake City, UT 1960).

Kahneman, Daniel, *Thinking, Fast and Slow*, Farrar, Straus and Giroux, New York, NY 2011).

Kehoe, Alice Beck, *America: Before the European Invasions*, (Longman, London, UK, 2002).

Kennedy, Roger G., *Hidden Cities: The Discovery and Loss of Ancient North American Civilization* (The Free Press, New York, NY 1994).

Largey, Dennis L., *Book of Mormon Reference Companion* (Deseret Book,

Salt Lake City, UT 2003).

Larson, Stan, and Passey, Samuel J. (Eds), The William E. McLellin Papers: 1854-1880, (Signature Books, Salt Lake City, UT 2007).

Little, Gregory L., *The Illustrated Encyclopedia of Native American Mounds & Earthworks* (Eagle Wing Books, Inc. Memphis, TN 2009).

Lund, John L., *Joseph Smith and the Geography of the Book of Mormon* (The Communications Company, Salt Lake City, UT 2012).

Mackay, Michael Hubbard and Frederick, Nicholas J., *Joseph Smith's Seer Stones* (Deseret Book, Salt Lake City, UT, 2016).

Mackay, Michael Hubbard, et al. (editors) *Producing Ancient Scripture: Joseph Smith's Translation Projects in the Development of Mormon Christianity*, (The University of Utah Press, Salt Lake City, UT 2020).

Mann, Charles C., *1491: New Revelations of the Americas before Columbus* (Alfred A. Knopf, New York, NY 2005).

May, Wayne (publisher), *Ancient American* (periodical)

May, Wayne, *THIS LAND: Only One Cumorah* (AAAF, 2006).

May, Wayne, *THIS LAND: They Came from the East* (AAAF, 2005).

Meldrum, Rod, *Exploring the Book of Mormon in America's Heartland*, (Digital Legend Press, Salt Lake City, UT 2011).

Miner, Alan C., *Step By Step Through the Book of Mormon*, online at https://stepbystep.alancminer.com/

Nibley, Hugh, *Lehi in the Desert and The World of the Jaredites* (Bookcraft Publishing Co., Salt Lake City, UT, 1952).

Nibley, Hugh, *Since Cumorah* (Deseret Book Company, Salt Lake City, UT, 1973).

Neville, Jonathan E., *Moroni's America* (Digital Legend Press, Salt Lake City, UT, 2017)

Neville, Jonathan E., *Letter VII* (Digital Legend Press, Salt Lake City, UT, 2016)

Neville, Jonathan E., *Whatever Happened to the Golden Plates?* (Digital Legend Press, Salt Lake City, UT, 2017)

Newell, Linda King, and Avery, Valeen Tippets, *Mormon Enigma: Emma Hale Smith* (2d Ed)., Univ. of Illinois Press, Champaign, IL 1994).

*New Perspectives on the Origins of Americanist Archaeology*, David L.

Browman & Stephen Williams (Eds) (University of Alabama Press, Tuscaloosa, AL, 2002).

Packer, Cameron J., "A Study of the Hill Cumorah: A Significant Latter-day Saint Landmark in Western New York," (Thesis) Religious Education, Brigham Young University, December 2002

Priest, Josiah, *American Antiquities: Discoveries in the West* (4th Ed.) (Hoffman & White, Albany, NY, 1834).

Parry, Jay A., *Treasured Testament: The Miraculous Coming Forth of the Book of Mormon*, Covenant Communications, American Fork, UT, 2019).

Quinn, D. Michael, *Early Mormonism and the Magic World View: Revised and Enlarged* (Signature Books, Salt Lake City, UT 1998).

Palmer, David A., *In Search of Cumorah: New Evidences for the Book of Mormon from Ancient Mexico* (Horizon Publishers, Bountiful, UT 1981).

Read, M.C., *Archaeology of Ohio 1896* (The Western Reserve Historical Society, Cleveland, OH 1879).

Ritchie, William A., *The Archaeology of New York State* (Harbor Hill Books, Harrison, NY 1980).

Seely, Jo Ann H.; Seely, David Rolph; and Welch, John W., *Glimpses of Lehi's Jerusalem* (2004). Maxwell Institute Publications. 39

Shipps, Jan and Welch, John W. (Eds), *The Journals of William E. McLellin: 1831-1836* (BYU Studies, Provo UT, 1994).

Smoot, S. Edgar, *Lost American Antiquities: A Hidden History*, Legends Library, New York 2013).

Squier, E.G., *Antiquities of New York* (Geo. H. Derby and Co., Buffalo, NY 1851).

Squier, Ephraim G., and Davis, Edwin H., *Ancient Monuments of the Mississippi Valley* (Smithsonian Institution, Washington, DC, 1848).

Sorenson, John L., *Mormon's Map* (FARMS, Provo, UT, 2000).

Sorenson, John L., *Mormon's Codex* (Deseret Book, Salt Lake City, UT 2013).

Sorenson, John L., and Johannessen, Carl L., *World Trade and Biological Exchanges Before 1492*, (iUniverse, Inc., New York, NY 2009).

Sorenson, John L., *An Ancient American Setting for the Book of Mormon*

(Deseret Book, Salt Lake City, UT 1985).

Trubowitz, Neal L., *Highway Archaeology and Settlement Study in the Genesee Valley* (Occasional Publications in Northeaster Anthropology, George's Mills, NH 1983).

Welch, John W., and Welch, J. Gregory, *Charting the Book of Mormon: Visual Aids for Personal Study and Teaching* (Foundation for Ancient Research and Mormon Studies, Provo, UT 1999).

Wulf, Andrea, *The Invention of Nature: Alexander von Humboldt's New World,* (Vintage Books, New York, NY, 2015).

Welch, John W. (Ed.), *Opening the Heavens: Accounts of Divine Manifestations 1820-1844* (2ⁿᵈ Ed.) (Deseret Book, Salt Lake City, UT, 2017).

Whitney, Orson, *Life of Heber C. Kimball* (Bookcraft, Inc., Salt Lake City, UT 1945).

Williams, Stephen, *Fantastic Archaeology: The Wild Side of North American Prehistory* (University of Pennsylvania Press, Philadelphia, PA 1991).

*The Worlds of Joseph Smith: A Bicentennial Conference at the Library of Congress* (BYU Studies, Vol 44, No. 4 2005).

Wunderli, Earl M., *An Imperfect Book: What the Book of Mormon Tells Us about Itself,* Signature Books, Salt Lake City, 2013).

## FARMS Publications (promote M2C)

*The Geography of Book of Mormon Events: A Source Book*

*The Book of Mormon Text Reformatted according to Parallelistic Patterns*

*Book of Mormon Authorship Revisited: The Evidence for Ancient Origins*

*Isaiah in the Book of Mormon*

*King Benjamin's Speech: "That Ye May Learn Wisdom"*

*Pressing Forward with the Book of Mormon: The FARMS Updates of the 1990s*

*Warfare in the Book of Mormon*

*Rediscovering the Book of Mormon*

*Reexploring the Book of Mormon*

## Academic Papers (sample)

Abrams, Elliot M., "Hopewell Archaeology: A view from the North Woodlands," J. Archaeol Res (2009) 17:169-204. This overview article cites 46 journal articles.

Brett, C.E., Ver Straeten, C.A., and Baird, G.C., 2000, "Anatomy of a composite sequence boundary: The Silurian-Devonian contact in Western New York State," New York State Geological Association, 72nd Annual Meeting, *Field Trip Guidebook*, p. 39-74.

Burks, Jarrod, "Geophysical Survey at Ohio Earthworks: updating Nineteenth Century Maps and Filling the 'Empty' Spaces," *Archaeological Prospection*, 21, 5-13 (2014).

Cowgill, George L., "On Causes and Consequences of Ancient and Modern Population Changes," *American Anthropologist*, 1975.

Dimitrov, Dimitar Alekseev, "North America's Ancient Cities," independent.academia.edu. (2020). This overview cites dozens of sources.

Keith, Scot, "The Woodland Period Cultural Landscape of the Leake Site Complex," Paper presented at the Southeastern Archaeological Conference, Lexington, Kentucky, October 2010.

Kohler, Timothy A., "Public Architecture and Power in Pre-Columbian North America," For the International Symposium "Power, Monuments, and Civilization" Nara, Japan, December 1997, Santa Fe Institute.

Nolan, et al., "Scale and Community in Hopewell Networks (SCHoN) Summary of Preliminary Results," *Encountering Hopewell in the Twenty-first Century, Ohio and Beyond. Volume Two: Settlements, Foodways, and Interaction* (2020).

Nolan, et al., "New Dates on Scioto Hopewell Sites: A SCHoN Project," *Current Research in Ohio Archaeology 2017*, www.ohioarchaeology.org

Pacheco, Paul J., et al., "Investigating Ohio Hopewell Settlement Patterns in Central Ohio: A Preliminary Report of Archaeology at Brown's Bottom #1 (33Ro21)," Current Research in Ohio Archaeology 2005.

Schwarz, Kevin R., The Great Hopewell Road: New Data, Analysis, and Future Research Prospects, *Journal of Ohio Archaeology* Vol. 4, 2016.

# Index